MW00440503

The Compleat Motherfucker

A Feral House book.
ISBN: 978-1-932595-41-3

Feral House
1240 W. Sims Way Suite 124
Port Townsend WA 98368
www.FeralHouse.com
Front cover design by Sean Tejaratchi
Book design by Jacob Covey

THE COMPLEAT MOTHERFUCKER

JIM DAWSON

fh
FERAL HOUSE

TABLE OF CONTENTS

INTRODUCTION

In early June of 2008, Dick Cheney—the imperial vice president who ran our country (into the ground) for eight years—admitted to reporters that he had Cheneys on both sides of his family, "and we don't even live in West Virginia." His snide implication required no further explanation. Thanks to stereotypes of moonshine-swigging Hatfields going back more than a hundred years, many Americans still believe that Appalachian hillbillies are the products of consanguinity, or shared blood, between cousins, siblings, or parents and offspring. As a West Virginia native who has spent most of his adult life in other states, I've fended off countless brother-sister/mother-son jokes, and assured plenty of folks that my family tree does indeed fork at every generation. Furthermore, to the best of my knowledge, I never knew anybody who was his own stepdad. Yet, even today, I can't shake that little childhood ditty rattling around in my head—a take-off on the popular pre–World War I song "Pretty Baby"—that we kids used to sing: "If your mother has a baby and the baby looks like you, motherfucker, motherfucker!"

Other than that, so far as I can recall, *motherfucker* wasn't part of my working or playing vocabulary. Even after I went out into the world in the early 1960s, the word never came up unless somebody was telling a joke about black people. There was the one, for instance, where you're sitting on an airplane as it's taxiing down the runway. The honeyed Kingfish drawl of the pilot comes over the intercom: "Well, hello deh, folks, we got us a fine day, a *fine* day, yessah, no clouds, no wind, it look like it gonna be smoove all da way to St. Louie. So y'all just kick back and relax and enjoy yo'selfs while I tries to get dis motherfucker off da ground."

This was just an updated minstrel routine about a slow-witted Negro—a "coon" in minstrel parlance—finding himself in a situation clearly over his head. The joke would have been pointless if the pilot had been white. (In her 1973 best-seller *Fear of Flying*, Erica Jong's "So I keep concentrating very hard, helping the pilot fly the 250-passenger motherfucker" just doesn't have the same impact.) The humor depended on the teller's talent for dialect and the listener's fragile sense of racial superiority, but if anyone were going to find it funny, the "trigger" word, the punch that defined the punch line, was *motherfucker*. Nothing else worked, because the joke played on the typical white listener's assumption that *motherfucker* was an all-purpose baseline word of the black idiom. Its presence reinforced the centuries-old idea that blacks were uncouth, for who else would slip references of fucking their mothers into everyday speech? But today the word's trigger value in that joke is practically meaningless, not only because minstrel humor sounds more dated than ever to reasonably educated people, but also because many whites now use *motherfucker* as liberally as blacks do.

Maybe you've noticed that Americans are regressing (some might say evolving) into a tonal English that's short on vocabulary and long on gestures, inflection, and the need for context. Take the word *dude*. Originally a New York fashion term for men's clothing in the 1880s—short for *subdued*—it became part of black hipster lingo in the 1920s and crossed over to white America in the form of "dude ranches" in the West, where city slickers paid good money to sleep in bunk houses and kick parched cow turds across the prairie. After California surfers picked it up in the 1950s, *dude* became the lingua franca of marijuana-puffing stoners who embraced repetitive and inarticulate utterances as if they were haiku. And so today we have a word with dozens of meanings, depending on how it's spoken. As *New York Times* writer Dave Itzkoff put it not long ago, "In the right circumstances dude can be a stern admonition to a co-worker ('Please stop tapping that pencil on your desk'), an entreaty to a teammate ('Pass me the basketball!'), or a subtle nudge to a friend ('Check out the scantily clad showgirls on that escalator')." In late 2007 Anheuser-Busch began a series of "dude" TV commercials for Bud Light beer, featuring an airhead (Jason Davis) and his pals dealing with each other and various situations with just a one-word vocabulary.

It's doubtful that we'll be seeing a Bud Light "motherfucker" commercial anytime soon, but the word has become even more elastic and all-encompassing than *dude*. Young suburban whites and old hippies say *dude*, but people from every age, race, and ethnicity say *motherfucker*. A lot of it has to do with the mass marketing of urban street culture over the past forty years. In 1973, in a comic riff called "White Harlem," George Carlin observed that if five young white guys and five young black guys start hanging out together, after a month the whites will be walking, talking, and standing like blacks, not the other way around, because black culture is more expressive and "in the moment." Later on, in an interview, Carlin rephrased his point: "If you mix an Irish neighborhood and a black neighborhood, it won't have any effect on the blacks at all. But in six months all the Irish kids will be finger-poppin' and doing the boogie and saying, 'Hey, what's happening, motherfucker?'" That pretty much sums up what occurred all over America—and beyond.

What I've written here isn't groundbreaking or revolutionary. An earlier book called *The F Word*, published by Random House, has already expounded at length on the word *fuck*. Its editor, Jesse Sheidlower, stated in his introduction, "[T]he increasing acceptance of fuck in American society is not a sign that its use should be encouraged—nor should this book be considered such a sign. Any sort of language has a time and a place appropriate to its use, and it is often unsuitable to use the word so thoroughly chronicled in this book. It would be as misguided to say that 'fuck' should be used everywhere as it would be narrow-minded to insist upon its suppression." That's exactly what I mean to say here. Just substitute *motherfucker* for *fuck*. Thank you, Mr. Sheidlower, for making my job easier.

But where we've taken "the MF word" to the next level is our use of its full, uneuphemized, unadulterated spelling in the title: *The Compleat Motherfucker*. Not MF, not Mofo, not Motherf%#$, but Motherfucker. Yes, it's going to limit the book's mainstream coverage. In August 2008, when Crown published humorist Sandra Tsing Loh's *Mother on Fire*, the *Los Angeles Times* omitted its subtitle—*A True Motherf%#$@ Story About Parenting*—in its review, even though critic Susan Carpenter did at one point call Ms. Loh a "cunning linguist." The message? In a family newspaper, a pun on the word for licking pussy is one thing, but a typographic bowdlerization for a mother-humping, mother-jumping, mother-bumping mother thumper is quite another. And we can be certain that the *Times* will not be extolling the considerable virtues and merits of *The Compleat Motherfucker* anytime soon.

But hey, we come to you with our principles, along with our subject word, fully intact, and how many other books can make that claim?

WORD TO YOUR MOTHER

"A boy's best friend is his mother!"

—Norman Bates, *Psycho* (1960)

Most people will agree that it's the mother of all dirty words.

Motherfucker!

In its current compound form, motherfucker has been around for roughly four decades. It is two separate Anglo-Saxon words—one sacred, one profane—locked together by constant usage like two pieces of dried soap, one fragrant (Çameo) and the other gritty (Lava). It should come as no surprise that contemporary usage of *motherfucker* is generally regarded as African American in origin. Though it's literally an accusation of committing one of nature and society's most powerful taboos, the word is rarely used in that sense. Sure, the U.S. Supreme Court (*Keefe v. Geanakos*, 1969) called it "a vulgar term for an incestuous son," which is "admittedly highly offensive," but that was forty years ago. *The American Heritage Dictionary of the English Language*, Fourth Edition (2000) defines the word—pronounced "moth-er-fuck-er," without any stressed syllables—as "vulgar slang" for someone thoroughly despicable or something unpleasant, frustrating, or despicable. A *Webster's Dictionary* poll found that *motherfucker* appeared only thirteen times out of a sample of one hundred million words spoken or written in English, which ranks it number 97,576 on the frequency-of-usage scale. Many Americans never say it because they believe it's a linguistic toxin that poisons the air whenever it's breathed aloud. Yet millions of others look upon it as neutral, or even positive. *Motherfucker* has come to mean almost anything, and nothing at all.

Anthropologists believe that incest taboos have been with us since our earliest days, because sex interferes with other traditional roles within a household and foments jealousies. Also, primitive tribal societies encouraged marriage between different families to form alliances.

Any way you look at it, incest is a dysfunction that creates rot from the inside. And since the bond between mother and son is the most intimate and powerful of all, ancient lawgivers assigned it special attention—though with qualifications. According to the Code of Hammurabi, written on a big stone slab nearly four thousand years ago, the Babylonians proscribed sexual relations between a widowed mother and her son. Law #157 declared: "If a man, after his father's death, has lain in the bosom of his mother, they shall both of them be burnt together." On the other hand, the penalty for a young man *schtupping* his stepmother was merely disinheritance. But nothing was mentioned about what might happen if a boy jumped his mother's bones while his father was still alive. Perhaps King Hammurabi's legal team considered it such an outrageous offense that its prohibition was a given.

Leviticus, the third book of both the Torah and the Old Testament, likewise has a loophole of omission for motherfuckers. Essentially a book of priestly rites and social rules separate from the Ten Commandments (which were handed down earlier, in Exodus), Leviticus contains two chapters of what are generally called Holiness Codes, a laundry list of sins and abominations given to the Jewish people by Yahweh himself. (Okay, rather than call him Yahweh or Jehovah, I'll use the more familiar *God* from now on, since God is a naturalized American citizen and loves the good ol' U.S.A. above all others.) Chapter 18 deals with sexual matters, from adultery to homosexuality to bestiality, and naturally God didn't forget motherfucking either. Addressing Moses in the wilderness after the Jews escaped from Egypt, God said (in verse 7): "None of you shall approach to any who is near of kin to him, to uncover their nakedness.... The nakedness of thy father, or the nakedness of thy mother, shalt thou not uncover: she is thy mother; thou shalt not uncover her nakedness." Furthermore, in verse 8: "The nakedness of thy father's wife shalt thou not uncover; it is thy father's nakedness." If this stilted Elizabethan prose from the 1611 King James version gives you a headache, here's the simplified text from the 1970 *New American Bible*: "You shall not disgrace your father by having intercourse with your mother. Besides, since she is your mother, you shall not have intercourse with her. You shall not have intercourse with your father's wife, for that would be a disgrace to your father."

What's curious here is that God spelled out two separate sins: getting naked with your mother and getting naked with your father's wife, i.e., your stepmother, because in those ancient days, when men often took extra wives and were obligated to marry their brothers' widows, stepmothers were as plentiful as aunts, and were considered a class unto themselves. And yet, when God got around to naming capital offenses in Chapter 20, he specifically described only the stepson/stepmother relationship (verse 11: "And the man that lieth with his father's wife hath uncovered his father's nakedness: both of them shall surely be put to death; their blood shall be upon them"). Did He forget about the crime of motherfucking? Or was it simply a given? After all, Reuben, the eldest son of the patriarch Jacob, had created a stepmother precedent by fucking one of his dad's wives, Bilhah, in Genesis 35, whereas there was no corresponding example within early Jewish history of a mother and son bumping uglies. But still, since even fucking one's mother-in-law was punishable by burning (verse 14), you'd think there'd be a special place in Holy Bible hell for a guy slipping Mom the old rod and staff. Perhaps God, despite his rep for being a really good multi-tasker, had something else on his mind that day.

(The great German dramatist Friedrich Schiller dealt with the sticky stepmother problem in his 1787 play *Don Carlos*, loosely based on a real sixteenth-century Spanish crown prince, whose love for the wife of his father, King Phillip II, brought the Catholic Church's Inquisition down upon him.)

In any event, according to Biblical scholar Calum M. Carmichael, "the incest rules of the Bible—in particular those found in the two chapters of Leviticus 18 and 20—have had the greatest effect on Western law than any comparable body of biblical rules." In 1603 the Church of England expanded the original list with its own Table of Levitical Decrees, which encompassed the prohibition of marriage not only among blood relatives, but also between in-laws. However, many of those laws were later struck down. Countries in the modern world have a wide range of tolerance of incest between consenting adults; it's indictable in Canada, for instance, but perfectly legal in France. In the U.S., both incest and age-of-consent laws vary from state to state: New York has nothing on the books to prosecute consanguineous adults, whereas the heavily Catholic Massachusetts will send even first cousins to prison for having sex, which probably reflects the Church's prohibitions against the marriage of first cousins. In fact, anthropologist Nancy W. Thornhill, of the University of New Mexico, after studying 129 societies from the sixteenth to the twentieth centuries, concluded in an article in the June 1991 issue of the journal *Behavorial and Brain Sciences* that most societies' incest laws are concerned with in-laws and cousins, not members of a nuclear family. Statistics show that when incest does occur, usually there's a stepfather or stepbrother involved with an underage girl or boy, which automatically moves the offense into the legal realms of pedophilia or statutory rape. Mother-son cases are extremely rare.

Possibly the earliest literary use of the term *motherfucker* was in the Ionic (i.e., Greek) poetry of Hipponax, who accused a sculptor who had insulted him of being a *metrokoites*—a motherfucker—in the fifth century B.C. Twenty-two centuries later, the Marquis de Sade, a smut writer and public nuisance who gave us the word *sadism*, was thrown into prison for torturing a prostitute and screaming that Jesus Christ was a motherfucker. But considering that the less offensive word *fuck* was outlawed in print—both in England (by the Obscene Publications Act of 1857) and in the U.S. (by the Comstock Law of 1873)—and barred from every dictionary since Samuel Johnson's until *The Penguin Dictionary* broke the ban in 1965, it's no wonder that *motherfucker* is even less documented. The earliest known examples occur in two Texas Court of Appeals reports, one in 1890 ("that God damned mother-f---king, bastardly son-of-a-bitch!") and the other in 1897 ("a mother-fucking son-of-a-bitch!"). As befits its uncharted subterranean status, *motherfucker* is a flexible and ungoverned word that was allowed to mutate into many contracted, abridged, disguised, and castrated forms. The most frequent spelling in modern usage is probably muthafucka, which American blacks use among themselves as an alternative to nigga—both words blunted at the end to reduce their volatility. Then there are muhfucka, mofugga, mofucka, mahfah, muddafucka, mofo, and any number of other permutations that, if fully listed, would fill the rest of this book and bore the shit out of everybody. There were even the initials *MF* (as in jazz trombonist Maynard Ferguson's early 1970s *M.F. Horn* albums) to give the idea of the word without also delivering its sting. (Since Ferguson's initials were actually MF, he could play the title either way, but self-respecting jazz fans considered themselves hip enough to know what the title really meant; likewise, when poet Amiri Baraka, in his *Autobiography of LeRoi Jones*, used them to refer to his father—"But somehow she ran into this big-eyed skinny dude (MF) My father"—he was engaging the reader in wordplay.) Less subtly there are BMF (i.e., Bad Mother Fucker, one of wrestling star Stone Cold Steve Austin's early 1990s characters, and now a subtitle on his Stone Cold WWE T-shirts), JAMF (jive-ass motherfucker, favored by Clint Eastwood's Dirty Harry character in the 1983 film *Sudden Impact*), and BAMF (an acronym for bad-ass motherfucker, popularized by comic Dane Cook as a track title on his chart-topping 2005 *Retaliation* album; one becomes a BAMF, says Cook, by cruising around in a goosed-up cement truck, similar to the one that Stone Cold BMF Steve Austin used to drive to his wrestling matches). Then there are the replacement terms that aren't very subtle, such as *mother-effer, mother-frigger, mother-farker, mother-frocker* (the subject of a 1959 Redd Foxx comedy routine), *mother-humper, mother-jumper, mother-hugger* (used in Billy Holiday's 1956 autobiography), *mother jiver* (a con man or jokester), *mother superior* (one of *Downbeat* magazine's approving jazz appellations), *mothersucker* ("He was up on his feet looking the mothersucking nigger in the face," wrote Cecil Brown in his 1969 *The Life and Loves of Mr. Jiveass Nigger*), *mammy-huncher, mammy-tapper, mamma jamma* (popular during the late disco and funk era thanks to the 1981 song "She's a Bad Mamma Jamma"), *motherfouler* (the term that novelist Ralph Ellison used in his landmark 1952 *Invisible Man*), and *motherferyer*, which jazz hipster Mezz Mezzrow dropped into his 1946 memoir *Really the Blues*. Then there are the one-off oddities like *mickyficky*—the word dubbed over all instances of *motherfucker* when film director Spike Lee's *Do the Right Thing* aired on network television—and Bill Murray's *mother-puss-bucket!* exclamation in the 1984 film *Ghostbusters*. And let's not forget the euphemistic typos such as Ken Kesey's 1968 poem *Cut the Motherf*****s Loose*, about his jail stint for drug possession, and *motherf%#$@*, which Crown Publishing used in the subtitle of humorist Sandra Tsing Loh's 2008 memoirs, *Mother on Fire*. To members of the Crips, one of Los Angeles's two major black gangs, the word is spelled *motherfuccer*, because to them "CK" means Crip Killer and therefore must never be written. Publishers over the years also created various abridgements of the word, as when black bandleader Preston Love, recounting his years on the road in the early 1950s, was stuck with *mother—ker*, and, going back even further, John O'Hara's 1934 novel *Appointment in Samarra* braved the censors with *mother-------*. We've also had the personified stand-ins like Mother Hubbard (a favorite of black comic Moms Mabley), Mother Fletcher (used in a recurring comedy bit by Jackie Gleason on his 1950s and '60s network TV shows, as well as the name of a notorious rock 'n' roll club in Myrtle Beach, South Carolina), Mother Trucker (the title of an Emmy-winning 1996 TV movie about Teamster boss Diana Kilmury, as well as a description—bad mother truckers—for participants in motor sports events featuring large pickups on balloon tires), and W.C. Fields's Mother o' Pearl (delivered through clenched teeth after he suffered some random humiliation). In the right context, an innocuous term can euphemize motherfucker, such as *motor scooter* (as in "He's a bad motor scooter and a mean go-getter," from the Hollywood Argyles' 1960 number-one hit record *Alley-Oop*), and *motorcycle* (used in various rock 'n' roll songs like the Storey Sisters' "Bad Motorcycle," the Crestones' "She's a Bad Motorcyle," and the Lost's "Mean Motorcyle," and by the emcees at many black theaters in the 1960s to describe some of the more sexually menacing soul singers of the time). Then there are the code terms for MF in the military alphabet of Alpha-Baker-Charlie, such as Maryland farmer, mustard farmer, melon farmer (network TV's most famous dub-in), muddy funster (a tongue-in-cheek British concoction), Mr. Franklin, and Mary Frances (perhaps a reference to a particularly nasty Catholic school nun or a ball-busting cheerleader). Strangely enough, however, neither Muckle Flugga (a small rocky isle in Scotland's Shetland Islands) nor Momofuku (the Japanese inventor of instant noodles in a cup, as well a series of trendy Japanese noodle bars in Manhattan) appears to be a stand-in for *motherfucker*, though they'd be perfect.

Even *mother* itself, and the more modern *mutha*, are often shorthand for motherfucker—as in Frank Zappa's legendary sixties rock group The Mothers, or King-Tee's seminal 1988 rap tune "Payback's a Mutha." Scriptwriters even managed to sneak a couple of *mothers* into Hollywood movies as early as the 1930s. Today, *mother* has attained the status of daily parlance—along with *bull* (short for bullshit)—evidenced by its recent use, for example, in such TV shows as *Law & Order* and *Monk*.

As if *motherfucker* weren't supercharged enough on its own, it often comes with a standard intensive to give it a little more oomph or nuance. For example, a motherfucker is often bad, bad-ass, crazy, tough, or mean—adjectives bestowing respect or gravitas. "Joe's a mean motherfucker" doesn't mean Joe is abusive and diddles his mom, but rather that you shouldn't fuck with him if you value your health. The respect especially given to a "bad motherfucker" is best illustrated in a Chris Rock comedy routine called "Tipping Your Hat to Whitey" from his 2005 *Never Scared* album, in which he marvels at how white settlers always managed to ruthlessly exploit and profit handsomely from every native culture they colonized—and then he caps each example with a mock-appreciative: "That Whitey's a bad motherfucker!"

Motherfuckers you should definitely avoid at all costs are dirty, nasty, stinking, or rotten. And the motherfucker you should avoid being is dumb, lazy, lyin', phony, and, worst of all, jive or jive-ass (which is a harsher way of saying lyin' or phony). A sweet motherfucker can be a lot of things, from a great person to a punk-ass faggot, depending on how well the speaker knows and likes whomever he's talking about. A good-looking man or woman is a fine motherfucker. Anyone handy with a punch line is a funny motherfucker—who can tell a joke like a motherfucker.

When you get down to it, really, a motherfucker can be anything. In his 1987 concert film *Raw*, comic Eddie Murphy used the word to mean a house ("I'm livin' up in this motherfucker"), his own anus ("You know what really makes me mad is when shit come halfway out your ass and go back up in that motherfucker"), Bill Cosby ("That Jell-O pudding-eatin' motherfucker"), the movie *Raw* itself ("You're all gonna be in the shit, only I'm getting' paid for the motherfucker"), and a standard of certainty ("A lot of housewives have to get jobs on the side to make ends meet, [but if your husband's] got $300 million, the ends are meetin' like a motherfucker"). Jazz composer Charles Mingus, in his 1971 autobiography *Beneath the Underdog*, saw it as a common description of the average put-upon or victimized African American when he complained, "Musicians are as Jim-Crowed as any black motherfucker on the street." On the other hand, Chris Rock, on *Never Scared*, used it as an admonishment against some of his fellow blacks ("Motherfucker come to court twenty minutes late; what kind of black man comes to court twenty minutes late?…This is court, motherfucker!").

Motherfucker can also be a formidable force ("That Chicago wind is a motherfucker"), something contemptible ("Now ain't that a motherfucker!"), a standard of excellence ("He plays guitar like a motherfucker!"), the ultimate ("It's cold as a motherfucker out there!") an event ("This motherfucker is wack, let's get the fuck outta this motherfucker"), an exclamation of awe ("Mother*fucker*!") or disappointment ("*Muh*ther*fuck*er!"), an object of endearment ("Man, I loved that little motherfucker!"), and a U.S. Army frankfurter (as in "motherfuckers and beans," the Vietnam-era term for the C-ration meal of little-finger-sized franks and baked beans). *Motherfucker* can mean absolutely nothing and absolutely everything at the same time.

In most instances it's a noun, but it can also be a pronoun ("Motherfucker walked in here like he owned the place!"). It can be an adjective, more or less synonymous with just plain *fucking* as a more intense version of the emphatic intensive *goddamn*, as in "You motherfucking asshole," or as a strong assent or agreement: "Motherfuckin' A," short for "Motherfuckin' all right." It's even a blunt-edged verb on rare occasions, as when Public Enemy's Chuck D., in the 1990 hit "Fight the Power," rapped: "Elvis was a hero to most, but he never meant shit to me…motherfuck him and John Wayne." The late comedian Bernie Mac illustrated *motherfucker*'s pliability and frequency within everyday black speech during one of his routines in the film *The Original Kings of Comedy* (2000): "When you're listening to one of our conversations you might hear the word *motherfucker* about thirty-two times. Don't be afraid of the word motherfucker.... I'ma break it down to ya.... If you're out there this afternoon and you see like three or four brothers talkin', you might hear a conversation and it goes like this: 'You seen that motherfuckin' Bobby? That motherfucker owes me thirty-five motherfuckin' dollars! He told me he gon' pay my motherfuckin' money last motherfuckin' week. I ain't seen this motherfucker yet. I called the motherfucker fo' motherfuckin' times, but the motherfucker won't call me back. I called his motherfuckin' momma the other motherfuckin' day.... She gonna play like the motherfucker wasn't there. I started to cuss her motherfuckin' ass out, but I don't want no motherfuckin' trouble. But I'll tell ya one motherfuckin' thang...the next time I see this motherfucker and he don't have my motherfuckin' money, I'm gonna bust his motherfuckin' head! And I'm *out* this motherfucka!'"

This is nothing new. As far back as 1960, one of New York City's black weekly newspapers, the *Citizen-Call*, noted the word's growing frequency in its July 30 edition: "Doctors, lawyers, businessmen and athletes, especially professional baseball players and jazz or cool school musicians, use the term, 'M...,' as lingual crutches." Nine years later, Black Panther founder Bobby Seale wrote in his memoir *Seize the Time*,

> Motherfucker is a very common expression nowadays. Eldridge [Cleaver] ran it down to me once when a number of people got upset over this vernacular of the ghetto. Eldridge said: "I've seen and heard brothers use this word four and five times in one sentence and each time the word had a different meaning and expression.... But today, check the following sentence: 'Man, let me tell you. This motherfucker here went down there with his motherfucking gun, knocked down the motherfucking door and blew this motherfucker's brains out. This shit is getting to be a motherfucker.'"

On a purely semantic level, the repetition of this one word, but with different meanings, within a sentence or paragraph can create confusion. In his autobiography *Seize the Day*, when Bobby Seale recalled the day that Malcolm X was assassinated, he wrote: "I went to my mother's house and I got six loose bricks from the garden. I got to the corner and broke the motherfuckers in half.... Every time I saw a paddy roll by in a car, I picked up one of the half-bricks, and threw it at the motherfuckers." Logically, he's saying that he threw his half-bricks at the bricks he hadn't broken in half yet. But of course he doesn't mean that at all, and the reader accepts that *motherfucker*'s meaning is fluid, that it's a shapeshifter from one sentence or phrase to the next.

Oftentimes the word provides nothing more than conversational cadence ("What the motherfuck is going on here?"), or a rhythmic fill in a hip-hop song (as in "Down 4 My Niggas," when Snoop Dogg raps: "It's getting' nutty in dis muthafucka, I got my buddy in dis muthafucka, leave a nigga bloody in dis muthafucker, we in da cutty, muthafucka, you done done too much, you got it comin', muthafucka"). The four syllables are a natural fit for music written in 4/4 time. The hard "k" in the third syllable also gives high-energy music an extra kick, particularly when the word is pronounced "muthafucka." It goes without saying that unless the speaker is really pissed off, only a total square would pronounce all four syllables and emphasize them equally, moth-er-fuck-er, as prescribed in *The American Heritage Dictionary of the English Language*, Fourth Edition.

The term was originally "mother fucker"—two separate words that remained apart for at least a couple of centuries. First there's *mother*, a Teutonic immigrant that entered Old English as *modor* and traded its "d" for a "th" sound in the sixteenth century. Then comes *fuck*, which didn't appear in English until the early sixteenth century or show its aggressive little face on the printed page until John Florio's *World of Wordes* (1598): "Fottere, to iape, to sard, to fucke, to swive, to occupy." There is no truth to the old joke that long ago, in Mother Africa, a king named Mutafuk made his subjects speak his name throughout the day, and that his tribesmen subsequently carried the tradition to America as slaves. If you believe that, I've got a mother in Brooklyn I'd like to sell you. She looks just like Marisa Tomei.

Given that God handed Moses a stone tablet demanding that we honor our mothers, it would seem that the Kosher Law would forever apply here. Just as dill pickles and vanilla ice cream—perfectly nice food items by themselves—should never be combined, so too should mother and fucker be kept apart on separate dishes. But that's not how it turned out. Mother and fucker fused together as one printed word in the crucible of the American Civil Rights movement and entered the national idiom with the Anti–Vietnam War movement—all within a few years in the 1960s. Its frequent, almost unapologetic use since then has been seen as a symptom of either a free-spirited, more informal citizenry or a growing coarseness in civil society. Within the black community, where *motherfucker* was once limited to the poorest and most unassimilated, and was looked upon with approbation by the working class (after all, Martin Luther King never said, "I've been to the motherfucking mountaintop!"), its presence reflects how over the past forty years African

Americans have rejected white society and its claims of propriety. Among whites, the word's frequency hints at either an overall dumbing-down of the English vocabulary or a growing linguistic complexity that depends on more context—vocal stress, gestures, and facial expressions—and fewer words. Take your pick.

Motherfucker's greatest purveyor within pop culture was probably Richard Pryor (more on him later), but the man who put the word on the map was George Carlin, thanks to his comic monologues on a couple of 1973 live albums: "Seven Words You Can Never Say on Television" on *Class Clown* and its "Filthy Words" sequel on *Occupation: Foole*. When a New York public radio station aired Carlin's "Filthy Words" in 1975, an angry citizen complained to the Federal Communications Commission that his young son had heard it, and who knows, it may have irrevocably damaged the lad. The FCC's sanctions against the station ultimately led to the U.S. Supreme Court's 1978 ruling that the First Amendment's right to free speech didn't protect Carlin's "vulgar, offensive, and shocking" use of the words. By that time, however, Carlin had already recited those seven words on television, albeit in a rarefied, non-broadcast universe called premium cable TV.

As Carlin pointed out in his original "Seven Words" routine:

> Yeah, there are four hundred thousand words in the English language, and there are seven of them that you can't say on television. What a ratio that is: 399,993 to seven. They must really be bad. They'd have to be outrageous, to be separated from a group that large.... You know the seven don't you? Shit, piss, fuck, cunt, cocksucker, motherfucker, and tits, huh? Those are the heavy seven. Those are the ones that will infect your soul, curve your spine, and keep the country from winning the war.

(Carlin's choice and word order may have been inspired by comic Lenny Bruce's last filmed performance, shot in a San Francisco club in late 1965 and released in art houses a year later, in which he read to the audience a section of the judge's opinion from his 1964 obscenity trial in New York: "In the latter two performances, words such as ass, balls, cocksucker, cunt, fuck, motherfucker, piss, screw, shit and tits were used about one hundred times in utter obscenity." For more on Bruce, see Chapter 8.)

Other offending expletives exist, of course, but they're what Carlin called "two-way words"—like cock, prick, and balls—with perfectly respectable alternate meanings that take the sour piss out of them. ("Yes, you can prick your finger, but don't finger your prick.") But the seven nasty sisters have no soft, equivocal side. "Under any circumstances you just cannot say them ever, ever, *ever*, not even clinically," said Carlin. "I mean, it's just impossible. Forget those seven, they're out."

But for my purposes, at least one of them, *motherfucker*, cannot be shaken free from memory. It's unforgettable. In fact, it's ubiquitous, easily worthy of at least a book.

BAD BLACK MOTHERFUCKERS!

"A black musician who had a white woman and a Cadillac was a bad motherfucker!"

—jazz pianist Hampton Hawes, *Get Up Off Me* (1973)

British and American whites most likely used the term "mother fucker" several hundred years ago, but we're hearing it in common parlance today because it found a special resonance among black American men. As actor Ving Rhames, portraying boxing promoter Don King in HBO's 1997 film *Only in America*, put it: "Black people don't get no credit for nothing. All we've got is one word. That word is *motherfucker*." Its popularity comes directly from the patois of early-twentieth-century ghetto hipsters and jazz musicians. They picked it up from their forbears.

But why did black men seize so passionately upon this particular linguistic pathology? Why did they have such ambivalent feelings of love and hostility toward their mothers—and women in general? Can it be traced to some residual resentment their ancestors harbored against the priestesses and matriarchs of West African societies, such as the powerful witches—called *iya wa*, or "the mothers"—of Nigerian Yoruba tribes who had been expelled from their polygamous families for not producing male children? Or did American slavery create its own twisted matriarchal arrangement by giving black women favored status over men?

Forty years ago, two black psychiatrists named William H. Grier and Price M. Cobbs wrote a book called *Black Rage* in which they elaborated upon the second explanation. Yes, black women did have a special place in the American South—as mothers, or as mother surrogates such as aunts and grandmothers—but theirs was not a traditional matriarchy. Since the father, if he were around at all, was laboring all day at some exhausting menial job and held no real power in the family, it fell upon the mother to rear and care for the children and to serve as an intermediary between them and the hostile, white-supremacist society outside their door. She was, according to Drs. Grier and Cobbs, "the culture bearer.... This is every mother's task. But the black mother has a more ominous message for her child and feels more urgently the need to get the message across. The child must know that the white world is dangerous and that if he does not understand its rules it may kill him."

This lesson was crucial under slavery, but its value hardly lessened during the harsh Jim Crow era when a black man could get lynched just for looking at a white woman with the wrong gleam in his eye, or at a white man with the wrong glint. "The black mother...must intuitively cut off and blunt his masculine assertiveness and aggression lest they put the boy's life in jeopardy." What she desperately did *not* want her child to become was a "bad nigger," overtly defiant against whites, because such a young man would almost certainly come to a bad end. "Even today [in 1968], the black man cannot become too aggressive without hazard to himself," the doctors wrote.

The result of this maternal crushing of the spirit was the compliant and accommodating "boy"—the word most Southern whites assigned to every black man, regardless of his age. Soul singer James Brown remembered in his 1986 autobiography how his Southern-born father related to whites: "He had a temper about white people, but he never showed it to *them*.... He'd call white people 'crackers,' curse 'em and everything when they weren't around, but when he was in front of them, he'd say, 'Yessir, nawsir.'" Likewise, novelist Richard Wright noted in *Native Son* (1939) how even in Harlem, far from the South, young black street hooligans avoided striking out against whites because it "trespass[ed] into territory where the full wrath of an alien white world would be turned loose upon them; in short, it would be a symbolic challenge of the white world's rule over them; a challenge which they yearned to make, but were afraid to."

Loving, protective mothers created these men by thwarting children's youthful aggression in myriad small ways—with a sudden verbal slash, the back of a hand across the mouth, a switch across the shoulders, or some other capricious and humbling cruelty. "What at first seemed a random pattern of mothering has gradually assumed a definite and deliberate, if unconscious, method of preparing a black boy for his subordinate place in the world," wrote Grier and Cobbs. "As a result, black men develop considerable hostility toward black women as the inhibiting instruments of an oppressive system. The woman has more power, more accessibility into the system, and therefore she is more feared, while at the same time envied."

The doctors observed that one result of this maternal wounding was that black men were susceptible to a sudden welling up of emotionless tears whenever they saw another man, such as an athlete, entertainer, or politician, "standing supreme in a moment of personal glory." As they explained this strange weeping: "The tears are for what he might have achieved if he had not been held back...by some inner command not to excel, not to achieve, not to become outstanding, not to draw attention to himself." The source of this command, the man realized, was his mother. "Only *she* was so concerned with his behavior and *she* was most concerned that he be modest and self-effacing. And when he sees that his grief is over lost achievement, relinquished at the behest of his mother, he becomes enraged with her."

There is an old joke, told mostly by blacks amongst themselves, about a little boy sitting in the kitchen watching his mother dip pieces of chicken into white flour before she drops them into the frying pan. He playfully pokes his fingers into the flour, dabs it all over his face, and says, "Look, Ma, I'm white!"

She looks up and asks, "What did you say?" As he's in the middle of repeating himself, her open hand flies out of nowhere and slaps his face. "Don't you ever say that again!" she warns him, with a bitter edge in her voice.

The boy runs crying from the kitchen into the warm, enfolding arms of his Aunt Nell in the next room. She murmurs, "Honey baby, what's wrong?"

"Mommy slapped me."

"Why did she do that?"

"'Cause I said I was white."

Aunt Nell slaps him across the face and says, "Don't you *never* say that again!"

Crying even harder now, he runs to his grandmother. Leaning over with deep concern in her kindly face, she asks, "What's wrong, little one?"

"Mommy and Aunt Nell slapped me!"

"Now, now, baby, tell your granny why'd they do something like that."

"'Cause I said I was white."

Granny slaps him even harder, almost knocking him down. Some of the flour comes off on her hand. "Don't you *never* say that again," she snaps. Then, in a calmer voice, she asks, "Now baby, what did you just learn?"

"I-I-I learned," he sniffles, "that I been white now for only two minutes and I already hate you black motherfuckers!"

James Baldwin perhaps said it best in his 1964 play *Blues For Mr. Charlie*: "manhood is a dangerous pursuit here." Just walking into a country store and asking for a can of Prince Albert tobacco without saying *Mister* Prince Albert (since a picture of a white man was on the label) could get a Negro into trouble. Baldwin based *Blues For Mister Charlie* on a 1955 murder of a black Chicago teenager whose mother hadn't properly schooled him on how to act around white Southerners. Emmett Till was visiting his relatives in Mississippi when he became too familiar with the young wife of a storekeeper. Three days later two men kidnapped him from a relative's house, beat him to a pulp, shot him, wrapped barbed wire around his neck, and dumped his body into a river.

In order to function under such intimidation, young black males—like anyone constrained by severe rules and demands—needed some means of expressing their rage and coming to grips with their own emerging manhood. That's why they admired the explosive, terrifying "bad nigger" their mothers had warned them about. The bad nigger, also called "crazy nigger," was bad for everybody all around, an ill wind that blew nobody any good. He stirred up all the trouble that lay just beneath the surface of everyday life. He was especially dangerous because his open defiance—his "bad attitude"—drew fire upon the other black people around him. And yet, since bad niggers "terrified the Negro community and in a sense provided a negative model for 'nice families,' such men had profound importance for the Negro community," said Drs. Grier and Cobbs. "They provided the measure of manhood for all black men."

Within that context, the word *bad*—coming off a protective mother's admonishing tongue—took on an ironic power of its own. *Bad* came to mean good, and *baad* was even better. As sociologist H.C. Brearley wrote in a 1939 essay in *The South Atlantic Quarterly* called "Ba-ad Nigger," "an emphasis on heroic deviltry is so marked that the very word *bad* often loses its original significance and may be used as an epithet of honor." A black man didn't just call "a local hero" bad, said Brearley; "he calls him 'ba-ad.' The more he prolongs the *a*, the greater is his homage." No wonder the first successful blaxploitation film, released in 1971, called *Sweet Sweetback's Baadasssss Song*, was actor-director Melvin Van Peebles's story of a black gigolo who kills two white cops while defending a Black Panther and makes a successful run for the Mexican border to save his *baad* black ass. As for the word *nigger*, it certainly had its own back-handed honor among blacks, but at the same time it was so laden with powerlessness and humiliation that something was needed to replace it. Since the young black anti-hero had to first stand up to the mother who represented the powerful system before he could defy the system itself, who better to put her in her place than a "bad motherfucker"?

But in order to survive and thrive, the bad motherfucker had to possess more finesse than the bad nigger. The bad nigger was too flat-out crazy, too brazen and reckless for his own good. Even the twentieth century's first famous bad nigger, heavyweight boxing champion Jack Johnson, had to flee to Paris to escape a one-year prison sentence under the 1910 White Slave Traffic Act, better known as the Mann Act, which Congress reportedly enacted with him in mind because of his notoriously extravagant taste for white women. As H. Rap Brown described the bad nigger in a 1969 essay called "Die, Nigger, Die," "He was rebelling against the way the deck was stacked against him, and even his rebellion was a stacked deck." He wasn't likely to grow into the eminence of old age. He lashed out, he made his point, maybe he fought the law and scared a few people and scored some high-falutin' pussy, but in the end he usually found himself up a tree in one way or another.

The bad motherfucker, on the other hand, had a chance of winning. Though the bad nigger may have had a few tricks up his sleeve, the bad motherfucker was a trickster to his core. He knew that white society held no future for him, so he made his own rules and spoke his own patois. Working a "slave"—a menial, low-paying job, generally for a white boss—was beneath him. His success had to come from gambling, pimping (either supplying women for other men or being a gigolo), selling dope, fencing stolen goods, and otherwise using his mother wit to game the white man's economic system by exploiting everyone around him. Better yet, he was a musician or an athlete, admired by other black men—and women. *Especially* women. As Charles Keil pointed out in 1966 in *Urban Blues*, the most popular blues/soul singers among women were the ones who, like Bobby Bland and Wilson Pickett, presented themselves onstage as bad motherfuckers. So the bad motherfucker wasn't just figuratively fucking his own mother; he was literally fucking other young men's mothers. He knew the ropes, the street, the con. He was quick and slick on his feet and, more importantly, quick and slick with his words, because words and ideas have real power in an environment where nobody owns much of anything. As H. Rap Brown put it, "In [our] world, the heroes were bloods who will never be remembered outside our Black community. Cats like Pie-man, Ig, Yank, Smokey, Hawk, Lil Nel—all bad muthafuckas. Young bloods wanted to be like these brothers. They were the men in our community. They had all the women and had made their way to the top through [local] sports and knowing the streets."

With the coming of the Civil Rights movement, the 1960s provided the bad motherfucker outside of the South with a new political avenue, in open defiance of white society and its kangaroo justice system. After a 1965 race riot devastated Los Angeles's Watts ghetto, two Oakland, California, college students named Huey P. Newton and Bobby Seale formed the Black Panther Party For Self Defense. Their rallying cry was "All power to the people," and since one of those powers, spelled out in the Second Amendment to the Constitution, was the right to bear arms, Newton and Seale recruited armed young men and women to protect Oakland's black neighborhoods from the city's police. Poet-activist Amiri Baraka, who was then known as LeRoi Jones, recalled how seeing photos of Seale and other Panthers "on the front page with their heat strapped on or in hand did something wonderful to us. It pumped us up bigger than life. Black men demanding democracy and justice and ready to fight about it. Those were heady times." These black John Waynes didn't call each other mere motherfuckers, because the word standing alone was reserved for their worst enemies, as when Panther leader David Hilliard claimed, "Fuck that motherfucking man. We will kill [President] Richard Nixon. We will kill any motherfucker who stands in the way of our freedom," and Bobby Seale wrote, "[Newton] never forgot about the people. He'd bring it right down to the food, and the bread and employment, decent housing, decent education—the way the motherfuckers, the President, and all, fucked over us." They referred to the U.S. government as "the imperialist motherfucker."

On the other hand, the Panthers themselves, everyone agreed, were *bad* motherfuckers, which flipped the word around completely, from contempt to admiration. Seale proclaimed Huey Newton to be "the baddest motherfucker ever to set foot in history," because he "stood up in the heart of the ghetto, at night, in alleys, confronted by racist pigs with guns and said...'I'm not going to allow you to brutalize me. I'm going to stop you from brutalizing my people.... If you shoot at me, I'm shooting back.'" Another Panther, George Jackson, said of fellow Panther James Carr: "Jimmy was the baddest motherfucker!" Unfortunately, as their mothers would have told them, the armed, in-your-face recklessness of the Black Panthers eventually brought the weight of the nation's law and order down upon them. Newton and hundreds of other Panthers went to prison, and twenty-seven were killed in battles with police and federal agents. Sometimes a bad motherfucker, like the earlier bad nigger, was too bad for his own good.

To understand the power of the word *motherfucker* in the black community, you have to look at the way a young male, from puberty to his late teenage years, traditionally established his virility—his badness—and his place in the neighborhood pecking order by playing a game called "the dozens," in which he challenged his friends and rivals by denigrating the morality, looks, intelligence, and skin color of their family members—especially their mothers. In fact, "playing the dozens" or putting someone "in the dozens" often meant verbally fucking or sexually shaming another guy's mother. The point was that if your mother was a lowdown dirty slut lacking even a shred of decency, what the fuck did that make you?

Some experts, such as Geneva Smitherman, speculate that the term came from the New Orleans slave markets, where deformed, crippled, and otherwise low-grade slaves were sold in lots of "cheap dozens"—a humiliation among the slaves themselves. Other sources say it comes from an original challenge requiring twelve insults, each worse than the one before, as in "I fucked your mama one, she said, 'You've just begun.'... I fucked your mama seven, she said, 'Lordy, I think I'm up in heaven,'" and so on up to twelve. (This game of twelve insults may have been the inspiration for the popular 1923 Trixie Smith blues song called "My Man Rocks Me (With One Steady Roll)," whose verses began with references to looking at the clock—such as "I looked at the clock and the clock struck three, I said, 'Baby, whooeeee!'"—from one to twelve. This song structure eventually led in 1954 to "Rock Around the Clock," rock 'n' roll's first million-selling record.)

H. Rap Brown recalled that he and his buddies "played the dozens for recreation, like white folks play Scrabble." An example:

> I fucked your mama
> Till she went blind,
> Her breath smells bad,
> But she sure can grind.
> I fucked your mama
> For a solid hour.
> Baby came out
> Screaming "Black Power!"

Anthropology Professor Roger Abrahams of the University of Texas quoted a similar rhyme in a 1962 article for *Journal of American Folklore*:

> I fucked your mother on an electric wire,
> I made her pussy rise higher and higher.
> I fucked your mother between two cans.
> Up jumped a baby and hollers, "Superman!"

Brown explained, "The real aim of the dozens was to get a dude so mad that he'd cry or get mad enough to fight. You'd say shit like, 'Man, tell your mama to stop coming around my house all the time. I'm tired of fucking her and I think you should know that it ain't no accident you look like me.' And it could go on for hours sometimes."

Amiri Baraka called the dozens "the African Recrimination Songs" that held lessons for every black kid: "How to rhyme. How to reach in your head to its outermost reaches. How to invent and create. Your mother's a man—Your father's a woman. Your mother drink her own bathwater—Your mother drink other people's. Your mother wear combat boots—Your mother don't wear no shoes at all with her country ass.... I fucked your mama under a tree, she told everybody she wanted to marry me. I fucked your mama in the corner saloon, people want to know was I fucking a baboon."

Richard Pryor dealt peripherally with the dozens during the filming of his 1983 concert movie *Richard Pryor Here and Now* in New Orleans. Momentarily caught off guard by someone shouting, "How's yo' mama?" he fired back, "Wh—how's my mama? I beg your pardon. I'll slap you in the mouth with my dick. One at a time, please. I'ma finish with this motherfucker ask me 'bout my mama. How's yo' mama? We be some mama-callin' motherfuckers this evening."

Yo' [your] mama, in fact, has become a catchphrase from the dozens that has spread into the general culture, as in "Yo' mama so ugly, they filmed *Gorillas in the Mist* in her shower!" or "Yo' mama is on my top ten list of things to do." (The contraction is nothing new: Kokomo Arnold, one of the first popular American blues musicians of the 1930s, recorded a song called "Twelves," in which he boasted about fucking an entire family: "I like yo' mama—sister, too.... Yo' mama, yo' daddy, yo' greasy greasy grandnanny.") The term has become so popular—some would say overused—that now it's mostly a defiant retort—"Yo' mama!"—that requires nothing further, except perhaps a clutching of the crotch for emphasis. In fact, over the last twenty years the mother-trashing aspect of the dozens has become an institution in American culture, with its own TV insult show (MTV's *Yo Momma*, which debuted in 2006), weekly *Saturday Night Live* routine (Chris Rock's "Mother Joke of the Day" segments during the 1993 season), books (James Percely's series of "yo' mama" *Snaps* joke books throughout the nineties, as well as Andrew Barlow and Kent Roberts's 2005 nerdy deconstruction of the dozens, including "Yo mama's so poor, her hierarchy of needs—determined per the definition of humanist psychologist Abraham Maslow—begins, like everyone else's, with water, food, and safety, but it does not go very far beyond 'safety' before it includes needs she cannot ever hope to meet," in *A Portrait of Yo Mama as a Young Man*), and recordings (such as the

Pharcyde's "Ya' Mama" and rap parodist MC Hawking's 2004 download "The Dozens," with lines like "Yo' mama's such a slut, the other night I had to park my dick on her ass and wait an hour to get in").

But why have the dozens been such an integral part of African American society over the past hundred years or more? In the late 1960s Swedish social anthropologist Ulf Hannerz studied ghetto boys playing the dozens in Washington, D.C., where the jousting was called "joning." Among the examples he recorded were:

> I fucked your mother on top of a wall.
> That woman had pussy like a basketball.
> I fucked your mother from house to house.
> She thought my dick was Mighty Mouse.

and

> I fucked your mother on a car.
> She said, "Tim—you're going too far."
> I fucked your mother in a Jeep
> She said, "Kenny—you're going too deep."

Hannerz theorized: "The boys have supposedly just found out that they have identified with the wrong person, the mother. Now they must do their utmost to ridicule her and thus convince everybody and themselves—but particularly themselves—of their masculinity and independence."

Roger Abrahams believed that playing the dozens was valuable for the black boy raised by a mother or other female family member, because "it has been a woman who has…threatened his potential virility with her values and her authority…. So he must exorcise her influence. He therefore creates a playground which enables him to attack some other person's mother, in full knowledge that that person must come back and insult his own. Thus someone else is doing the job for him, and between them they are castigating all that is feminine, frail, unmanly."

In 1939 Yale psychologist John Dollard, in an article called "The Dozens: Dialectic of Insult" for the magazine *American Imago*, took the subject into more forbidden territory when he wrote that

> the point of the game seems to be to bring up matters painful to the other person. The physical self of the addressed person is derogated; he is sometimes accused of incestuous behavior; adulterous acts are alleged on the part of persons "sacred" to him,

> i.e., those toward whom the accused does not himself have conscious sexual wishes.... It is evidently this element of exposure of the other person's unconscious wishes which is crucial. When the taunting speaker hits his unconscious mark he describes a repressed wish struggling for expression in his hearer.

At the same time, said Dollard, the speaker's "verbal expression of forbidden acts are in themselves gratifying," and his "accusations...represent in most cases repressed wishes of his own."

Hannerz was convinced that boys and young men were using the dozens to work through their conflicted feelings toward their mothers, because they generally abandoned the game by the time they reached adulthood and turned their attentions elsewhere. "It is clear in this case that the boys are not modeling themselves closely on the pattern of adult males, as the latter have stopped rhyming about their mothers," he wrote. Once the young man has reached an age where he's out from under his mother's authority, he no longer has the unconscious desire to goad other boys into insulting her.

But he doesn't leave the dynamics and the skills of the dozens behind. They've simply trained him for the next stage of development: standing up for himself in a more refined ritual, called "signifying." In its basic form, signifying is the elaborate use of innuendo to insult, tell on, or manipulate someone else by saying one thing but meaning another. The most famous illustration is the so-called "signifying monkey" of black folklore. The monkey is a little trickster who tells his jungle neighbor, a lion, that a local elephant has been saying terrible things about his family; if the lion was hip, he'd know that the monkey was just fucking with him, but instead he falls for the ruse and angrily heads off to challenge that dirty motherfuckin' elephant. As you might expect, the larger, more powerful pachyderm stomps the lion's sorry ass into the ground, which the lion deserves for being a chump, and the monkey gets a little jungle cred for setting it all into motion.

In the real world, black men signify not so much to stir up trouble between their neighbors (called "selling woof tickets"), but rather to show off the wit and verbal agility they've picked up from all those young years of playing the dozens. According to H. Rap Brown, "Signifying is more humane [than the dozens]. Instead of coming down on somebody's mother, you come down on them." One form of signifying is the rap, where a silver-tongued narrator puts himself into a scenario where he's the baddest cat around—out-fucking, out-fighting, and outsmarting everybody else (including the listener). As an example, Brown (who got his nickname from his rapping ability), recalls one of his own routines:

> Rap is my name and love is my game,
> I'm the bed-tucker, the cock* plucker, the motherfucker,
> the milkshaker, the record breaker, the population maker,
> the gun-slinger, the baby bringer,
> the hum-dinger, the pussy ringer...
> Women fight for my delight.
> I'm a bad motherfucker.
> * Cock here has its Southern meaning: a girl's vagina.

Then there's the more epic and hyperbolic version of signifying, called "the toast," which Roger Abrahams describes as "a narrative poem" recited "in a theatrical manner.... The subject treated is freedom of the body through superhuman feats and of the spirit through acts that are free of restrictive social mores (or in direct violation of them), especially in respect of crime and violence." They were basically street ballads, spoken rather than sung. In a culture dependent upon oral traditions going back to the *griots*—tribal historians and genealogists—of Western Africa, the heroes of the toast were often the ultimate bad mammy-jammers, the archetypes of motherfuckerdom. And the silver-tongued dudes who told these tales, confined only by the limits of their imaginations and oral skills, shared in the glory and infamy of these fantastic characters as they ran them through their epic paces. The toast's most famous, baddest motherfuckers were Shine, Stagolee, and Dan Tucker, archetypes created during slavery and later, in the case of Shine and Stagolee, inserted into historical events.

For example, when the British luxury liner R.M.S. *Titanic* sank in 1912 and carried fifteen hundred poor souls to the bottom of the Atlantic, many American blacks felt a sense of relief—and comeuppance. Since there were no Negroes among the crew or passengers, they didn't have to give up their seats on the lifeboats and go down with the ship, which under normal circumstances would have been their fate. But in the media storm that followed the tragedy, a popular toast began to spread through black American neighborhoods detailing what might have happened if a certain slick motherfucker named Shine had been aboard. The story had taken form in the late nineteenth century, sometime after Reconstruction, when blacks began migrating to Northern cities. But its roots went farther back into slavery. For example, one version of "Shine on the Titanic" began with the line "It was 1849 when the great *Titanic* went down." Anthropologist Neil A. Eddington offered another version that began "The 30th of May was a hell of a day, that's the day when the *Titanic* sunk"—even though the ship went down on April 14. Street chroniclers had simply updated the story by making it more newsworthy, without bothering to change the date of what had been some earlier disaster on an American lake or river.

"It was hell, hell, it was some fucked-up times, when that *Titanic* hit that iceberg and began to go down," went one version of the story. Shine was either a cook in the scullery or a boiler room worker in charge of one of the *Titanic*'s powerful engines; in either case, he went topside to warn the captain that water was pouring in below. Though the captain assured him that it was okay to return to his post because the giant pumps would keep the water out, Shine was having none of it: "I'm gon' take my chances in jumping overboard.... I'm going overboard when that water reach my ass." Before long, as it dawns on everyone else that the situation is dire, the captain's wife says, "Shine, Shine, please save poor me, I'll give you all the pussy you can see." But Shine tells her, "I got pussy on land, I got pussy on sea, I got twenty-five motherfuckers in New York just waitin' on me." Then the captain's pregnant young daughter begs, "Shine, please save poor me; I'll name this kid after thee." Shine says, "Bitch, you went and got knocked up, that's fine, but you got to hit this water just like old Shine." Then the millionaires beg, "Now, Shine, oh, Shine, save poor me, we'll make you wealthier than one Shine can be." But Shine, hip to their empty promises, tells them, "You hate my color and you hate my race; jump overboard and give those sharks a chase."

At that point Shine leaves the sinking ship. "Say, Shine hit the water with a hell of a splash, and everybody wondered if that black sonovabitch could last. Say, the Devil looked up from hell and grinned, say, 'He's a black, swimmin' motherfucker. I think he's gon' come on in.'" In one version, on the way to shore he fucks a forty-foot whale's blowhole. In another version a shark pulls up next to him and says, "Shine, Shine, you swim so fine, you miss one stroke and your black ass is mine." Shine replies, "You may be king of the ocean, king of the sea, but you gotta be a swimmin' motherfucker to out-swim me."

When he reaches a port town (in one variation it's Harlem), Shine heads straight for a bar, kicks down the door, and demands a hot rum toddy. In one toast he decides to fuck everybody in the place, male and female, and cuts a swath through them as efficiently as that iceberg had sliced through the *Titanic*'s steel hull; in another he gets too drunk before he has a chance to fuck anybody, and then "a little green fly flew up Shine's ass and tickled Shine to death." At that point Satan down in hell says, "All you bitches, you better climb the motherfuckin' wall, 'cause Shine gon' come back down here and fuck us all."

According to author Langston Hughes, in a 1951 *Negro Digest* article called "Jokes Negroes Tell on Themselves," the stud motherfucker in hell was a common motif in black jokes and folklore. "No sooner did the Negro set foot in hell than he grabbed the Devil's daughter and ruined her. Ten minutes later he enticed the Devil's wife behind a hot rock and ruined her. About this time the Devil's mother came along. The Negro grabbed her and ruined her. The Devil suddenly became aware of this mighty despoliation. Trembling, for the first time since he had been ruler of hell, he fell to his knees and called on God for help, 'Lord, *please*, take this Negro out of here before he ruins *me*!'"

Hughes, of course, had to clean up the toast's colorful prose for publication, and by so doing he also destroyed the meter of its poetry. In their 1968 Columbia University research project, detailed in a paper called "The Use of Language in the Speech Community," William Labov and his colleagues discussed the toast's elaborate rhythms and internal rhymes in the hands of a veteran street storyteller.

> The word *motherfucker* is used over and over again in just this way [to break up the regular meter]; by itself it would occupy a full half-line *A motherfucker*, but it is never used this way. Instead we have such intricate rhythms as:
>
> Shine said, "You round here lookin'
> like a pregnant pup.
> Go find that motherfucker that
> knocked your ass up."

Following another example, this time of the signifying monkey, the researchers state:

> Again, *motherfucker* is a decoration on the basic rhythm which prevents any reversion to a doggerel meter.
>
> He said, "He's a big burly motherfucker, weigh about
> ten thousand pounds,
> When he walk, he shake the motherfuckin' grounds."
> Say, "He a big peanut-eatin'
> motherfucker, big long flappy ears,
> Been turnin' out these parts for the last ten years."

Probably the most famous toast is for Stagolee—or Staggerlee or Stackerlee or Stack Lee—who has been celebrated in countless blues recordings going back to the 1920s, not to mention Lloyd Price's sanitized R&B paean ("Stagger Lee") that stayed at number one on America's pop charts for four weeks in 1959. But mostly he was the center of an oral soap opera that black people regaled each other with around a fire, a dinner table, or a bottle of whiskey at the end of another hard and humiliating day in Jim Crow America. Cecil Brown, the author of *Stagolee Shot Billy*, recounted that when he was a boy on a North Carolina tobacco farm in the late 1950s, "to young black field hands sitting in the shade of a tree at the end of the tobacco road, Stagolee was as impulsive, as vulgar, as daring, and as adventurous as they wanted him (and themselves) to be. My uncles, who were my male role models, and their friends recited their rhymed, obscene praise of Stagolee's badness."

The real Stagolee was a thirty-one-year-old pimp, nightclub proprietor, and riverboat line owner (the *Stack Lee* was one of his boats) named Lee Sheldon, who shot a local grifter named Billy Lyons in a St. Louis saloon on Christmas day of 1895. Because Sheldon and his victim were both well known in the black community, his trial got a lot of press, even in the white papers. Sheldon was sentenced to the Jefferson City Penitentiary for thirteen years. After a brief parole in 1909, he returned to prison for another crime and died there of tuberculosis in 1912. Though his murder of Lyons was well documented, it's anyone's guess how much of the various Stagolee toasts were based on his own exploits and what was borrowed from earlier folk ballads. Certainly his milieu—St. Louis's thriving whorehouse district—made him an ideal figure for black folklore, thanks in part to the growing presence of blues-singing levee camp workers, muleskinners (dirt graders), and steamboat roustabouts working up and down the Mississippi River, who used the basic template of his story as a framework for their own defiance, imagination, and wishful thinking. It didn't take long for "Stack Lee" Sheldon to morph into bad-ass superman Stag Lee, loved by women, respected by black men, feared by white men, and causer of trouble wherever he went.

In one well-known version, he stopped in at a dive called the Bucket of Blood for a bite to eat and got offended when the bartender slid "a stale glass of water" and "a fucked-up piece of meat" onto the bar.

> I said, "Raise, motherfucker, do you know who I am?"
> He said, "Frankly, motherfucker, I just don't give a damn."
> I knowed right then that chickenshit was dead.
> I throwed a thirty-eight shell through his motherfucking head.

Musicologist Alan Lomax discovered "Stagolee" in ballad form during a field trip down the lower Mississippi around 1910, while Sheldon was still alive. From 1924 to the present, the song has been recorded more than two hundred times, but perhaps the most definitive version is Mississippi John Hurt's 1928 Delta blues classic, "Stagolee." Stagolee had a reputation as "a bad motherfucker" in the song's informal street versions. In fact, "I'm a bad motherfucker" was traditionally the final line. But Hurt and the other blues singers who told his story on wax couldn't say those words, so something very primal and integral to Stagolee's story was always missing.

There were many other bad motherfuckers immortalized in street poetry, such as Joe the Grinder, Pimpin' Sam from Alabam, Stavin' Chain, Dolomite, and Petey Wheatstraw the Devil's Son-in-Law, but the most successful within the commercial music business was Dan Tucker, or Bad Man Dan, who possessed such verve and prowess that women instantly fell under his spell. Dan could fight with his fists or his gun, but he was generally too busy romancing the most beautiful and rich women in town, black and white. Of course, whenever his story was presented for public entertainment beyond the street corner and neighborhood bar, Dan had to be toned down and his trysts restricted to the dark side of the tracks, where he couldn't commit any transgression like fucking the white mayor's daughter in the ass. Dan Tucker popped up everywhere in the early music industry. In nineteenth-century minstrel shows he was Dan Tucker, Dan Cupid, or Jim Dandy. (Dandy would show up again in 1956, when R&B singer LaVern Baker praised his various rescues on the national pop charts.) In the 1890s May Irwin recorded a hit called "Crappy Dan," with the lyric: "My name is Crappy Dan, I'm a spo'tin' man" (a "sportin'" man, i.e., a pimp). Sheet music exists for a 1921 song called "The Lady's Man, Dapper Dan from Dixieland," notable for a section in which Dan, a Pullman porter (a prestige job for blacks in those days), shouted the names of passing towns where he had various women waiting for him. Several years later, blues empress Bessie Smith sang his praises in "Hustlin' Dan" and "Kitchen Man"—"wild about his turnip tops, like the way he warms my chops." In 1937 Georgia White revealed the exploits of "Dan the Backdoor Man"—a common reference in blues music to a stud sneaking in the back door as the woman's boyfriend or husband is heading off to work. Songwriters welcomed Dan as a handy man to have around, if only because his name rhymed with handy man, or lover man. But Dan *Tucker* the baddest mother*fucker*, well, songwriters couldn't be seen with him in Tin Pan Alley. On the 1957 single "Deacon Dan Tucker," singer-songwriter Jesse Belvin had to settle for "I'm Deacon Dan Tucker, and I'm looking for a pretty girl."

Dan did make his way near the top of the pop charts in 1951 when a polished black vocal group called the Dominoes recorded a million-selling song—co-written by a middle-aged Jewish woman and a young black choir leader—called "Sixty-Minute Man." In a basso profundo, singer Bill Brown boasted, "Listen here, girls, I'm telling you now, come up and see ol' Dan. I rock 'em, roll 'em, all night long, I'm a sixty-minute man." Radio stations wouldn't spin it, because Miss Anne might hear it and get her ears singed, and then the FCC would bust through the doors and rip their broadcasting licenses off the walls, but thanks to the ever-present jukebox, "Sixty-Minute Man" got steady play around the country.

But to truly be a bad motherfucker, a black man had to sing his own praises without hiding behind Dan Tucker or Jim Dandy. One of the first successful artists to toast himself on a commercial record was Ellas McDaniel, known as Bo Diddley, so named because as a boy he built and played his own homemade guitar, known among Mississippians as a diddley bow. Along with recording a boastful hit record in 1955 called "Bo Diddley," he introduced the dozens on an even bigger hit four years later called "Say, Man," and toasted himself on songs like "Who Do You Love?" ("I walked forty-seven miles of barbed wire, I use a cobra skin for a necktie, I got a brand new house on the roadside, made from rattlesnake hide"). Diddley based the song on the verse of an old toast called "The Great MacDaddy," whose lines went: "I've got a tombstone disposition, graveyard mind. I know I'm a bad motherfucker, that's why I don't mind dyin'"; on vinyl Diddley re-imagined it as "Tombstone hand and graveyard mind, just twenty-two and I don't mind dyin.'" Not until the 1970s could a bad motherfucker put it out there loud and clear. His name was Rudy Ray Moore, and he called his superhuman alter ego Dolemite. But I've saved him for another chapter.

When gangsta rap burst on the scene in 1988, like a fusillade from an AK-47, with N.W.A.'s (Niggaz With Attitude) *Straight Outta Compton* album, the group rebottled the old toasts in new raps. One of their numbers, "Something Like That," featured member Lorenzo Patterson introducing himself by name as MC Ren…

> and for the street it's Villain,
> and strapped with a gat, it's more like Matt Dillon
> on *Gunsmoke*, but not a man of the law.
> I'm just the baddest motherfucker that you ever saw.

> See, I peep and then I creep on a fool,
> get my blood pressure high but still stay cool.
> Dig a grave of a nigga lookin' up to me,
> that really had the nerve that he could fuck with me...
> You know, it's MC Ren kickin' mucho ass.

Nowadays most black recording artists, along with more than a few sports heroes, present themselves to the world as bad, pimped-up, superhuman motherfuckers—or "sucker-motherfucker stoppers," to quote N.W.A.'s Dr. Dre—possessing all the money, bling, and compliant young bitches that any man could wish for. To paraphrase the title of ex-basketball star Dennis Rodman's autobiography, they're "bad as they wanna be." They're standing at the center of a glitzed-out, blitzed-out celebrity culture that screams "Bad motherfucker!" even in the rare instance they don't want to say it out loud themselves.

But despite their gains in show business, African Americans today are still relatively powerless in the greater scheme of things. Until the fundamentals change, the wounded pride of the young black male will continue to require the balm of the bad-motherfucker myth.

SIGGY & ED: A COMPLEX TALE

"What's up, motherfucker?"

—Josephus (Gregory Hines) greeting King Oedipus (Ronny Graham)
in Mel Brooks' *The History of the World: Part I* (1981)

In case you're not familiar with Oedipus, here's a verse by satirist Tom Lehrer that sums up his historical predicament:

> There once lived a man called Oedipus Rex.
> You must have heard about his odd complex.
> His name appears in Freud's index,
> Because he loved his mother!

I mean *really* loved his mother. We're not talking about some poor mama's-boy schlub like that rocket scientist in the Mike Nichols and Elaine May comedy sketch from the 1960s who's reduced to cooing baby-talk when his mother emotionally pounds him into a puddle of guilt. No, this is the real thing. A real motherfucker.

In fact Oedipus, the mythical king of Thebes who married his own mother and sired four children with her, is the most famous motherfucker of them all. Sigmund Freud named his most important stage of psychosexual development after him. But the fable of Oedipus, as presented by Greek playwright Sophocles and others, had little to do with incest and more to do with fate and its inexorable hold on our lives. Oedipus and his wife Jocasta didn't know they were related, and when they eventually discovered their transgression, their self-punishment completed what Aristotle would later call one of the greatest tragedies of them all.

Besides Sophocles's play *Oedipus Tyrannus* (*Oedipus the King*, or *Oedipus Rex*) from circa 425 B.C., there are many references to Oedipus that suggest he may have been based on a historical character. In the eighth century B.C., Homer noted in Chapter XI of the *Odyssey* that during Odysseus's journey through the underworld, he "saw fair Epicaste [Jocasta], mother of King Oedipus whose awful lot it was to marry her own son without suspecting it. He married her after having killed his father, but the gods proclaimed the whole story to the world; whereon he remained king of Thebes, in great grief for the spite the gods had borne him; but Epicaste went to the house of the mighty jailor Hades, having hanged herself for grief, and the avenging spirits haunted him as for an outraged mother—to his ruing bitterly thereafter." Every Greek playwright worth his salt, from Euripides to Aeschylus, later essayed the Oedipus legend, but Sophocles's classic—among the few that survived extant—is the one that people read today.

So how do a mother and her son marry each other without realizing what they've done? Well, in Greek mythology, with all its oracles and crazy coincidences, anything could happen—and did. Here's how Sophocles laid it out, partly through a series of flashbacks. Since Greek is Greek to me, my reference is Francis Storr's 1912 translation.

When the Oracle of Delphi tells Laius, the king of Thebes, that his newborn son will grow up and murder him, Laius and his wife Jocasta decide to thwart destiny by piercing the baby's feet and ordering the court shepherd to abandon the crippled infant to the wolves in the forests of nearby Mount Cithaeron. (In those days folks often left unwanted or deformed babies in the wilderness.) Instead, the shepherd, figuring nobody will ever be the wiser, passes the baby along to another shepherd in Corinth, on the other side of the mountain. This shepherd in turn delivers the baby to Polybus, the king of Corinth, whose queen has been unable to give him an heir. Polybus takes to the boy immediately and names him Oedipus (pronounced *oy-DEEP-us*) because of his swollen feet. (*Oed* means "swelling" and survives today as edema, or tissue swelling, which is spelled *oedema* in British English; and *pus* is the Greek stem for foot—look no further than the eight-tentacled octopus.)

All right, now that the story needs a goosing, along comes another oracle. (Oracles were generally old women who hung out at shrines, which were also called oracles, and channeled prophecies, which were also called oracles, from deities. The main job of oracles was to inject a new plot development whenever a playwright wrote himself into a box or simply ran out of ideas.) It's roughly eighteen years later when a drunk at a banquet confides to Oedipus, "Thou art not true son of thy sire." Oedipus is naturally shocked by this revelation, but just to make sure this isn't some shit-faced shenanigan, he heads for an oracle to confirm his parentage. The oracle can't tell him anything about that, but she's getting this other text message directly from Mt. Olympus that says Oedipus will someday kill his father and schtup his mother. This discombobulates Oedipus so much that he decides on the spot to never return home again, just to make sure that the prediction doesn't accidentally come true. But as destiny would have it, he starts hobbling on his walking stick towards his true birthplace, Thebes, where his real parents still live. Descending from Mount Parnassus to the foothills, he meets an imperious older man with a retinue of several people at a crossing of three highways. When the man rudely orders him off the road, Oedipus declares that no heir to the throne of Corinth will move aside for anyone. The man either strikes Oedipus in a serious case of road rage or runs over one of his already sensitive feet, and that really pisses off our hero. So perhaps by using his staff like some deadly Ninja stick, he does a Bruce Lee act on everybody, including the old man, leaving only one survivor to run away. Oedipus then continues on his merry way to Thebes and thinks no more about it.

He settles down there and prospers by solving a local problem called the Riddle of the Sphinx. (Sophocles doesn't go into detail about this riddle because he doesn't want the Sphinx, a querulous bitch who's a real pain in the ass for everyone, to get in the way of his story, but other writers tell us that the riddle was "What animal has four legs in the morning, two legs at noon, and three legs in the evening?" Oedipus answers "Man," because babies crawl on all fours and old folks use a walking stick, just like Oedipus does [hence his insight into the riddle].) After this correct answer sends the Sphinx packing, Creon, the interim ruler of Thebes since King Laius's recent murder at the hands of marauders, turns the crown over to Oedipus and offers him the hand of his sister Jocasta, Laius's widow.

Again years pass. King Oedipus and Jocasta have four children, and since none of them look like inbred hillbillies from Toadsuck, West Virginia, nobody's the wiser. Everything is going very well because, as Mel Brooks put it in *The History of the World: Part I*, "It's good to be the king." In other words, it's time for another oracle to fuck things up. (Actually, this is the part of the story where Sophocles begins his play, and we learn all the previous information in narrative flashbacks.) When a deadly plague suddenly hits Thebes, Oedipus sends Creon to Delphi to ask the oracle what's causing it. Creon returns with the news that the plague is punishment for the murder of Laius. "This stain of blood makes shipwreck of our state," Creon reports. Oedipus places a curse on the killer, whomever he may be, because "I his blood-avenger will maintain [Laius's] cause, as though he were my sire." For good measure, if the murderer has somehow ingratiated himself to Oedipus and escaped punishment right under his nose, "I pray the curse I laid on others fall on me." Oops, bad idea. And then Oedipus makes another mistake by demanding the presence of the local prophet Teiresias. When the old man at first refuses to talk, Oedipus threatens him with death, which prompts Teiresias to tell him, "Okay, asshole, you asked for it" (my words, not Sophocles's) and fesses up: "Thou art the man, thou the accursed polluter of this land…thou art the murderer of the man whose murderer thou pursuest." Then he adds, "I say thou livest with thy nearest kin in infamy, unwitting in thy shame." Rather than believe Teiresias, Oedipus accuses him and Creon of cooking up this story to put Creon on the throne. Teiresias wisely heads for the hills while he's still got his head, but not before he delivers a parting shot that "the dogging curse of mother and sire one day shall drive thee, like a two-edged sword, beyond our borders, and the eyes that now see clear shall henceforward endless night." Jocasta intercedes for her brother Creon by reassuring Oedipus that oracles are unreliable. Why, she and Laius had once been told by the Oracle of Delphi that their own son would kill his father, and look what happened: Laius was murdered instead by highwaymen at a crossroads, long after his only son had died in infancy. So much for oracular credibility! But Oedipus tells her that he himself once killed a man at a crossroads. What if the victim were Laius? Jocasta assures him that a witness reported to her that robbers had done the deed. But Oedipus isn't satisfied with this answer. He sends for the lone survivor. Maybe the guy had simply been ashamed to admit that only one dude, and a cripple at that, was able to kick everybody's ass.

At this point in the story, perhaps Greek audiences would have been clamoring for more confusion, so when Sophocles introduces a new character to the court, it's not the witness Oedipus has summoned, but rather a messenger from Corinth to tell Oedipus that his father Polybus has peacefully died in his bed. That means that Oedipus is now not only King of Thebes but also King of Corinth. If one crown, to quote Shakespeare's Richard II, is a "heavy weight" upon the head of a monarch, imagine how two must have felt, especially in the days before chiropractors. The message also means the oracle had wrongly predicted Oedipus's patricide, "[u]nless the longing for his absent son killed [Polybus] and so I slew him in a sense." Oedipus then wonders aloud, "Must I not fear my mother's marriage bed?"

Oedipus's question evokes an answer from Jocasta that would become one of Sophocles' most controversial passages. "This wedlock with thy mother fear not thou. How oft it chances that in dreams a man has wed his mother! He who least regards such brainsick phantasies lives most at ease." Sigmund Freud himself probably marked those words with the late-nineteenth-century's equivalent of a yellow highlighter in his well-thumbed copy of *Oedipus Rex*.

"But my fear is touching her who lives," says Oedipus. "'Tis no secret Loxias [Apollo] once foretold that I should mate with mine own mother."

The messenger, who's been standing by listening to all this, asks Oedipus, "Who may this woman be whom thus you fear?"

"Merope, wife of Polybus," Oedipus tells him.

"But there's nothing to fear," the old messenger says, letting the cat out of the bag. "She wasn't your mother, nor was Polybus your father." He explains that he had once been a mountain shepherd, and that "a herdsman of the king" from Thebes had personally delivered Oedipus to him as an infant, and he in turn had "loosed the pin that riveted [his] feet" and given him to the king. Jocasta, suddenly realizing in horror that Oedipus is her son, cries, "Ah mayst thou ne'er discover who thou art!" and rushes out of the room.

Next, the herdsman to the royal household is brought in, and the Corinthian messenger recognizes him as the shepherd who brought him the infant Oedipus. Coincidentally, this shepherd *also* happens to be the lone survivor and witness to Laius's murder at the crossroads, which he now admits was not committed by robbers but rather by one man. Now Oedipus, like Jocasta, knows the truth. He rushes off to find her, but she has already hanged herself. Distraught, he takes the golden brooches from her robe and jabs their pins into his eyes, blinding himself. Creon crowns himself king, and Oedipus goes into guarded seclusion, insisting that he should be left to die in Cithaeron's wilderness as the gods had originally intended. Sophocles later brought him back in a sequel called *Oedipus at Colonus*, but he was simply a blind old man in a supporting role to his daughter, Antigone.

Homer was more forgiving: In the *Odyssey* he wrote that Oedipus continued his reign after Jocasta's death. But mostly the Greeks wanted punishment without redemption, because the ultimate crime was patricide and the penultimate crime was mother-humping, unless it was the other way around. It doesn't matter, because Oedipus was guilty of both, and his culpability was 100 percent because under Greek law a guilty act didn't require a guilty mind, if you're following along with the *CliffsNotes*. Intent was irrelevant.

Oedipus's story has been retold and re-jiggered many times in every medium. In the seventeenth century John Dryden wrote a popular drama about him. Italian film director Pier Paolo Pasolini updated the story to the twentieth century in his 1967 *Edipo re*. Steven Berkoff, in his play *Greek*, set the story in London's East End during the Margaret

Thatcher era, with Eddy standing in for Oedipus and poverty for the plague and a more forgiving morality for the heartless Greek code. But the guy who put Oedipus into the modern history books and medical texts was that wild and crazy Viennese guru of neuroses himself, Sigmund Freud.

Since Oedipus had no discernable mommy issues or grudges against his father, and since he had in fact left Thebes in the first place to avoid even the possibility of fulfilling the dreaded prophecies, he was not a very good poster boy for Freud's famous infantile sexual complex. No matter. Freud, like the Greeks, didn't care about intent. Oedipus did the deed, and since there weren't any other convenient mammy-jammers in history or myth, that was good enough.

According to Freud, the human mind is like a little house with a great big dark cellar. (I'm purposely avoiding the iceberg that's usually floated out to illustrate his theories.) Most of it is belowground, out of sight, a hidden cache of images and emotions—the unconscious—that motivates most of our waking thoughts and determines our behavior, even though this subterranean entity was fully formed by events that occurred before we were five year old. Freud developed psychoanalysis as a way of probing into this abyss, uncovering dreams and phobias and figuring out what went wrong. One of his most important postulations was that to become a happy human being, every child first must pass through several stages of sexual development—and any poor soul who flunks anywhere along the way is doomed to pathological relationships, psychic traumas, and gnawed-to-the-nub fingernails. Out of this came what Freud called the *Oedipus complex*. "Every new arrival on this planet is faced by the task of mastering the Oedipus complex," Freud wrote in *Three Essays on the Theory of Sexuality* (1905); "anyone who fails to do so falls a victim to neurosis." (Freud originally applied Oedipus to both sexes; only later did his acolyte, Carl Jung, call the female counterpart the Electra complex, based on another Greek myth that Sophocles also wrote about, even though Electra didn't have sex with her father but rather avenged his assassination by assisting in the murder of her mother. Lot's two daughters might have been a better example if the Book of Genesis hadn't left them nameless.)

Anyway, here's the Oedipus complex in a nutshell. During every boy's psychosexual development (roughly between ages three and five), he wants to bang his mother, but first he has to get rid of that big lug standing in his way, i.e., Dad. At the same time, the boy (projecting his own murderous desires) fears that his rival is likely to punish him first by cutting off his little love-bestirred tallywhacker that's creating all the trouble.

If all is going well during this stage, our sybaritic toddler will back down, give up his carnal designs on his mother, and resolve that if he can't fight the old man, he might as well join him—and thus assume his father's masculine identity. But if he continues with this emotional dilemma, says Freud, the little fellow will forever side with his mother against his father and become one of those mama's boys who's still living at home and eating her cooking when he's fifty. Worse, he could become a homosexual who's still living at home, eating mama's cooking, and listening to Céline Dion records. (Girls who don't navigate through the Electra complex properly develop "penis envy.") How this happens, according to Freud's paradigm, is that a dominant, over-affectionate, or seductive mother will play along with the child's sexual fantasy, not by actually having sex with him, but by bringing him as a confidant into her own troubled, adversarial relationship with her husband or with men in general.

Being an avid student of Greek literature, Freud connected Oedipus with infant sexuality as early as October 15, 1897, when he wrote his friend Wilhelm Fliess that "I have found, in my own case too, falling in love with the mother and jealousy of the father, and I now regard it as a universal event of early childhood.... If that is so, we can understand the riveting power of *Oedipus Rex*." In his first major work, *The Interpretation of Dreams* (1899), Freud observed: '[I]t is the fate of all of us, perhaps, to direct our first sexual impulse towards our mother and our first hatred and our first murderous wish against our father. Our dreams convince us that this is so. King Oedipus, who slew his father Laïus and married his mother Jocasta, merely shows us the fulfillment of our own childhood wishes." It would be another decade, however, before he would borrow Carl Jung's idea of "complexes" and specifically identify an Oedipus complex in a paper called "A Special Type of Object-Choice Made by Men" (1910). In the early 1920s, when he put together his "developmental theory" of how a little boy's "erotogenic zones" change from oral to anal to phallic, Freud rolled the Oedipal struggle into the "phallic stage" and revised his theory, claiming that as a boy enters puberty he solves his sexual conundrum not by moving past his desire to fuck his mother but rather by repressing it. In other words, all future sexual objects are stand-ins for Mom (if the boy has successfully traversed the phallic stage) or Dad (if he hasn't).

One guy who may have suffered from Oedipal angst was Julius Caesar. A century and a half after Caesar's death in 44 B.C., biographer Suetonius Tranquillus noted in chapter VII of his *Life of Julius Caesar*: "In the stillness of the night...[the young Roman emperor] dreamt that he lay with his own mother; but his confusion was relieved, and his hopes were raised to the highest pitch, by the interpreters of his dream, who expounded it as an omen that he should possess universal empire; for that the mother who in his sleep he had found submissive to his embraces, was no other than the earth, the common parent of all mankind." Another biographer, the Greek historian Plutarch, repeated the same episode. As fate would have it, one of Caesar's assassins, Marcus Brutus, may have been similarly afflicted with Oedipal yearnings; he was the son of Servilia, Caesar's early mistress and longtime love, known for being a really hot babe. Plutarch believed that Brutus was Caesar's illegitimate son, which added a much deeper, darker meaning to Caesar's last words, "Et tu, Brute," as the younger man fiercely plunged his dagger into Caesar's heart. (Apropos of nothing, Caesar also fathered a child with Egyptian Queen Cleopatra VII, a daughter of siblings; her mom was her aunt and her dad was her uncle, and she had only one set of grandparents.)

As the cornerstone of Freudian psychoanalysis, the Oedipus complex has taken a lot of lumps over the years. Most people, especially conservatives, don't want to think about semi-flaccid infantile hard-ons, mother-lust, or a subconscious determinism that trumps free will; America's evangelical Christian right has condemned Freud as Satan's agent for even bringing it up. At the same time, most liberals today prefer to believe that the homosexual framework has a genetic origin, thanks to the work of Simon LeVay, Ivanka Savic Berglund, and others, and therefore dismiss Freud's paradigm altogether. Regardless, the Oedipus complex has assumed a life all its own, and poor Oedipus will be taking the rap for being history's quintessential motherfucker for time immemorial.

In conclusion, let's end where we started, with Tom Lehrer's "Oedipus Rex," from a live album that sold very well in 1959:

> So be sweet and kind to Mother, now and then have a chat.
> Buy her candy or some flowers or a brand new hat.
> But maybe you had better let it go at that!

BABY SAID

HALF A WORD!

"Trouble he's a mutha, no he ain't mine to tame
money is his lust, confusion is his game"

—poet Wanda Coleman, "Trouble on My Doorstep Blues" (1987)

"ONE TOUGH MOTHER!" screamed the electronic billboard above Sunset Boulevard in Hollywood, ballyhooing a new (May 2008) E! Channel reality series called *Living Lohan*, starring Dina Lohan, mother of errant, erring party-girl actress Lindsay Lohan. The ad line captured the three definitions of the word *mother* as we know it today.

Yes, Dina is Lindsay's biological mother (that's the first meaning), but the big flashy MOTHER hovering above heavy traffic was also mocking motherhood (the second, ironic meaning), because the bottle-blonde wench with the winch-tightened face had become a tabloid symbol of the destructive stage mother—called "pimp mama" in today's dishy parlance—who struggles to compete with her celeb daughter and in the process enables all sorts of bad habits and risky behavior. When Mingling Moms, a social network of Long Island yentas with too much time on their hands, hailed Dina as their "Mother of the Year" on Mother's Day 2008, bloggers and media wags acted as if the Red Crescent had honored Hezbollah for its humanitarian efforts. One columnist noted that nobody could tell if the Mingling Moms were kidding because their deadpan expressions—the result not of any poker-strategy classes but rather their "Botox-plugged faces"—betrayed nothing. TMZ.com more succinctly put it: "dina-lohan-is-a-good-mutha-alright." So long, Mother Goose; hello Mommie Dearest, you rotten mother.

This use of *mother* as a pejorative takes us to *mother*'s third meaning, which is really a nuance of the second meaning, to wit: an abbreviated, socially acceptable *motherfucker*—with the "fucker" as silent as the "ts" in *beaux-arts*. How socially acceptable? Well, nobody complained about that MOTHER beaming from billboards all over Los Angeles. And television audiences apparently didn't blink an eye when New York detective

Cyrus Lupo (Jeremy Sisto) on NBC's legacy drama series *Law & Order* told a kidnapper whose female victim survived in an early 2008 episode, "You're one lucky mother," or when a member of Snoop Dogg's posse on basic cable's TNT network's *Monk*, in a 2007 episode called "Mr. Monk and the Rapper," told Adrian Monk (Tony Shalhoub), "I hate that motherffff.... I hate that fella."

Just to be sure I've made my point here, let me reiterate: *Mother* is short for *motherfucker*. And though it's as unresolved as a knuckle-rapped "shave and a haircut" without the "two bits," we've become very comfortable with it. Everyone's heard the old joke about the black infant gurgling "Mother" and sending the overjoyed father running to his wife yelling, "Honey, baby done said half a word!" Just as President George W. Bush could utter "As we say in Texas, that's bull!" in front of TV cameras without conjuring offensive images of steaming piles of pasture poop, you're now free to call somebody a motherfucker as long as you cut the word in two and leave the second half implied. It could be said that all three meanings of the word apply equally to Mrs. Lohan, if by *motherfucker* we're talking about a formidable force of nature.

The near respectability of this abridged form owes a little to Saddam Hussein, Iraq's baddest mother, who boasted on January 6, 1991, that foreign troops who dared to march into Kuwait, which Hussein's army then occupied, would be immolated in *Umm Al-Ma'arik*, or "the Mother of all Battles"—a reference to a bloody Arab victory over the Persians nearly fourteen hundred years ago. Since "mother of" is an Arabic figure of speech that means ultimate or greatest, Hussein was threatening a fiery destruction that looked like something out of the Book of Revelation. But when the U.S. and its coalition of allies sent Hussein's vaunted war machine scrambling in a panic toward Baghdad, the expression overnight turned into a joke (the Mother of All Retreats) and has remained so ever since. What hard-partying frat boy hasn't boasted at one time or another of blasting the Mother of All Farts? What put-upon husband hasn't suffered from the Mother of All Mothers-in-Law? When a temperamental TV actress (Shannen Doherty in one case) and a celebutante (let's make her Paris Hilton) verbally clash in a hoity-toity nightclub, the *New York Post* is likely to report it as "The Mother of All Catfights." And sometimes the joke can get very dark, as when Pentagon generals named their powerful new 21,000-pound firebomb the Mother of All Bombs, or MOAB; the Army's public relations office, fearing the designation was dangerously frivolous, quickly declared that the acronym actually meant the more awkward Massive Ordinance Air Blast bomb, which should have been MOABB. (Apropos of nothing, the biblical Moab was the offspring of his grandpa Lot, a daughter-fucker, though it must be said that Lot, like Oedipus, was an innocent party.) More recently, people often drop the "all," as when National Public Radio reporter Tovia Smith in May 2008 called the conspicuously gigantic Chevy Suburban "the mother of SUVs." This in turn corrupted the earlier English idiom "mother of," meaning progenitor or antecedent, as in "necessity is the mother of invention" or a certain giant sequoia is "the mother of the Big Sur forest." Now that we had a perfectly respectable meaning for mother that was roughly the equivalent of the short form of motherfucker, "you mother" and "nasty mother" and any other dirty rotten mother was ready for primetime. Even *The Scientist*, a respected publication that bills itself as "The Magazine of Life Sciences," felt free in July 2006 to give a story about the ruthlessness of Mother Nature the title "A Nasty Mother." *Motherfucker* has thus been transformed and downgraded into one of George Carlin's "two-way words" (prick, balls, et al) rather than the deadliest of the seven deadly words you can't say on television—as long as you only pronounce the first two syllables. Everyone knows what you mean, but pretends not to.

It may come as no surprise that this is not completely new. Take, for example:

"You *mother*!"

The curled lip, the arms akimbo, the bitter emphasis on the second word, the line's enclosure within a medium close-up shot inserted into the scene specifically for its delivery—all of it leaves no doubt that what the female star of Warner Bros.' *Night Nurse* means to say is "You motherfucker!"

What makes it so shocking is that the nurse is a young Barbara Stanwyck.

The year is 1931.

Though Hollywood's infamous Production Code Administration already existed that year, its restrictive rules concerning what was unacceptable in film entertainment wouldn't kick in for another three years, when the Catholic Church decided, through its Legion of Decency, to appoint itself America's moral guardian of the movies. The studios in 1931 were enjoying what is now called their "pre-Code era," and Warner Bros. more than the others was known for pushing boundaries. Still, the creative minds behind *Night Nurse*—director William A. Wellman, screenwriter Oliver H.P. Garrett, and dialogue specialist Charles Kenyon—had to be careful how they handled this scene. The setup was that Stanwyck's character, a private nurse, was trying to alert an alcoholic socialite (Charlotte Merriam) that the people around her were trying to starve her daughter to death in order to plunder the child's trust fund. When it becomes obvious that the drunken woman doesn't care, Stanwyck calls her "a cruel, inhuman mother.... Why do poor little children have to be born to women like you?" She knocks her to the floor, and that's when the director cuts to the medium close-up and Stanwyck spits out her line. Sixty years later, when *New York Times* critic Pauline Kael wrote a thumbnail review of Night Nurse's videocassette reissue, all she could talk about was that "memorable moment." When I saw a clean print of the film in 2006 at a crowded American Cinematheque screening at Hollywood's Egyptian Theater, the audience gasped and tittered. And no wonder; seen today in its early black-and-white context, Stanwyck's "You *mother*!" has more impact, more outright shock value, than an effusion of *motherfuckers* in *Snakes on a Plane Meet the Bad Mamma Jammas.*

Censorship enforcer Joseph Ignatius Breen of the PCA put a stop to that in 1934, but he didn't completely foil the infrequent writer or director from sneaking one past the gatekeepers. In 1952, at RKO Studio, Richard Fleischer shot a spare little B-movie called *The Narrow Margin* about a tough cop (Charles McGraw) accompanying a lady (Marie Windsor), who he thinks is an equally tough mob widow, on a train from Chicago to Los Angeles. At the beginning of the film, when McGraw takes possession of the witness and walks her toward the door, Windsor tells the Chicago cop who's been minding her, "So long, mother," again with a biting, hard-bitten emphasis on the word. The kiss-off could be taken as her parting shot at the overprotective bodyguard she resented, but with a dame this nasty the other meaning also applied. The line almost certainly wouldn't have passed muster at Warner Bros., Paramount, or MGM in 1950, but RKO was an edgy studio whose eccentric king, Howard Hughes, didn't always play by the rules.

If anyone put the unadorned-but-pregnant-with-meaning "mother" on the cultural map, it was Richard Buckley, known to connoisseurs of cool as Lord Buckley, a white comic who delivered monologues in black hipster patois shaped within an exaggerated King's English. Born in California's Mother Lode gold country in 1906, Buckley gigged in mob speakeasies during the 1930s and soaked up the speech rhythms of jazz musicians. He developed a kind of *Amos 'n Andy* act that by 1950 crystallized into his bohemian Lord Buckley shtick of reciting incidents from history, literature, and mythology in jive. In a conversation with Michael Monteleone and Walt Stempek, Buckley pal Vaughn Marlowe recalled the restrictions Buckley faced in those days.

> His real shocking piece, the underground piece, was Jonah and the Whale, because it came as a surprise. Talking in public about marijuana on a stage was an absolute no-no. You never heard anyone do that. And to realize that he had this whole story built around a guy smoking dope in the belly of a whale was funny, it was hilarious because it was forbidden. He couldn't have gotten an audience's attention any faster if he'd say motherfucker, which of course was also an absolute no-no. Lenny Bruce did die for our sins.

(For an elaboration on that last thought, see Chapter 8.)

So Lord Buckley limited himself to the first half of the word to keep out of trouble. In a 1951 performance of Lincoln's Gettysburg Address, he referred to the Civil War killing ground—"the hassle site of some of the worst jazz blown"—as "Gettys-mother-burg." In a 1958 routine called "Supermarket" he ranted that the giant stores had originally kept prices low by making shoppers do all the work schlepping their carts through the aisles, and yet even after the markets later raised their prices, "you're still pushin' the mother cart. Still workin' for 'em. And you'll even take carts and push them into other carts."

In another routine called "The King of Bad Cats," recorded in 1960 just before his death, Buckley retold the Marquis de Sade's tale of Prince Minski, a nineteenth-century Hannibal Lector whom Buckley called a "mad mother": "Prince Minski was a cat that been with it, he gave it away, he took it back, he put it down, he picked it up, he jumped it, he tumped it, he ripped it, he wrapped it, he tapped it, he papped it, he rigged it, he gigged it, he danged it, he donged it, he blanged it, he jumped around, he split it, he made every mother scene there was to make!"

Minski lured a couple of hungry paupers to his island castle with the promise of a sumptuous feast (which turned out to be human flesh). The first thing they came to was a wall

> about eleven-hundred-damn-ninety-two foot high. A cloud-pushin' mother and God knows how thick. With a small uranium door in it, you know what I mean. And the boat slide up to it and Minski take his big old long stalk leg and he kick the big button and the door swung open, and *whooosh*, they go through and *kabang*—that mother slammed like doomsday's break! And they finally come to another big deep underground.
>
> *Boom*, that one slam and they come to a drawbridge.
>
> *Brrrrt*, up and down. They cross up back. Now they

> come to a wall so tall it take seventeen French acrobats to see the top of this mother with a small rang-a-dang door in it. And they open that door and *boom*, they slipped through and *boom* that mother blammed and the minute it did he turned to them and he said: "I'm the baddest cat in this world! There ain't nothin' I ain't done."

In part because Lord Buckley was their patron saint, 1950s beatniks embraced the word *mother*. In a popular 1958–1961 NBC-TV detective drama called *Peter Gunn*, which featured Henry Mancini's cool-jazz soundtrack and a stable of Beat characters, everybody hung out at a club called Mother's, loosely based on hipster joints like San Francisco's hungry i, where impresario Enrico Banducci was known to berate hecklers and belligerent customers with "You noisy bunch of mothers!" and throw them out. (The formidable Mother in *Peter Gunn* was played by Hope Emerson, a 230-pound actress who stood over six feet tall.) And thanks to a beatnik character, "mother" was cleverly dropped into a teenage pop single in 1959. Voiceover specialist Bob McFadden, who would later become the voice of a sixties TV cartoon character named Cool McCool, linked up with budding poet Rod McKuen to cut a silly novelty called "The Mummy." The record was simplicity itself. McFadden, in his best schlemiel voice, whined, "I'm a mummy, I scare people. Watch what happens when I walk up to somebody. 'Hi, I'm a mummy!'"—followed by the screams of an unwary passerby. After a couple of these, he approaches a beatnik (McKuen) and announces, "I'm a mummy!" The hipster responds with a deadpan "That's cool."

"I'm a *mummy*!" McFadden insists.

"You mean you're a mother."

"No, I'm a *mummy*! Aren't you gonna scream?"

"Oh yeah. Like, 'help.'"

"The Mummy," credited to Bob McFadden & Dor (Rod spelled backwards) and released on Brunswick Records, slipped into the Top 40 without anyone complaining.

Even traditional Catskills nightclub comics like Belle Barth, who spritzed double-entendre jokes between croaky workouts of creaky show tunes, were tossing *mother* around like a rag doll in the early sixties. "Sayonara, mother!" Barth shouts to one customer leaving the room during her act. Poking fun at another member of the audience, she quips, "She's the mother of the year, isn't she? She kiddin'? I've been called a mother for ninety years." When the company that released Barth's party records teamed her with another Borscht Belt veteran named Pearl

Williams, it called the LP *Battle of the Mothers*. Neither one of the old broads looked the least bit maternal.

Jazz magazines put the word into national parlance. The November 1961 issue of *Metronome*, for example, described the popular New Orleans artist Al Hirt thusly: "Make no mistake, Hirt is a talent. A brilliant trumpeter. Not a Miles, not a Clark Terry. Not a jazz trumpeter. But a mother, nonetheless." In other words, the writer liked him. Among jazz players and aficionados, a mother was a cat who could really blow. Blow like a motherfucker.

By 1966, as the word motherfucker was popping up more frequently in mainstream American speech, *mother* became a marketing problem for Verve Records, a subsidiary of MGM Records, when it wanted to sign an eccentric new rock artist named Frank Zappa. Verve demanded that Zappa do something about the name of his band. "The record company that finally signed us didn't want to sign a group called The Mothers," Zappa told a Finnish TV interviewer in 1974.

> Because—do you want the real reason or the television reason? In the United States the term "mother" is short for "motherfucker" and the term "motherfucker" can be used in a variety of ways. One way, it means somebody who stuffs it up their mother, and in another way it means a musician who is supposedly good on his instrument. And at the time, in the place where we were working, all the guys who were in the group were the best available in Pomona.... So I thought we should call the group The Mothers. As I explained, short for the other word. The record company said, "No, you'll never be able to sell any records like that," and they said, "If you don't change the name of the group we're not going to give you a contract." They wanted to call it The Mothers' Auxiliary, which is a name that is usually attached to parent organizations in the States. So I said, "No, out of necessity, we will become The Mothers of Invention."

But that newly minted panhandle took prominence only on the cover of their first album, *Freak Out!* (1966). The inside of the LP's foldout jacket identified Zappa as "leader and musical director of THE MOTHERS of Invention," and on the back cover, one "Suzy Creamcheese" began her liner notes with "These Mothers is crazy.... None of the kids at my school like these Mothers." When Zappa got contractual control of designing his subsequent LP covers, he made certain that "The Mothers," in giant flowery letters, dominated his second album, *Absolutely Free*; he tucked the words "of Invention" underneath, in tiny print. Outside the offices of Verve Records, the group remained known as Frank Zappa and The Mothers.

(Incidentally, during an East Coast tour in 1967, Zappa and The Mothers were asked to lip-synch along with their recording of "Son of Suzy Creamcheese" during an appearance on a WOR-TV show called *From The Bitter End*, shot at a famous Greenwich Village folk club. Staring into the camera, Zappa mouthed the words "you're a motherfucker" over and over rather than mime the lyrics. As soon as the station producer realized what was going on, he cut to a "Please Stand By" sign. Fortunately for everyone, the song was less than a minute and forty seconds long. The performance is available on various DVDs and on YouTube.)

Woody Allen made his own point on the matter and turned the word into a punch line in a scene near the end of his 1971 comedy *Bananas*, when a South American prosecutor calls former Miss America Sharon Craig (Dagne Crane) to the stand to testify against Allen's character, Fielding Mellish, in a spoof of mindless beauty pageant blather.

> Prosecutor: Tell the court why you think he is a traitor to this country.
>
> Sharon Craig: I think Mr. Mellish is a traitor to this country because his views are different from the views of the president and others of his kind. Differences of opinion should be tolerated, but not when they're too different. Then he becomes a subversive mother.

By the early 1970s, as the rebel ethos of the anti-Vietnam movement was taking hold in working-class America, a Texas coffeehouse troubadour named Ray Wylie Hubbard wrote an indictment of the nation's heartland called "Up Against the Wall, Redneck Mother," inspired by LeRoi Jones's famous 1967 line—though Hubbard worked an actual mother into the lyric to de-fang the word. One of Hubbard's touring buddies, Jerry Jeff Walker, liked "Up Against the Wall, Redneck Mother" so much that he recorded it in 1973 for what turned out to be a successful album called *Viva Terlingua*. The song became such a popular progressive country music anthem that many other artists jumped onboard, including Bobby Bare, Kinky Friedman, the Riders of the Purple Sage, and the Hemorrhage Mountain Boys (singing the song in Pig Latin).

> He was born in Oklahoma [West Virginia, in Wylie's original],
> His wife's name's Betty Lou Thelma Liz

> And he's not responsible for what he's doing
> 'Cause his mother made him what he is.
> And it's up against the wall, redneck mother,
> Mother, who has raised her son so well.
> He's thirty-four and drinking in a honky-tonk.
> Just kicking hippies' asses and raising hell.
> Sure does like his Falstaff beer,
> Likes to chase it down with that Wild Turkey liquor;
> Drives a fifty-seven GMC pickup truck;
> He's got a gun rack; "Goat ropers need love, too" sticker.

This barroom sing-along tapped into a growing malaise among blue-collar Americans. They sensed that the good ol' U.S.A., having lied to them a few years earlier and packed them off to a pointless war, was peaking as a world power and had nowhere to go but down. Vietnam was already in the shitter. The crippling 1973 OPEC oil embargo let everyone see that the fist squeezing Uncle Sam by the short 'n' curlies belonged to a cartel of Arab rag-heads. And the growing number of German and Japanese cars and pickups on the road reminded them daily that manufacturing jobs were slipping away. As young white guys gazed into their uncertain future, they smoked marijuana and listened to antisocial hard-grind rock and the bitter "outlaw" country music of Waylon & Willie and David Allen Coe. It was cathartic to stand with your redneck brethren in a honky-tonk with a few mugs of beer under your DEATH BEFORE DISHONOR belt buckle and sing "Up against the wall, redneck mother*fucker*." FM radio and jukeboxes couldn't play *that*, but the shorthand version was perfectly okay, and everyone still got the cruel joke.

In fact, *mother* was being tossed around so casually that everybody from black funksters to rock 'n' roll white nationalists adopted the more informal *muther*, or *mutha*, which removed it even further from *motherfucker*. (Incidentally, India's sewage-ravaged Mutha River, which runs through the tangy city of Pune, has no connection to what we're talking about here.) In a refreshing exception to all the social misunderstandings, blacks and whites across the political spectrum could get together on *something*. For example, a 1970s all-white Minnesota jug band called itself the Sorry Muthas. Writing liner notes for a CD many years later, Garrison Keillor noted, "The Sorry Muthas were successful too, though they were careful not to overdo it and to break up before they could make too much money." By 1977, when Polydor Records released a James Brown album called *Mutha's Nature*, the word was solidly R&B.

In 1980 both spellings had reached Great Britain, as evidenced by *Metal For Muthers*—the name of two anthology albums of 1970s British heavy metal bands—and a twelve-inch compilation EP of four thrash rock groups called *Muthas Pride*. In 1982 a New Jersey punk and hard-rock promoter created Mutha Records to market his groups' recordings. The 1990s gave us the metal bands Heavy Sonic Muthers and the White Trash Muthers, hip-hopping Poison Clan's *2 Low Life Muthas* CD, and British electronica artist Substance's "Nasty Muthas" track. In case some dim bulb out there didn't get the picture, George Clinton and Digital Underground rerecorded Funkadelic's funky "(Nut Just) Knee Deep" on a 1996 *Greatest Funkin' Hits* CD as "Knee Deep (Deep as a Mutha Funker Remix)." In 2000 La Wanda Paige, best known as Aunt Esther on Redd Foxx's 1970s sitcom *Sanford and Son*, explained it further with the title of her comedy album *Mutha Is Half a Word*. More recently, a New Zealand rock band called Flight of the Conchords put a fine point on it by recording a song called "Mutha'uckas," lamenting that in the course of your business day, "there's too many mutha'uckas 'uckin' with [your] shi—."

Early on, there were two different films called *The Muthers. The Muthers* (1968) was seventy-four minutes of cheesy, peekaboo sex drama starring polyester & lace queen Marsha Jordan and late-fifties *Playboy* Playmate Virginia Gordon as a couple of suburban lounge lizardesses swapping and swinging in hotly-lit splendor, while their busy husbands are off making money in the city and their kids smoke dope on the poolside patio. As in any good morality tale, they all pay for their sins in the end. *The Muthers* was a typical example of the soft porn that died out as soon as the hardcore theatrical stuff emerged in the early 1970s.

Eight years later came a second outing called *The Muthers*, a girls' prison blaxploitation flick shot in the Philippines by writer-director Cirio H. Santiago, a protégé of B-movie king Roger Corman. Again a former *Playboy* Playmate was recruited: Jeannie Bell of TNT Jackson fame, starring as half of a braless, bouncy, modern-day pirate duo (with Rosanne Katon) that rescues Jeannie's sister (Trina "Thumper" Parks) from the clutches of a slave trader. The tag line says it all: "Out of the steaming slave markets come the ravaging sea-savages…the Muthers!" Typical dialogue is Parks's line after a snake bites one of her ample boobs: "Just like every other snake I ever met—can't leave my tits alone." Dame Judy Dench couldn't have delivered it any better.

Nowadays the preferred spelling is *mutha*, and it practically defines the current repackaging of the 1970s blaxploitation era, when many of the kick-ass protagonists were ballsy, titular (as in eponymous, not physical endowments) women such as *Coffy* and *Foxy Brown* (both Pam

Grier) and *Cleopatra Jones* (Tamara Dobson). Melvin Van Peebles, the filmmaker who practically invented the genre with his 1971 opus *Sweet Sweetback's Baadasssss Song* (which codified the word *bad-ass*), wrote and directed a 2008 adventure spoof called *Confessionsofa Ex-Doofus-ItchyFooted Mutha*. Meanwhile, *Bad Muthaz* and *Bad Brothas Mean Muthas* are two separate DVD series that are reissuing seventies black films starring Fred "The Hammer" Williamson and others.

The name has even been attached to products, like Harley Davidson's Dyna bub two-inch Step-Muthers, i.e., exhaust pipes for the 1991–98 Dyna models. And Evisu, an upscale Japanese designer of denim and footwear, has a brand of sneakers called Muthas Head.

Then there's the successful *Big Mutha Truckers* video game (introduced in 2002 and upgraded since then) that puts you in the cab of an eighteen-wheeler, trying to win "A Trial by Truckin'" in Hick State County, where bikers, truck-jackers, and the corrupt police are all out to disable your truck and get a piece of your profits. (*Mother trucker* had already gained the tolerance of middle-America; as early as 1996, *Mother Trucker: The Diana Kilmury Story* was an Emmy-winning TV movie about a modern female Teamster leader who bucked the system.) Also, if you need accessories (camping shells, etc.) for your pickup truck in California, you can visit one of several Mother Truckers stores (*mothertruckers.com*).

Writing in *Black Journalism Review* (*blackjournalism.com*), Askia Muhammad calls this mainstreaming of *mutha* and *mother* the new "M.F. Culture." As he sees it, "The influence of Black life on America has greatly expanded the boundaries of what's now permissible in polite White society." Muhammad contrasted today's cross-the-board entertainment with Redd Foxx's "licentious" but relatively tame party records from fifty years ago. "Redd Foxx...only gave the suggestion that his humor was forbidden.... Today, the forbidden is no longer forbidden.... I recently saw an advertisement for a tractor-pull contest—loosely defined as a "motor sports" event—on a children's cable channel that described the competitors as some 'Bad Mother-Truckers.' That's about as close as I can imagine anyone coming on your basic kid-accessible television to saying the once-forbidden M-F-word."

Some might call it black America's payback—and it's a mutha. (Quick, hold that thought and turn to the next chapter.)

PAYBACK'S A MUTHA!

"Yeh, payback is hard, hmmm, a head rolling in the streets!"

—Amiri Baraka, —*The Autobiography of LeRoi Jones* (1984)

New Jersey homegirl Wahida Clark was doing time at Alderson Federal Prison in West Virginia for conspiracy, fraud, and money laundering when she mouthed off at the wrong person and landed in solitary confinement for eight months. Don't do the crime if you can't do the time, right? Well, Wahida put her downtime to good use and wrote a novel about a smokin' little diva who sleeps her way into the world of glamour, glitz, and guns. She called it *Don't Knock the Hustle*, but her publisher retitled it *Payback's a Mutha*, a term popular in hip-hop music since the 1980s. When the book became a bestseller in 2006, the press dubbed Wahida the Queen of Thug Love Fiction.

What "payback's a mutha" is really saying, of course, is "payback's a muthafucka." But what does that mean, and where did it come from?

Payback itself is a late-twentieth-century compound noun from the verb phrase "to pay back." Paying back generally meant the return of a loan, but the Book of Romans in the New Testament (or more specifically its seventeenth-century English translator) has preserved a darker meaning: "'Vengeance is mine; I will repay,' saith the Lord." Thanks to several generations of movie gangsters going back to Edward G. Robinson in *Little Caesar* and Jimmy Cagney in *The Public Enemy* (both 1931), the King James Bible seems to have won out. Paying back is now an American synonym for "getting back at." But to qualify for what has evolved into modern payback, retribution couldn't be merely "tit for tat" or the ancient Code of Hammurabi's "eye for an eye." No, it had to be an almost superhuman force or a collective punishment on the level of a backlash, or blowback, or "the chickens coming home to roost" (an unpopular allusion that Malcolm X made in 1963 following the assassination of JFK). Payback isn't just giving muthafuckas what they deserve, it's giving it to them in wrathful spades, which means that when this payback comes, it won't be just bad—it'll be as bad as a motherfucker. It will in fact *be* a motherfucker!

Take this recent exchange on a website, when a white blogger who complained about how blacks treated him in Atlanta was answered by an African American: "The feeling that white people feel in atlanta is the feeling that black people feel in iowa or anywhere that is mostly white, payback is a mutha!"

"Oh, so it's acceptable for black people to be racist then, in the name of 'payback,'" the blogger responded. "Tell me, how do you go about discerning which white people are deserving of 'payback'?"

Or take Amiri Baraka's comment to interviewer Kalamu ya Salaam on the June 22, 2003, page of online *African American Review*, as he remembered back when he was still LeRoi Jones, perusing the mostly glowing first reviews of his 1964 play *Dutchman* in New York's mainstream newspapers: "A strange sensation came over me; the sensation was 'Oh, you're going to make me famous,' but then I'm going to pay all of you [white] people back. I'm going to pay you back for all the people you have fucked over. That was clear. There was no vagueness about that.... When I got that feeling, it was a terrific feeling. It was like some kind of avenger or something. It was: Now, I'm going to pay these motherfuckers back!" Jones soon afterward abandoned his Beat career and white wife in Greenwich Village and migrated uptown to Harlem to begin his Afrocentric, anti-Western, "black arts" movement.

Black payback as comeuppance went national in 1995 after the mostly black O.J. Simpson jury acquitted the ex-football celebrity despite overwhelming physical evidence that he murdered his wife and her boyfriend. Pundits asked in print, "Was this payback for all the black men who were railroaded into prison by white juries over the past hundred years?" Likewise, the race riot that had left sections of Los Angeles in flames three years earlier was payback not just for a jury acquitting four Los Angeles cops who mercilessly beat a small-time criminal named Rodney King on videotape, and not just for a local Korean grocer being slapped on the wrists for shooting black teenager Latisha Harlins to death (also on videotape), but for all the shit that black people had to put up with. "We wanted to hurt [Korean store owners] physically, economically, raise their insurance rates—anything we could for payback," black activist Najee Ali told the *Christian Science Monitor* in late April 1992. Or as hip-hop militant Sister Souljah (Lisa Williamson) explained it in "The Hate That Hate Produced": "They say two wrongs don't make a right, but it damn sure makes it even."

Los Angeles rapper Ice-T (Tracy Marrow), fronting a heavy metal group called Body Count in 1994, expressed this racial resentment in "Masters of Revenge": niggaz were "masters of payback, inciters of chaos, messengers of rage, all we wanna do to you is what you did to us. All we wanna take from you is what you stole from us. You took my past, I want your future.... You took my parents, we want your children.... Payback, muthafuckas!"

Payback got its first public airing three decades ago on a revenge record by the Godfather of Soul himself, James Brown. It was the early 1970s, after the Civil Rights movement had hardened into Black Power; ghettoes around the country had gone up in flames, and blacks were talking about the big payback for all those years of oppression. Brown had been turning street slogans into musical riffs for years, such as "Say It Loud—I'm Black and I'm Proud" and "I Don't Want Nobody to Give Me Nothing (Open Up the Door, I'll Get It Myself)." In 1973, with an album from four years earlier called *It's a Mother* already under his belt, Brown recorded a number one R&B (and number twenty-six pop) funk hit called "The Payback (Part 1)."

Brown knew how to hedge his bets in even his edgiest songs. In the opening lines of "The Payback," he appealed to his black listeners' resentment toward the power structure: "Hey! Gotta gotta pay back! (*Vocal chorus*: the big payback!) Revenge! I'm mad! (*Chorus*: the big payback!) Got to get back! Need some get-back! Payback! (*Chorus*: the big payback!) That's it! Payback! Revenge! I'm mad!" Then he turned the song on its head by reducing the lyric to a plaint of black people wronging each other rather than being wronged by The Man. "Get down with my girlfriend, that ain't right! Hollerin', cussin', you wanna fight, payback is a thing you gotta see, brother, do any damn thing to me, sold me out for chump change (*Chorus*: yes you did!).... Get ready, you mother, for the big payback (*Chorus*: the big payback!)"

That the payback would be a muthafucka, or at least a mutha, was implied. Fourteen years later, in 1987, straight outta Compton came gangsta rap co-founder King Tee (Roger McBride), who removed the ambiguity by recording a song for Capitol Records called "Payback's a Mutha." For King Tee the term was a modern equivalent of George Herbert's observation from four hundred years ago that "Living well is the best revenge," and he rubbed it in with a little bit of signifying: "See, not long back when I was seventeen, when I walk in the jam, suckers look at me mean, they wouldn't give me respect, told girls I was wack. You shouldn't have did that, brother. I'm here for the payback.... See, money I got, 'cause I'm a pro at this trade, you thought you got away, but you're about to get paid, you told girls I was wack, shouldn't have did that, brother. Look, I'm King Tee and my payback's a mutha.... Ya better get ready, my payback's a mutha." Five years later, King Tee's rap inspired the title of an album by the group No Face called *Payback (Is a Mutha)*. This refined definition of the term seemed to sum up black America's obsession with 1980s super-flash bling-bling culture and its over-conspicuous over-consumption as a means of getting over on everybody else and erasing those earlier years of humiliation.

Most middle-class white parents today would probably concede that black America got its payback through the viral success of hip-hop culture, with all its fashion accouterments and antisocial attitude adjustments. As early as 1988, when N.W.A. (Niggaz With Attitude) were selling millions of gangsta albums to suburban whites—especially the sons of divorced mothers who were miming the Oedipal dysfunctions of no-daddy ghetto boys—and injecting words like *bitch*, *ho'*, *muthafuckas*, and *yo' mama* into the national teen lexicon, payback was already on its way to muthahood. Ice-T might complain that these legions of white youngsters crip-walking in baggy pants with their baseball caps turned backwards were "the aural equivalent of voyeurs, thrilled by this crazy world that has nothing to do with their experience," but rap was immersing them in Askia Muhammad's "M.F. Culture" and creating a whole new multi-billion-dollar business opportunity for the Ice-Ts of the world.

Once a catchy phrase gets into the language, there's no stopping it—especially on the music charts. By the mid-nineties payback had shed its political tint and turned into bad karma for cheating lovers. R&B singer Gerald Levert, at the end of his 1998 pop hit "Thinkin' Bout It," bemoaned how all those years of treating women like crap were coming back to haunt him now that he'd found a special lady to fall in love with. "For the life of me I just can't conceive, why I just can't leave you, why you do this to me, baby. I feel like a fool but what can I do, your love gots me weak, baby. Why must I endure your constant greed, your endless need to be so damn freaky. Now I understand, 'cause it once was me, yes payback's a mother, baby.... Guess payback's a mother."

Nowadays, of course, payback's no longer just a mutha or a mother because there's no reason to hide the complete word. That's why Lil' Kim, in "Heavenly Father" (2003), rapped: "You ain't promised tomorrow. Karma's a motherfucker.... Payback's a motherfucker, put that on the Stuy." That's why Jake the Flake & the Flint Thugs titled a song "Payback's a Muthafucker" (2006), and why Sublime, a punk-ska trio from Long Beach, California, introduced "New Song" that same year with the lines: "I heard that payback's a motherfuckin' bitch, but I won't stress and I won't switch, and I would not take my life.... Payback's a motherfuckin' blast."

Loose in the culture, it also became a staple of film dialogue. As early as 1985, in the low-budget *Stryker's War*, a returning Vietnam vet (Robert Rickman) takes on a murderous American cult. Holding up a dead rat he had stabbed with his bayonet, he announces, "This sucker's confirmed! Payback's a motherfucker!" And just ten years later, the phrase had become so familiar—and so worn out—that in the comedy *Friday*, Chris Tucker's character, Stormy, goofed on it by taking it back to its roots: "Gimme my goddamn money.... Yeah payback's a motherfucker, nigga." (Cable television's USA Network later cleaned up [i.e., overdubbed] "payback's a motherfucker, nigga" for middle-American tastes by transforming it into the perfectly respectable "payback's a mother, ain't it. Peace.")

It's that respectability that's threatening to kill the expression altogether, especially among blacks, who tend to reject anything as soon as whites embrace it. African American novelist Jervey Tervalon, author of *Dead Above Ground*, remembers his Los Angeles boyhood as being "filled with wonderfully expressive phrases but few with as much impact as 'Payback is a mutha.' But now the term is passé. Nowadays you hear 'payback's a bitch' far more frequently than 'payback's a mutha'. For whatever reason anything with mutha seems forced or dated."

In other words, now that payback's just a bitch, only revenge can be a muthafucka.

MAMMY,
HOW I LOVE YA,
HOW I LOVE YA!

"Mammy—the term of endearment used by white children to their negro nurses and to old family servants."

—*Bartlett's American Dictionary* (1859)

Of all the words we have for mother, none is more pregnant with dark emotions than *mammy*, a variant of *mama*. (It is less frequently spelled mammie.) With all its associations of maternal love mixed with humiliation and subjugation, the word crosses the American color line like no other. The *Oxford English Dictionary* places its benign origins in early-sixteenth-century England and Ireland, most likely a child's diminutive taken from the word mam, which itself is related to mammary, since the tit is usually a child's earliest, most intimate contact point with its mother. But mammy as we know her today comes from the early-eighteenth-century South, where female slaves were not only the heart of the black family, but also the caretakers and wet nurses for the children of their white masters.

Though many prosperous families continued to keep full-time black nannies and housekeepers well into the twentieth century, whites generally abandoned the word *mammy* in the 1930s, even though full-bodied mammy figures trudged into modern pop culture as devotional objects of Tin Pan Alley minstrelsy (e.g., Al Jolson's "My Mammy"), film and TV characters (Mammy in the 1939 film *Gone With the Wind*—which garnered Hattie McDaniel an Oscar for Best Supporting Actress—and Beulah in the postwar radio and TV shows of the same name), corporate mascots (Quaker Oats' Aunt Jemima), and kitschy figurine collectibles like salt 'n' pepper shakers and cookie jars.

For African Americans the dehumanized *mammy*, like the word *nigger*, was so tinged with shame and in dire need of reclamation that they kicked her around and turned her on her head, so that today mammy survives as a pejorative, without any sentimentality, to mean mothers and grandmothers. "It's another one of those words that we [blacks] can use but you'd better not," says Gloria Stanford, a retired California social worker in her seventies. In *Pimp: The Story of My Life*, a 1967 memoir, ex-whoremonger Iceberg Slim (Robert Beck) recalls how one of his street mentors told him, "Any sucker who believe a whore loves him shouldn't a fell outta his mammy's ass." Another pimp named Weeping Shorty greets him later with, "Well kiss my mammy's dead ass, if it ain't Macking Youngblood." Slim later hears that before Shorty died of an overdose, his last words were, "Well kiss my dead mammy's ass if this ain't the best 'smack' I ever shot." Black prostitutes referred to johns looking for older women as "mammy freaks." Because of the mammy's traditional role as the Miss Fix-It of the house, anything cheap and slapped together with whatever materials are handy is called "mammy-rigged," a variant of jerry-rigged. And wealth is "money's mammy," a kind of "mother of" reference, as when novelist Langston Hughes, in a 1950s essay, lamented the financial difficulties of being a black writer competing with whites "[w]ho wrote the best selling plays and novels and thereby made money's mammy."

Along with mother, mammy—specifically *your* mammy—naturally came in for her fair share of abuse whenever young black men played the dozens. In 1938, when jazz pioneer Ferdinand "Jelly Roll" Morton recorded an interview for the U.S. Library of Congress, he sang a song called "The Dirty Dozen," which he remembered picking up in a Chicago whorehouse "about nineteen-eight." Based on the dozens, it relied on mammy for the punch line. "The main theme was the mammy [who] wouldn't wear no drawers," Morton told interviewer Alan Lomax between verses he played on the piano. "I thought it was a very disgusting mammy that wouldn't wear some underwear."

> Oh, you dirty motherfucker,
> you old cocksucker,
> you dirty son of a bitch,
> you're a bastard,
> you're everything,
> and yo' mammy don't wear no drawers.
> Yes, you did me this, you did me that,
> you did your father,
> you did your mother,
> you did everybody you come to,
> 'cause yo' mammy don't wear no drawers.
> That's the dirty dozen,
> oh, the dirty lovin' dozen,

the dirty dozen,
yes, yo' mammy don't wear no drawers.
So I had a bitch,
wouldn't fuck me 'cause she had the itch,
yes, she's my bitch,
oh, yo' mammy wouldn't wear no drawers.
Said, you dirty motherfucker,
you old cocksucker,
you dirty son of a bitch,
oh, everything you know,
oh, you're a low bitch,
yes, yo' mammy won't wear no drawers.
I went one day
out to the lake,
I seen your mammy
a-fuckin' a snake.
Aw, she tried, she tried to shake,
aw, she shuck, shake on the cake,
Mammy don't wear no drawers.

The moral of the song? If your mammy is a dirty low-down slut that don't wear no underwear, what the fuck does that make *you*?

The insult has a long pedigree, going back at least four-hundred-plus years to William Shakespeare, who wrote in Act I Scene 1 of *Timon of Athens*:

> Painter: Y'are a dog.
> Apemantus: Thy mother's of my generation. What's she, if I be a dog?

And what does that make you?

In 1930, when popular blues artist Memphis Minnie recorded "New Dirty Dozen," she naturally had to clean up the lyrics considerably, leaving everything, even yo' mammy's drawers, to the imagination:

I know all about your pappy and your mammy,
your big fat sister and your little brother Sammy,
your auntie and your uncle and your mas and pas,
they all got drunk and showed their Santa Claus.

Sociologist John Dollard, in a 1939 article called "The Dozens:

Dialectic of Insult," gave this example:

> If you wants to play the dozens
> play them fast.
> I'll tell you how many bull dogs
> your mammy had.
> She didn't have one,
> she didn't have two,
> she had nine damned dozen,
> and then she had you.

Mammy certainly got no respect when the popular rhythm-and-blues group the Clovers made an underground recording in 1954 called "Rotten Cocksuckers Ball," with the opening line: "Cocksuckin' Sammy, get your motherfuckin' mammy, we're goin' downtown to the cocksuckers ball." I should point out that "cock" in this context, as in Jelly Roll Morton's "The Dirty Dozen," was the Southern strain, meaning a vagina rather than a penis.

According to writer Zora Neale Hurston, the phrase "Dat's your mammy" was the black equivalent of a then-popular white insult rejoinder, "So's your old man," with its unspoken addendum "And what does that make *you*?" In Hurston's 1942 "Story in Harlem Slang," one of her characters, a sporting cat named Sweet Back, challenges another pimp with, "If you trying to jump salty, Jelly, that's your mammy."

Though "yo' mammy" has been superseded today by "yo' mama," she occasionally still pops up to take her lumps. In the 2004 book *Yo' Mama!: New Raps, Toasts, Dozens, Jokes & Children's Rhymes From Urban Black America*, editor Onwuchekwa Jemie offers this one:

> I fucked your mammy from Baltimore,
> she had hairs on her pussy that swept the floor,
> she had bumps on her ass that would open the back door.

Mammy also has her own section in the motherfucker dictionary. Among the variations are mammy-tapper, mammy-jumper, mammy-humper, mammy-thumper, mammy-rammer, mammy-huncher, and mammy-lover—the last two being favorites of John Oliver Killens's black middle-class characters in his popular 1971 novel *The Cotillion*. But the term that gained the greatest pop-culture appeal was mammy-jammer, thanks to its alliterative rhyme. Jazz clarinetist Mezz Mezzrow used the line "Those Jim Crow mammy jamming whites" in his 1946 memoir *Really the Blues*, and listed "mammy jamming" in the glossary along with "motherferyer," defining each one as "an incestuous obscenity." We're not talking here about mere screwing; mammy jamming required humongous male endowment stuffing mammy's jellyroll, leaving not a millimeter unfilled, in what could best be described as action-packed fucking.

In 1964, when every R&B artist in Los Angeles was coming up with a new dance step in the wake of the Twist, the Pony, and the Mashed Potato, musicians Don Harris and Dewey Terry, who were better known for their crossover compositions ("I'm Leavin' It Up to You" and "Big Boy Pete") than their Don & Dewey singles, recorded a song about doing the mammy jammie, with lyrics like: "You ought to see my pretty girl Annie, when she back up and do the mammy jammie at the hootenanny." But singing about jammin' mammy must have been a little too suggestive for public taste, because Specialty Records didn't get around to releasing the recording until 1970, and even then it blunted the title on the label to "Mammer-Jammer," which by then seemed to be the preferred pronunciation in the neighborhood.

But since modern blacks have a habit of replacing "er" with "a" at the end of words like *nigger* and *mother*, it didn't take them long to settle on mamma (perhaps a compromise between mama and mammy) and jamma—still two separate words but without the hyphen. Nobody was fooling anybody, of course, because a mamma jamma was rarely just a mamma jamma; he, she, or it was a "bad mamma jamma." Like a bad motherfucker, a bad mamma jamma started off as a mean stud or a tough situation, but by 1980 it had been flipped on its head to describe a perfectly built, well-endowed young woman who in all respects was the antithesis of the traditional mammy. In other words, voluptuous and sassy Pam Greer in a mini-skirt and platform heels had replaced roly-poly, googly-eyed and rag-headed Hattie McDaniel. (Though it must be said that McDaniel's Mammy was a tough cookie, belligerent with all the black men on the plantation and acerbic with Miss Scarlett and Rhett Butler.) Leon Haywood, a Los Angeles pianist and producer, wrote a slammin' bass-heavy song called "She's a Bad Mamma Jamma (She's Built, She's Stacked)" for a young Detroit vocalist named Carl Carlton. Perhaps worried about radio stations and retail chains complaining about *mamma jamma*, the record company changed the spelling on the label to "She's a Bad Mama Jama (She's Built, She's Stacked)" to create a little distance between it and any hint of incest, even though Carlton clearly pronounced it mamma jamma on the track.

Her body measurements are perfect in every dimension,

she's got a figure that's sho' 'nuff gettin' attention.
She's poetry in motion, a beautiful sight to see,
I get so excited viewin' her anatomy.
She's a bad mamma jamma,
just as fine as she can be, hey,
she's a bad mamma jamma, oh,
just as fine as she can be.

The record was a huge disco-funk hit—both as a 45-rpm single and as a two-sided ten-inch dance mix—that kept black clubs (and maybe a few white ones) rocking in 1981. It spawned several covers (all using the more common spelling of "mamma jamma") by Stevie Wonder, the Ohio Players, Parliament, the Gap Band, and Rick James, among others, and later became one of those heavily anthologized tracks that exemplify their era. In rapper Foxy Brown's 1997 "Big Bad Mama," her producer sampled and remixed a few of Haywood's original instrumental lines and overdubbed them with the R&B-soul vocal group Dru Hill:

She's a bad mamma jamma,
just as foxy as can be.
Hey, she's a bad mamma jamma,
just as foxy as can be.

Carlton's recording later showed up on the soundtrack of *Undercover Brother*, a 2002 spoof of black movies from twenty years earlier. Even *The Parkers*, a black-themed TV show on the UPN network, ran an episode called "She's a Bad Mamma Jamma" in its fourth season, on April 28, 2003.

Most whites understood that *mamma jamma* was a stand-in for *motherfucker*, though many of them probably missed the mammy connection, and they likewise picked up on its definition as a perfectly built, 10-rated woman. But more than blacks, whites generalized the term to describe cars, guns, guitars, amplifiers, and any other cherished personal items that might be characterized by the pronoun *she*, often prefaced by the word smokin', as in: "This old sunburst Stratocaster is a smokin' mamma jamma."

Still, mamma jamma isn't always ready for white-themed prime time. TV writers have often fallen back on "mama yama" (pronounced *mahma yahma*), a term that originally surfaced in the 1950s with a rhythm & blues record called "Yama Yama, Pretty Mama" by Los Angeles artist Richard Berry, who's best known today for writing "Louie Louie." On *Seinfeld*, Cosmo Kramer (Michael Richards) sometimes described slutty-looking women as “mama-yamas.” And on *Buffy the Vampire Slayer*, a beautiful lesbian witch named Willow Rosenberg (Alyson Hannigan) sometimes referred to herself as “a hot mama-yama,” as in a 2001 episode called “All the Way” in which she mused, “Hard to believe such a hot mama-yama came from humble, geek-infested roots.” It's even harder to believe that mama-yama came all the circuitous way from motherfucker-infested roots.

But beyond these weak and distant cousins, mammy has disappeared from white culture, and there are many black folks wishing the word would leave the American vocabulary altogether. History professor Deborah Gray White, in *Ar'n't I a Woman*, wrote that mammies were hardly the mythological figures they've been made out to be. “In reality, the household mammy's work was never done and she was often worked past exhaustion.... In addition, the myth would have us believe that mammy was a respected and revered servant who was almost a member of the family; in truth, when mammy became too old she was oftentimes turned out of the house with very little regard for her survival. This precise atrocity occurred to Frederick Douglass' mother, a mammy who had outlived her usefulness and was then left in a mud hut in the forest to perish.”

R.I.P., mammy.

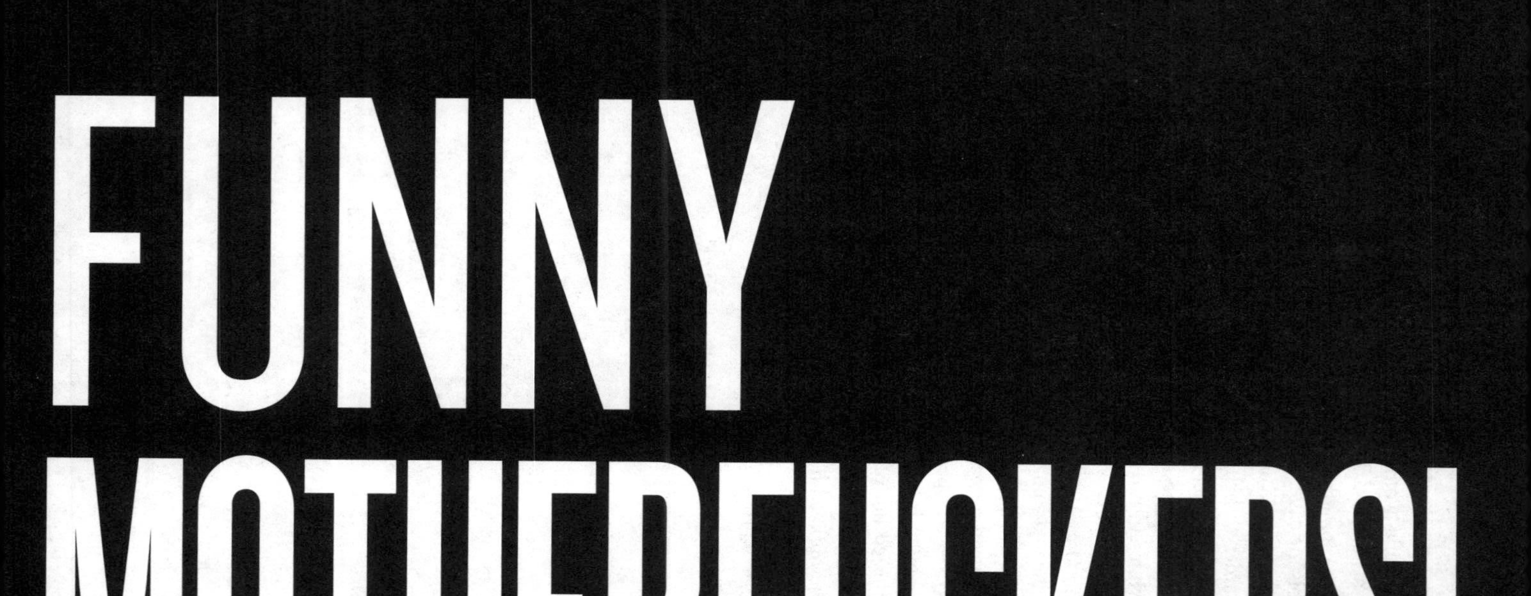
FUNNY
MOTHERFUCKERS!

"If you use blue material, you slip back into being that Negro stereotype comic."

—comedian Dick Gregory (1964)

"That's right, I said shit," comedian Redd Foxx told an audience at the Apollo Theater in Harlem. "If you would tell the truth, everyone here said shit. You ain't never said shit before, come out in the parking lot with me and let me slam my car door on your hand. You'll say shit, *and* motherfucker. '*Shit, motherfucker!*'"

Redd Foxx had been making "party records"—live albums laced with innuendos and double entendres—since 1954, but he didn't come right out and tell his "shit, motherfucker" joke until 1975, on his MF Records LP *You Gotta Wash Your Ass*. (MF was Foxx's own company, and yes, it was short for motherfucker.) That was still a time when *motherfucker* was reserved for the punch line because it could shock a laugh out of an audience. Now those days are gone. Black comics (and many young white ones) load their jokes up with *motherfucker*s not to get a laugh but simply to flavor the joke and move it along, knowing that anyone who goes to see them at a club or tunes into their cable TV specials is not likely to be offended. If anything, the modern audience is disappointed when *motherfucker* isn't used at all.

The closest that Redd Foxx got to *motherfucker* in the old days was "mother frocker," from a routine on his 1959 *Sidesplitters Vol. 2* album. It goes like this: "There were two factories in New York City. One of them made maternity frocks for expectant mothers, so they were called the Mother Frockers. The factory across the street made corks for wine bottles. They had to soak the corks before they could put them into the bottles, so they were called the Cork Soakers. One day a Cork Soaker didn't soak a cork long enough and it flew out of one of the bottles and hit one of the Mother Frockers in the eye. That made all the Mother Frockers mad at the Cork Soakers, so they went outside and had the biggest Mother-Frocking Cork-Soaking fight you ever saw." This bit remained such a popular part of his act that Foxx continued using it in its G-rated form long after he could say *motherfucker* without repercussions; at one recorded Las Vegas show in the 1970s, Foxx relocated the mother-frockers and cork-soakers fight to a convention hall just down the street.

Back in the fifties and sixties, Foxx had to coax the word out of the audience's own imagination, as with his joke about a guy who accidentally stepped on New York Congressman Adam Clayton Powell's foot and elicited a comment that Foxx recalled with mock ingenuousness as something that sounded like "Mother's Day." In another early routine about playing the horses at Santa Anita, he complained that a nag he'd bet on had let him down. "The race track officials called him a mudder [a horse that runs well on a wet, muddy track], and that's what I called him when I lost my money: you slow *mudder*!" Foxx's most sensational gag in the fifties was a mock commercial on his first album for a new product called Fugg soap ("When he comes home all dirty and nasty... tell him to go Fugg hisself"). The word *fug* had already been bandied about in literary circles because John Steinbeck and Norman Mailer had used it as a substitute for *fuck* in two best-selling novels in the 1940s (see Chapter 10), but Foxx's record producer, mindful that discretion was the better part of valor, innocuously titled the track "New Soap." Not until many years later, when Foxx's early albums were reissued, was Fugg ever printed on the jacket or the label. He couldn't even say *shit*; he had to hide it in a routine about different types of sneezes: the barnyard sneeze was "*Horshhhtttt!!!*"

Considering that Lenny Bruce was getting arrested in the early 1960s for saying *motherfucker* and *cocksucker* in all their un-euphemized glory, black comedians were wise to back off, even within the chitlin clubs where most of them were still relegated. Never mind uttering anything into a recording machine that could be used later as Exhibit A on a morals charge. Walter "Dootsie" Williams, a black Los Angeles record company owner who began producing slightly off-color party records around 1950, said that back in the day, long before he recorded Redd Foxx's first LPs, he had to remove his Central Avenue address from his album jackets because the police kept showing up at his door, threatening to haul him off to jail simply because one of his artists, a baggy-pants comic named Billy Mitchell, sang snicker bait like "The Song of the Woodpecker," which relied on the word *pecker* for its humor. Today those recordings would barely raise a giggle out of grammar school kids, but back in the 1950s they were a kick in the pants to the chaste, good-natured slapstick that passed for American mainstream humor. They were also among the few examples of black comedy that a white person could hear, and probably the easiest for him to understand.

African American humor, like African Americans themselves, has existed in a parallel universe for four hundred years. Born into a brutal system of servitude that tried to strip them of humanity, blacks had only three choices of behavior: defy, capitulate, or deceive. Defiance was fatal, and capitulation was death to the soul. Their only alternative was to always be on guard against revealing their rage, and to communicate with whites in circumspect ways that were non-threatening and seemingly guileless. According to cultural historian Mel Watkins, blacks learned to project a self-protective "public image of ever merry, frivolous, happy-go-lucky 'Sambos' in the minds of the majority white population," even while they seethed under their breath. An old blues lyric summed up their dilemma: "Got one mind for white folks to see, and another for what I knows is me." Later on, writer-activist W.E.B. Du Bois called it "double consciousness." The only steam vent for such a dichotomy was humor, but such humor also had to be double-edged and ironic, coded to mean one thing for insiders and something else for all others. According to Swedish social anthropologist Ulf Hannerz, "the complex ploy of masking genuine feeling with mirth and indirection seems to have become a characteristic aspect of the black lifestyle."

According to Robert Gold in his 1964 *Jazz Lexicon*, the word *hip* came from the idea that when shit started getting too deep, you had to put on your hip boots—the thigh-high gear traditionally worn by men who worked in sewers or around water. To be hip meant that you were wise to society's rivers of bullshit, including racism and all its hypocrisies. Urban black hustlers were certainly hip, and so were many jazz musicians, both black and white. But the comic fool who dared speak the absolute truth, regardless of who it offended and how it might come back and kick him in the ass, was the hippest of all.

The earliest professional black comedians found work after the Civil War in minstrel shows by stepping into the ridiculous stock Negro characters—city-slicker Zip Coon, fleet-footed Jim Crow, lazy and stupid Sambo—that had already been invented by white performers in blackface. The institution of minstrelsy was basically one joke: blacks were grinning, shucking, happy-go-lucky lay-abouts or tricksters, always giggling and cackling, always happy to sing and dance for the white folks, and completely satisfied with the status quo. It was exactly what white audiences, especially those in the South, wanted to see. But as black performers gradually took over these roles, they invested them with more expression and humanity, and in some cases made them even more flamboyantly ridiculous in order to show the absurdity of minstrelsy itself—a dangerous gambit because, while it greatly amused black audiences, it reinforced white prejudices. These entertainers also defused many of the old anti-Negro jokes by turning them into personal jibes. For example, in the former, all-white minstrel shows, a character might have insulted the purity and sanctity of black motherhood by saying, "Dem mammies can't be trusted when massa come down by the shack." But the black minstrel would change it by saying to another character, "Your mammy can't be trusted when massa come down by the shack," thus lifting the onus from the race itself and placing it upon the other man's mother—and indirectly upon him, making *him* the butt of the joke instead of black mothers in general. It was a small victory, but a victory nonetheless. Those late-nineteenth-century black minstrels may have been the originators of what became the dozens.

As minstrel shows were gradually absorbed into vaudeville at the turn of the century, the first famous Negro comedian, and one of America's first major recording stars, emerged. He was a British West Indies–born New Yorker named Bert Williams, whose songs and monologues touched gently on black folklore, but with enough genteel polish to make them palatable to whites. Though he died relatively young in 1922, Williams inspired the next generation of Negro comedians, including Dewey "Pigmeat" Markham, Butterbeans and Susie, Tim Moore, Jackie "Moms" Mabley, John Mason, and Leroy & Skillet. But unlike Williams, they were chitlin circuit performers confined to segregated tobacco barns and rundown ghetto theaters, where they didn't have to tailor their humor to white audiences. Though they continued to leaven their humor with bumpkin gags and good-natured fatalism, they broke away from the google-eyed, self-disparaging coons and Sambos and made pointed observations about the fucked-up world they had to deal with. But even then, unless they were in an anything-goes dive, they still conformed to a modicum of decency. All that survives from those days is a handful of ultra-low-budget movies shot exclusively for black audiences, and by necessity they were tame affairs that wouldn't spook a white theater manager or a Southern sheriff who might drop in to see what the local *nigras* were watching. Rarely do we get a glimpse of what unmentionables might have been uttered in a Harlem hole-in-the-wall or a Birmingham juke joint, away from the prying eyes and ears of outsiders. The closest we'll probably ever get to an early *motherfucker* reference is in a 1948 all-black musical comedy called *Killer Diller*. Moms Mabley—whom actor Ossie Davis once called "the mother of all black comics"—introduced a gag about Old Mother Hubbard and her kitchen cupboard with just the right inflection to let her audience know what she was really talking about. "Don't believe in them fairy tales in the first place," she said. "That Mother *Hubbard*—going to the cupboard after dog bones and stuff like that, that never happened. Mother Hubbard had her *gin* in the cupboard."

Then along came high-yellow, henna-headed Redd Foxx with the mischievously blue material. Born John Sanford in St. Louis, Missouri, he began his career as a washtub bass player in a Southside Chicago blues group and, in 1946, recorded a couple of singles as a vocalist. But his real bent was stand-up comedy, a fairly young art form created by tummlers, or professional enthusiasm generators, at Jewish resorts in New York's Catskill Mountains, and then taken up by burlesque joint barkers who needed short bursts of aggressive patter to keep audiences occupied between strippers. In the early fifties Foxx moved to Los Angeles and met Dootsie Williams, who was cashing in at the time on the nascent rock 'n' roll craze by producing R&B (later called doo-wop) songs like the Penguins' million-selling "Earth Angel." But Williams was growing weary of the increasing costs of payola to promote teenage singles, and he was ready to get back to making party records on the side, because they were cheap and didn't require radio promotion. He turned Foxx into an underground star by pulling his 1954 Fugg soap routine off an album and releasing it on a single. But ever mindful of those cops who had once pounded on his door in the middle of the night, Williams never let Foxx go beyond nudge-nudge humor and goofy word games like "mother frockers." A typical cutting-edge gag was Foxx suggesting a budget version of the new bikini bathing suit: "Two Band-Aids and a cork. Okay, *two* corks."

By the early 1960s, as white Americans from coast to coast were getting a daily dose of Southern brutality against Negroes on their TV sets, black comedy veered in the direction of social commentary, thanks to Dick Gregory, a cool Chicago cat in a Brooks Brothers suit who sat on a stool, blew smoke rings at the audience, and intoned lines like "I know a lot about the South. I spent twenty years there one night." Gregory didn't tell jokes so much as make bittersweet observations, such as: "What a country! Where else could I have to ride in the back of the bus, live in the worst neighborhoods, go to the worst schools, eat in the worst restaurants, and average $5,000 a week just talking about it." This was traditionally the type of self-deprecating but whitey-slapping material that black comics delivered to black audiences. In the old days, if a group of slumming whites had stumbled through the door, the comic probably would have toned it down some. But now, daily media images demonizing the Jim Crow South had changed the atmosphere. By taking some of the scorn out of his voice and letting white audiences think he was including them as liberal sympathizers against bigotry, Dick Gregory became America's first crossover black comic. The only touchy word he ever played with onstage was *nigger*, which turned out to be the title of his 1964 autobiography. (In its dedication to his mother, he wrote, "if ever you hear the word nigger again, remember, they're advertising my book.") In effect, he was doing Lenny Bruce's infamous "any niggers in here?" act, but on a national scale, without the word *motherfucker*, or any other obscenity. But Gregory did sparingly drop it into his book. His white co-writer and typist, Robert Lipsyte, later reported that Gregory's only complaint to him was, "You've hyphenated motherfucker. It's one word."

As the Civil Rights movement heated up, an emboldened Gregory sacrificed his show business career for a more militant activism that stretched the thin tolerance of his new audience. "I'm a Negro before I'm an entertainer," he said; "comedy without purpose [is] just another way of black guys dancing for white people." But he had already opened the door for black stand-up comedy in the wider world, and lots of young comics like Bill Cosby and Flip Wilson were happy to step through and dance. Even old-timers like Redd Foxx, Pigmeat Markham, Nipsy Russell, Slappy White, and Moms Mabley revived their careers. The price of their success, however, was that they had to soften their humor for a general audience.

But there was one black comic willing to stay on the fringes, below white society's radar. Rudy Ray Moore, at age thirty-one, had moved to Los Angeles from the Midwest in 1959 with the idea of becoming an R&B vocalist. After recording a couple of nowhere singles on tiny labels, he landed a job as emcee at a popular black club where he could say pretty much whatever he wanted between music and comedy acts. One day in 1961 Dootsie Williams asked him to record a party album. Moore was ecstatic to join a roster that included his hero Redd Foxx, but as he would say much later, Foxx's albums "didn't have the explicit language on them. They had adult-style phrases, double-meaning words, you know. But he never said 'motherfucker' and all that on records." And neither could Moore. Williams restricted him to R-rated jokes about penis size and word-play routines like the one about a Chinese man named Foo King. Any obscenities he dropped into his jokes were edited out of the tape.

But Rudy Ray Moore had an entrepreneurial streak. After recording several modest-selling albums during the sixties, he decided to go into business for himself. By now he was working as a manager of Dolphin's of Hollywood, a twenty-four-hour record shop at one of black Los Angeles's busiest corners, so he knew the ins and outs of local record distribution. As it happened, the sidewalk outside the store was a hangout for a middle-aged wino named Rico, who had a remarkable facility for delivering elaborate toasts, especially after he'd guzzled down a few refreshments from the liquor store next door. Rico's favorite character was a super-bad motherfucker named Dolomite. One day, while the juicehead was rhyming about Dolomite's exploits and keeping a small crowd of listeners in stitches, Moore wondered why nobody was putting genuine stuff like this on party albums instead of bullshit jokes that didn't meaning anything. He paid Rico to let him record some of his foul-mouthed routines, and then he went back and learned them himself, mimicking Rico's personal delivery. He also brushed off all those toasts he'd heard growing up, like "Shine and the Great Titanic" and "The Signifying Monkey." When he felt he was ready, he gathered friends at a local recording studio with "some liquor and finger sandwiches and beer and stuff. And I'd get them in a good rejoicing mood and crack these jokes and people would laugh right on track." He pressed up his own album called *Eat Out More Often*, featuring the Dolomite toast, which began: "Some folks say that Willie Green was the baddest motherfucker the world had ever seen, but I want you to light you up a joint and screw your wig on tight, and let me tell 'bout the bad little motherfucker named Dolomite." In fact, on the cheesy homemade album jacket, he dropped his real name and dubbed himself Dolemite, changing the spelling slightly from the original dolomite (which is actually a calcium-magnesium carbonate often used in vitamin supplements). The album caught on like wildfire around Los Angeles's black neighborhoods, enough to spend four consecutive weeks on *Billboard*'s soul charts in 1970. With his first royalties he produced another album, *This Pussy Belongs to Me*, which also charted, and after a couple of years he bankrolled his own painfully low-budget movie, *Dolemite*, starring himself as the karate-kicking super-pimp, spouting outrageous dialogue like "You no-business, insecure, rat-soup eatin', junkyard motherfucker!" that had black audiences screaming with laughter.

Moore, of course, was the beneficiary of the sixties culture wars, a time when the restrictions on obscene material were unraveling. As writer-critic Mel Watkins explained it, "The bluest, often profane street vernacular in which folk humor was frequently couched, often an integral part of the style and meaning of the tales or jokes presented, was not tolerated in popular culture before the 1960s." Moore later told writer Adam Bulger, "I'm the first one to use all of the four-letter words, motherfucker." He would eventually, in the early nineties, go so far as to utter *motherfucker* on comedian Arsenio Hall's syndicated late-night TV show by ending one of his raps with "Dolemite is my name—and I'm out of this motherfucker!"

At roughly the same time as Dolemite's breakthrough, a young Georgia songwriter-producer named Clarence Reid was reinventing himself as a character called Blowfly, so named because his grandmother had once told him, after hearing some of his dirty lyrics, "You're a disgrace to the black race. You're no better than a blowfly." Reid's Blowfly character, like Dolemite, was larger than life and as bad as he wanted to be, beginning on the day he was born: "The doctor smacked me on my ass. I yelled, 'One more time, motherfucker, I'll stick that rubber glove up yo' ass!'" (In that same vein, Dolemite's first words to his father as he popped out of the womb had been "Okay, *I'm* in charge now, cocksucker.") But unlike Dolemite, Blowfly added musical parodies to his toasts (for example, he sang "Raindrops Keep Falling on My Head" as "My Baby Keeps Farting in My Face"), backed with the same professional funk musicians he used on his R&B hits like Betty Wright's "Clean Up Woman." His first album, *The Weird World of Blowfly* (1971), was an instant hit with black audiences.

But throughout Rudy Ray Moore and Clarence Reid's prime years in the 1970s, there was a price to be paid for having a dirty mouth and a 100 percent ghetto point of view: segregation. Though many top rap artists would later commandeer a lot of their material, Dolemite and Blowfly never reached a mainline audience. Their material was always too black, too coded, too crude; they didn't, or couldn't, compromise to reach out to a larger audience. That left the job of bringing raunchy, profane, and honest black comedy to the masses—an antidote to Bill Cosby's whimsical, colorblind humor that had suddenly become popular—to a young, irreverent comic from America's everytown—Peoria, Illinois—named Richard Pryor.

Like Moore and Redd Foxx, Pryor had been hamstrung on his first albums, which were released in the late 1960s by small Los Angeles independent labels. His characters weren't fully formed and he wasn't yet speechifying in the fully inflected ghetto patois. *Nigger* popped up now and then in those early days, but the all-purpose *motherfucker* was nowhere to be heard. In retrospect, any of Pryor's fans who go back and visit those early murky albums will feel its absence. Young Richard's attempts at maintaining the rhythmic verisimilitude of street jive simply don't work without it.

Unlike the hyperbolic personas of Dolemite and Blowfly, Richard Pryor presented himself as an everyman: at times cool, at other times discombobulated, or frightened, or flat-out angry. A spectrum of human emotions could cross his face within the span of an idea. Unlike Redd Foxx, he could impersonate almost anyone in the neighborhood—even the white cop—with expressive intimacy and vulnerability. He could also be brutally honest, not only in his bittersweet observations about black-on-black or white-on-black interactions, but in his use of the rawest street language to pull it off. Calling him a comic is playing him short. Satirist, or humor activist, more correctly defined Richard Pryor. His genius, if you want to call it that, was taking all the inside stuff— the self-loathing, the odd tics of black folks, the excoriations of white folks and their wickedly silly ways—that black comics would normally reveal in front of an exclusively black audience and announce them in front of a mixed audience, with almost everybody laughing too hard or too nervously to be offended. Taking King Lear's line that "Many a truth is said in jest," he slipped razor-edged barbs into his jokes that white people might not have wanted to hear, but needed to.

But that came later. During most of the 1960s he was Richie Pryor, a mild and gentle comedian with processed hair and an insouciant cuddliness that calmed white audiences. He made his first national appearance in 1964 on aging crooner Rudy Vallée's *Broadway Tonight*, mugging for senior citizens and middle-aged women. He let everybody know he was grateful to be there. Yet even then, an inner rage was eating away at his personal life and occasionally bursting out in public. His career mirrored the double consciousness of being black, having to appeal to two completely different sensibilities, with black audiences waiting for the hostile bad-ass and whites expecting a safe, happy clown. Trying to contain two such personalities within one body became increasingly difficult for him. Eventually he suffered an emotional meltdown onstage at a Las Vegas hotel and exiled himself to Berkeley, California, where he lived for a time as an eccentric pothead, ambling through the streets in a kimono and talking to himself. What saved him from dereliction was falling in with a local cadre of emerging black intellectuals and writers, including Ishmael Reed and Claude Brown, who inspired him to get back to his cultural roots and find the real voice of a black man in the post–Malcolm X era.

When Pryor left Berkeley and returned to comedy he was a different artist. To establish his credibility as a denizen of the streets, Pryor began peppering his monologues with the most meaningful and volatile vocabulary of that environment, revealing what Mel Watkins described in his 1994 book *On the Real Side* as "that unique, previously concealed or rejected part of African American humor that thrived in the lowest, most unassimilated pattern of the black community."

His savvy new characters and routines made him a hit not only with belligerent urban blacks who wanted to laugh at their own predicament, but also with middle-class blacks rediscovering their roots within the late-sixties embrace of African culture and racial empowerment. Many young whites, temperamentally disenfranchised by Vietnam-era politics and the unraveling of Richard Nixon's imperial presidency in the early seventies, also felt a bond of brotherhood with him. As Pryor biographers John A. Williams and Dennis A. Williams put it, "an irreverent, bad-mouthed, apparently half-mad man, shrieking 'motherfucker this, motherfucker that,' or 'nigger this, nigger that,' or (in the face of militant feminism) 'bitch this, bitch that'—a penis-holding, gyrating, staggering, dope-stiffened, ambling street apparition, certainly was no more obscene than what was going on in Washington, or in the news from Southeast Asia still flickering on the TV every night at 7 P.M." Additionally, the greater mainstream white audience rediscovered him as he crossed over to film stardom in what had previously been a haphazard side career in Hollywood, especially after his breakout role as Gene Wilder's manic sidekick in Twentieth Century Fox's 1976 blockbuster *Silver Streak*. Pryor was suddenly the hottest bad-cat black man in America, a genuine cultural leader who said whatever was on his mind with an aggressive black attitude. Everybody wanted to hear what he had to say, as if he were a window looking directly into the hearts of black folks. And the two most powerful words in his vocabulary, the words he enshrined in his everyday black man speech, were *nigger* (which he disowned years later, in 1979, after a trip to Kenya) and *motherfucker*. Pryor put these two forbidden expletives out there like they had never been out there before, flashing in neon blue. White people knew the first word, of course, but not in the badge-of-honor way that Pryor employed it, as a bond between blacks and an obstacle to everyone else. The second word was more foreign, more disturbing. Some people ran for their hipster dictionaries; others just ran.

Here are just a few examples of Pryor's dependence on his favorite, most flexible four-syllable word.

- Spoofing a charlatan ghetto preacher uninterested in tending to the afflicted: "I'd like to say to the crippled peoples that come here—can't you find another church to go to?... An' you deaf and dumb motherfuckers, you motherfuckers that can't talk, we don't need you here."

- Commenting on the falling white fertility rate: "Shortage of white people lately. Y'all stop fuckin'? There will be no shortage of niggers. Niggers is fuckin'.... We got to have somebody left to take this motherfucker over."

- Answering a stock question about why black men always stand around groping themselves: "White guys always ask, 'Why do you guys hold on to your things?'....You done took everything else, motherfucker."

- Praising a black boxing champion: "That Sugar [Ray Robinson] fight so good, make ya dick hard. Sugar *git* in a motherfucker's ass. Ask Jake LaMotta."

- Explaining why black men are careful with traffic cops that pulled them over: "Nigger got to be talkin' about 'I am reaching into my pocket for my license,' 'cause I don't wanna be no motherfuckin' accident."

- Complaining about middle-class whites preferring bland copycat musical acts: "Jackson Five be singin' they ass off, [but whites] be talkin' 'bout the Osmond Brothers.... Mother*fuck* a Osmond Brothers!"

- Relating his experience with lawyers: "Lawyers is some expensive motherfuckers. I got a lawyer, first week the motherfucker brought me a bill for forty thousand dollars. I say, 'Motherfucker, I just met you!' Them motherfuckers will keep you outta the penitentiary and outta the courts—but it's gonna cost a lot! I had a guy...motherfucker took me hook, line and sinker!"

- Imparting ghetto wisdom through his character Mudbone: "You don't git to be old bein' no fool, see. A lotta young wise men, they deader 'n a motherfucker, ain't they?"

- Recalling his first heart attack: "I woke up in a ambulance, right? And there wasn't nothin' but white people starin' at me. I say, Ain't this a bitch. I done died and wound up in the wrong motherfuckin' heaven. Now, I gotta listen to Lawrence Welk the rest of my days."

- Challenging men who brag that they can fuck all night: "You some lyin' motherfuckers.... I can make love for about three minutes."

- Giving non-black situations a funny black perspective, as in his routine about a wino meeting Dracula: "Say nigger—you wit' the cape! What you doin' peepin' in them people's window? What's your name, boy? Dracula? What kind of name is that for a nigger? Where you from, fool? Transylvania! I know where it is nigger—you ain't the smartest motherfucker in the world, you know. Even though you *is* the ugliest."

Unfortunately, Pryor as an artist never made it out of the 1980s. Drug and personal problems, a tepid run of Elvis-quality movies, and finally the gradual debilitation of multiple sclerosis brought him down from the heights a full, agonizing fifteen years before his death in late 2005. He left as his legacy two generations of black comics (along with a few white ones) who felt no compunction about screaming "nigger!" and "motherfucker!" almost every time they opened their mouths. In fact, Comedy Central aired a loving memorial just prior to his death called *I Ain't Dead Yet, Motherfucker*—named after Pryor's own website—in which a dozen comics, from Whoopi Goldberg and Robin Williams to Chris Rock and Dave Chappelle, tried to put him in historical perspective.

Not everyone felt that Pryor's influence was entirely positive, of course. Dick Gregory told John A. and Dennis A. Williams that Pryor's barrage of ghetto gutter speech had been more subversive than anyone had foreseen. "When people used to bring out Redd Foxx records, all the good Christian folks had left. With Richard, we all heard his genius, not his profanity. It was an act of love to bring his records out. You didn't tell the children to leave the room. But children hear what you say, not what's behind the words. They heard the profanity. Every other comic thought the only way they could be successful was by using profanity."

For black entertainers of every medium it was more important that Pryor had changed the rules by dropping the emotionless mask, the glamour pose, the canned-for-the-white-folks patter that was de rigueur before he came along. Now artists could be as angry and as confrontational as they wanted to be, as long as they were modestly talented. And for comics in particular, it meant that unless they were on regular network or standard cable TV, *motherfucker* was a malleable, all-purpose fall-back for whenever they needed a few syllables to keep up the level of hilarity. Many comics, such as superstar Eddie Murphy and the *Def*

Comedy Jam wannabes who followed him, seemed determined to out-motherfucker every other motherfucker standing behind a microphone. Even the girls, like Millie Jackson and Wanda Sykes, liberally tossed the word around. By the late eighties it was also the lingua franca of rap music, blaring in the ears of every kid under twenty. Whites in particular responded to *motherfucker* because, unlike *nigger*, they could say it around blacks without starting a fight. And once they made *motherfucker* a part of their vocabulary, white kids began to speak a different language that seeped into other parts of their personalities. It wasn't quite what Norman Mailer was talking about back in 1957 when he introduced the idea of the "white Negro," but there was no doubt that white America was undergoing a "Negroization."

It was that very dovetailing of ghetto comedy and gangsta rap that resuscitated the career of Rudy Ray Moore's Dolemite. N.W.A.'s Eazy-E and Big Daddy Kane invited him to record with them. Other artists, including 2 Live Crew, sampled his records. And in 2008, not long before he died, Moore reprised his character Petey Wheatstraw the Devil's Son-in-Law on a record with Blowfly. It was all a testament to those Shine and Stagolee toasts from a century earlier, outrageous and hyperbolic tales of bad-ass black motherfuckers trying to get a little respect (and some pussy) in this white man's America.

LENNY DIED FOR
YOU MOTHERS!

"My mother-in-law broke up my marriage. My wife came home and found us in bed together."

—Lenny Bruce (1964)

"Are there any niggers here tonight?" comedian Lenny Bruce asked in one of his more infamous routines:

> "Oh, my god, did you hear what he said? Are there any niggers here tonight? Is that rank! Is that cruel! Is that a cheap way to get laughs?" Well, I think I see a nigger at the bar talking to two guinea owners....
>
> Now why have I done this? Is it only for shock value? Well, if all the niggers started calling each other nigger, not only among themselves, which they do anyway, but among others; if President Kennedy got on television and said, 'I'm considering appointing two or three of the top niggers in the country to my cabinet'—if it was nothing but nigger, nigger, nigger—in six months nigger wouldn't mean any more than good night, god bless you. When that beautiful day comes, you'll never see another nigger kid come home from school crying because some motherfucker called him a nigger!

Onstage, Lenny Bruce was a verbal bebop jazzman whose pessimistic takes on drugs, sex, political power, religion, and the sleazy backside of middle-class propriety slipped far beyond the bounds of the mother-in-law jokes and Borscht Belt patter that passed for American comedy in the mid-twentieth century. Popular Jewish stand-ups like Buddy Hackett, Jack Carter, Joe E. Lewis, and Henny Youngman sometimes worked a little "blue" after the blue-haired *bubelehs* went to bed, but nothing too *shmutsik*. Then along came Lenny Schneider, better known as Lenny Bruce, who'd been slogging through years of on-the-job training in dingy strip clubs—"toilets," he called them—competing with half-naked women for the audience's attention by riffing on whatever bizarre or filthy thoughts popped into his head, and occasionally even stripping off his own clothes to introduce the next girl. By the time he got his act together around 1956 or '57, his shtick, according to critic Nat Hentoff, was "an evocative spray of Yiddishisms, Negro and show-business argot, and his own operational semantics"—including forbidden words and images spiked to challenge audiences to deal with their personal and cultural hypocrisies. He disclosed in public what others would dare say only in private, mocking not only his audience but—with deadly mimicry—blacks, homosexuals, celebrities, and any other group that caught his jaundiced eye. In 1958 his own record company titled his second album *The Sick Humor of Lenny Bruce*. When TV variety show host Steve Allen introduced Bruce to a national audience in April 1959, he called him "the most shocking comedian of our time."

But Bruce's real shock value didn't hit sleepy America until the 1960s, beginning with two obscenity trials in California—one in San Francisco (where in 1962 he was acquitted of calling a transvestite a "cocksucker") and another in Los Angeles (where he was convicted by an assistant D.A. named Johnnie Cochran for saying "you dwarf motherfucker" at West Hollywood's Troubadour in 1964). Bruce was also arrested at the Gate of Horn club in Chicago, where, according to a police report, he uttered, "They say we fuck our mothers for Hershey bars" and "I want to fuck your mothers. Oh, thank you, thank you, thank you." A tape of his monologue, however, showed that what he actually said, in an uneasy riff about how Europeans must have felt about American occupation troops, was "They hate Americans everywhere. You know why? Because we fucked all of their mothers for chocolate bars"; and "You know what those Americans did to your poor mothers? They lined her up, those bastards…that master sergeant *schtupped* your mother for their stinking coffee and their eggs and their frigging cigarettes…. 'There's the fellow who fucked my mother—oh, thank you, thank you, thank you. Thank you for doing that, and for giving us candy.'" This was a far cry from the polite analyst-and-oedipal-patient routines that his fellow "sick" comics like Shelley Berman and Nichols & May were doing. Bruce was found guilty, but the case was dropped on appeal.

As it turned out, his downfall came in America's most liberal bastion, Greenwich Village. On March 31, 1964, as the thirty-eight-year-old comic was spouting "cocksucker" and "shit" and calling Republican presidential aspirant Barry Goldwater a "motherfucker" from the stage of the Café Au Go Go on Bleecker Street, a New York City licensing bureau inspector named Herbert Ruhe sat in the audience taking notes. Next morning, April Fool's Day, the bureaucrat duly submitted his report to Assistant District Attorney Richard Kuh, who passed it along to District Attorney Frank Hogan, a faith 'n' begorrah Irish Catholic unsympathetic to all sins cardinal and venal and certainly not kindly disposed toward this Yid bastard who not only spat upon the blessed robes of the Church, but had the gall to denigrate the sainted Jackie Kennedy in one of his routines—accusing her of "hauling ass" out of that limo convertible as Lee Harvey Oswald's bullets were spraying her husband's brain all over Daley Plaza. Since Hogan wasn't expecting any rapists or muggers to be out prowling the streets that night, he sent several spare police officers to the Café Au Go Go with a hidden tape recorder, in order that a transcript could be hurriedly typed up in time to be presented to twenty-three grand jurors the next morning. As nearly every *Law & Order* script has told us over and over again, a grand jury can indict a ham sandwich, so this one instantly handed down a non-kosher indictment against the comic for violating the city's penal code (Section 1140-A) prohibiting "obscene, indecent, immoral, and impure drama, play, exhibition, and entertainment...which would tend to the corruption of the morals of youth and others." For each of the three charges against him, Bruce faced a maximum of three years in prison. The following night, April 3, as a crowd of paying customers waited to catch his ten o'clock performance, a phalanx of flatfoots rushed backstage and hauled him away in handcuffs.

Bruce thumbed his nose at Hogan by returning to the café's stage four days later to recount his legal travails in explicit detail, and again there was a policeman in the audience with a tape recorder, catching even more damning sputters of *cocksucker*s and *motherfucker*s. The law had him dead-to-rights this time.

The crowd that turned up at the Criminal Courts Building for the opening of Bruce's trial on June 16, 1964, was large enough that the circus had to be moved to a three-ring courtroom. Instead of a jury, he faced three judges, with John Murtagh presiding. Bruce's attorney was Ephraim London, one of the country's top First Amendment lawyers, famous for fending off obscenity cases against explicit novels like *Lady Chatterly's Lover*, but London handed off the day-to-day courtroom examinations to his young associate, Martin Garbus, a Lenny Bruce fan with several censorship cases under his belt. Following the tack that Bruce was being prosecuted (or more precisely, persecuted) for "his attacks on religion and public figures, rather than because of his use of dirty words," Garbus presented him to the judges as a latter-day Jonathan Swift whose commentary had literary and social value beyond mere obscenity. *Obscenity* was the operative word here, the cornerstone of the city's case, because the U.S. Supreme Court had deemed seven years earlier, in *Roth v. U.S.*, that obscenity, which appealed only to "prurient interest and is without redeeming social importance," was the one type of speech not protected by the First Amendment. Even though another recent Supreme Court decision in *Jacobellis v. Ohio* more closely defined obscenity as "utterly without social value" (this was the case in which Potter Stewart said famously that he wouldn't attempt to define hardcore pornography, "but I know it when I see it"), the prosecution only had to convince the judges that Bruce's use of dirty words served no good purpose whatsoever.

That's why Assistant D.A. Richard Kuh characterized Bruce's routines as "cumulatively nauseating word pictures interspersed with all the three- and four-letter words and more acrid ten- and twelve-letter hyphenated ones, spewed directly at the audience"—unredeemed by any artistry or social criticism. "There is no unity of purpose, no cohesion… no common theme but filth," he told the triumvirate.

Lenny Bruce knew he was in trouble when the prosecution's key witness, Inspector Ruhe, read from the notes he'd taken at the club on the first night. Visibly uncomfortable and clammy with sweat, Ruhe essentially delivered a lousy performance of Bruce's act. "I'm going to be judged by his bad timing, his ego, his garbled language," Bruce groused afterward. "He doesn't miss a dirty word; he doesn't get too much of the rest.… All he says are dirty words. *His* act is obscene."

After just three days of police testimony, the prosecution rested.

When the trial reconvened, Martin Garbus trotted out several experts, including a psychiatrist who pooh-poohed the idea of Bruce's words sexually arousing anyone, media experts averring that Bruce hadn't offended local community standards, and pundits insisting that his expiating humor was healthy in a free society. But the star witness was a Broadway columnist for New York's *Journal American* named Dorothy Kilgallen, nationally known as a panelist on a long-running TV quiz show called *What's My Line?* in which the most difficult question was likely to be "Is it bigger than a breadbox?" Kilgallen had favorably reviewed Bruce's act in the past, but more important, she was a proper Upper-East-Side socialite, not a Village beatnik or a Columbia radical. Garbus later called her "as unlikely an advocate of public profanity as one might hope to find."

Kilgallen "projected the image of a woman with drawing-room manners who would be more at home sipping tea," rather than watching Lenny Bruce muttering profanities in a dim café. She was also, like

D.A. Frank Hogan, a high-profile Irish Catholic and a personal friend of Cardinal Spellman. When she told the court that Bruce was "a brilliant satirist" whose "social commentary, whether I agree with it or not, is extremely valid and important," it seemed like a reasonable opinion that even the pope himself might bless.

Here's a part of Garbus's direct examination:

> Garbus; Are the words 'cock sucker,' 'fuck,' 'shit' and 'ass' and 'mother fucker' used in the transcripts?
>
> Kilgallen: Yes, they are.
>
> Garbus; In what way are they used?
>
> Judge Murtagh: I think the transcripts speak for themselves, Counselor…
>
> Garbus; Miss Kilgallen, is there an artistic purpose in the use of language as set forth in transcripts in People's—
>
> Kilgallen: In my opinion, there is.
>
> Garbus; In what way?
>
> Kilgallen: *Well, I think that Lenny Bruce, as a night-club performer, employs these words the way James Baldwin or Tennessee Williams or playwrights employ them on the Broadway stage: for emphasis or because that is the way that people in a given situation would talk.*
>
> Garbus; Miss Kilgallen, did you see *Blues for Mister Charlie*?
>
> Killgallen: Yes.
>
> Garbus; And are some of those words used in Mr. Bruce's transcripts used in the play?
>
> Kilgallen: I believe almost all of them…
>
> Garbus: Have you heard the word 'mother fucker' used before?
>
> Kilgallen: Yes.
>
> Garbus: And in this context how is the word used?
>
> Kilgallen: Sometimes it was used as an epithet, a term of opprobrium, and sometimes I have heard it used among show business people, who sometimes speak rather frankly and roughly, as a term of endearment.

[Author's note: Garbus's reference to "the word mother fucker" indicated that for him it was a compound word, but for the court reporter it was two separate words. In the cross-examination below, Assistant D.A. Kuh referred to motherfucker as "the words" and "the phrase." He considered *cocksucker* also to be two words. This being 1964, the printed forms of these words were still in transition, and Garbus, hipper to underground culture than the other officers of the court, would have used the more modern spelling.]

> Kuh: You stated [earlier] those are words you don't use. Can you tell me if the prevailing portion of the community finds them repugnant in terms of usage in mixed company, in public performances?
>
> Kilgallen: I cannot speak for the majority of the community; I can only speak for myself, but I believe that certain words are valid and are not objectionable if they are used in the proper context and if they seem right at the time and if they are said in the proper manner. Some people can be offensive without using what we would call a dirty word. Some people could use a dirty word and not be offensive.
>
> Kuh: Can you tell me how the words or the phrase on page 2, 'shit in your pants,' and on page 2, 'cock sucker,' are used in a way that blend artistic merit, that demonstrate Mr. Bruce's moral character and that are inoffensive?
>
> Kilgallen: Mr. Bruce sometimes uses those words almost as a throwaway.
>
> Judge Murtagh: Almost as what?
>
> Kilgallen: A throwaway.
>
> Judge Murtagh: What does that mean?
>
> Kilgallen: That's show-business parlance I'm afraid, your Honor. It's an offhand thing that you almost don't hear.
>
> Judge Murtagh: How is the fact that words such as that are offhand, how does that make it proper if it is improper otherwise?
>
> Kilgallen: Well, your Honor, to me words are just words, and if the intent and the effect is not offensive the words in themselves are not offensive.... It depends on how it's done. I have seen entertainers who didn't use these words, but were offensive nevertheless, and I can give you examples. I have criticized them.
>
> Judge Murtagh: Did you hear him on these two occasions?
>
> Kilgallen: No, but knowing his performances I can almost picture the way he said them....
>
> Kuh: Are you familiar with any of Bruce's phonograph records?

Kilgallen: I think I have one.

Kuh: Now, you mentioned before something about Mr. Bruce's bit—or something—at the Palladium. Is that on that record?

Kilgallen: No, I'm not so sure. It's so long since I heard the record I really couldn't tell.

Kuh: Was that bit, so called, about the Palladium, a rather lengthy bit?

Kilgallen: Yes.

Kuh: Quite lengthy?

Kilgallen: For him it is.

Kuh: And except for one word at the very end, which I think is the word 'urination'...except for that, do you know of any other four-letter words or combinations, and I apologize, Miss Kilgallen, such as 'cock sucker' throughout this lengthy bit?

Kilgallen: I don't know it by heart. I only know the general idea and that I found it very amusing, at least to show people. I don't know whether it would be to the average audience, but I know Milton Berle laughed a lot when he heard it.

Kuh: Thank you. If I tell you that that record contains no vulgarity, none of the words that Mr. Garbus used so far in examining you, would you dispute that contention?

Kilgallen: No, sir; that makes sense.

Kuh: And so you recognize that Mr. Bruce can be amusing, even to Milton Berle, without utilizing any of these four-letter words or combination of them?

Kilgallen: Yes, I'm sure he can, because I think he's a near genius....

Kuh: Would you say that Bruce is able to get his social satire, his moral values, his artistic ability across fully and ably and unimpeded without the use of these words that I think you recognize, you, yourself, you indicated were not used?

London: I object to that. This trial is about these transcripts, not about anything else.

Judge Murtagh: Objection overruled.

Kilgallen: I don't know whether he can get his meaning across fully, because some of these words, which are objectionable, as you put it, are terms that are used by people in real life, and I think to be more graphic he must use them, just as a playwright or a novelist would use them.

Kuh: Let me read you this—and I'm reading from page 22 of

the April 1st performance…he says, "That's the way all of us feel, shitty all the time and low because we're no good, 'cause we run away but nobody ever stays, it's all bullshit, none of you mother fuckers ever stayed one time in your life, you never stayed and that's why you can sit and indict." Do you feel that that language is necessary to the effectiveness of that portion of that script?

Kilgallen: I think he felt it was necessary and perhaps it was. He was expressing the fear that all humans feel and he was sympathizing with it.

Kuh: And do you believe that words 'mother fucker' and 'shitty' and so forth were necessary to that expression, apart from what he might have felt, was necessary—do you feel that that was necessary, you as a person who is critical and is here as an expert on criticism?

London: I would object to that, your Honor.

Judge Murtagh: Objection overruled.

Kilgallen: I really can't judge that, because I didn't hear the way he said it.

Kuh: Well, will you recognize, Miss Kilgallen, that there are at least an appreciable number of persons in the community who would find that language highly repugnant?

Kilgallen: I'm sure there are.

Kuh: Can you tell us how the use of this language, not in Mr. Bruce's eyes, but in your eyes, as a critic, a person who was qualified here as an expert witness, will you tell us how the use of this sentence that I read is necessary to the artistic unity, if you will, of the Jackie Kennedy story?

Kilgallen: I do not underwrite anything that Mr. Bruce may have said. I'm just saying that what I have read does not offend me.

Kuh: Then you concede, as a critic and as an expert in criticism, that these words may be unnecessary to this story, that you personally cannot find a justification for them although you personally do not object—is that what you are telling us?

Kilgallen: I believe that if Mr. Bruce in his routine felt it was necessary, then it was necessary.… I feel it is in Mr. Bruce's style, just as *Blues for Mister Charlie* is in James Baldwin's style and *Tropic of Cancer* is in Henry Miller's style. He has the right to use the words he feels are fitting and pertinent and perhaps dramatic.

Forrest Johnson, a Presbyterian minister who attended Bruce's April 1 performance at the Café Au Go Go, also testified that he didn't consider the comedian's language inappropriate. On cross-examination Kuh asked Johnson, "Would you say the phrase, and you'll excuse me, Reverend, for using this language, but the phrase 'mother fucker' is in accord with [the Fourth Commandment, 'Thou shalt honor thy Father and thy Mother'?"

Johnson answered, "I don't think the term 'mother fucker' has any relationship to that Commandment."

Kuh countered, "To the uninitiated, to the unsophisticated, to persons other than reverends, Mr. Johnson, might someone understand the words 'mother fucker' as having to do with mothers and fucking?"

Newsweek drama critic Richard Gilman also testified that Bruce's words had no sexual connotation. "No more than when one individual calls another a mother fucker," Gilman said. "It's common parlance and does not mean that the individual is being accused of having had intercourse with his mother."

It was clear to Bruce and his lawyers that the case was going against him. Though Murtagh was one of three judges, he had taken charge of the proceedings and seemed to be working with the prosecution, overruling almost all of the defense's objections. Murtagh also let stand Kuh's offhand suggestion that a performance in front of a cloistered audience of paying adults was subject to the same standards as a nationally distributed recording of a performance by a record company, even though the commercial realities of 1964 would have prohibited the release of such an album. (Kuh, whose dislike of Bruce's impropriety wasn't just a courtroom act, explained later in his memoirs that he considered it "particularly appropriate that live shows, whether or not restricted to an admission-paying audience, are as subject to obscenity restrictions as are books [and records]." The way he saw it, "When pornography has provided the path to…prosperity and filth has fostered…adulation, whether or not the young are permitted to witness a specific performance, they are certain to learn something of how the entertainer's success was grasped.")

The court did not announce its verdict for another ninety-nine days. Bruce spent some of the intervening period firing his lawyer and writing a bizarre letter to Judge Murtagh in hopes, perhaps, of mollifying him. Bruce included his own analysis of the "literal" and "contemporary" usage of his "purple vocabulary" and told the judge, "Ninety-eight percent of the words I used are correct words in *Webster's Third New International Dictionary*." Bruce ended his missive by claiming that his desire was not "contempt," but rather "communication."

When judgment day finally rolled around in early November, Judge Murtagh, speaking for the court, found both Lenny Bruce and Café Au Go Go owner Howard Solomon "guilty as charged." The court's per curium opinion concluded that Bruce's act "appealed to prurient interest," was "patently offensive to the average person in the community," and lacked "redeeming social importance." In other words, it was obscene. Saying *motherfucker* or *cocksucker* or *shit* out loud in front of a group of adult New Yorkers—even ones willing to pay for the privilege—was a crime. One of the three judges dissented.

Though sentenced to "four months in the workhouse," Bruce remained free on bond to appeal the decision. There would be no vindication in his lifetime. Not even the *New York Law Journal* would publish Murtagh's opinion because the editors refused to reprint the so-called obscenities, and omitting them would have made the opinion incomplete and unusable by law journal standards. Bruce spent what was left of his life in a narcotic haze, obsessing over his legal problems, filing a series of pointless civil suits, and sending audiences toward the exits with droning soliloquies and readings from the transcripts of his trial. He had devolved from comedian to just another crank on a soapbox. Quotable remarks—such as "Take away the right to say fuck and you take away the right to say fuck the government!"—came infrequently now. When one of his early supporters, San Francisco *Chronicle* columnist Herb Caen, chided him for mistaking his personal problems for nightclub entertainment, Bruce self-destructively fired back by calling him "a cocksucking motherfucker." Maybe if he had hung on for a couple more years and not torched all the bridges behind him, Bruce would have seen light at the end of the tunnel ahead: his disciples like Richard Pryor and George Carlin waving torches of free speech as they lampooned America's obsession with dark religion and the evil power of dirty words. But instead, on August 3, 1966, Bruce took a powder. Cops found him crumpled next to the toilet in his Hollywood Hills home on the wrong end of a needle. *Playboy* eulogized him best in a single headline: "Dead. At forty. That's obscene."

The law had marshaled powerful forces to stop Lenny Bruce from being a potty mouth in public. In all, police arrested him eight times, and four cities brought six court cases against him. The trials took over four years, required eight state judges and more than a dozen state attorneys, and prompted Bruce's appeals in federal and state appellate courts in New York, Los Angeles, and San Francisco that wasted the time of twenty-five judges who all must have had much better things to do.

One of the New York prosecutors, Assistant D.A. Vincent Cuccia, later expressed regret over his role in the Café Au Go Go case. "I feel terrible about Bruce. We drove him into poverty and bankruptcy and then murdered him. I watched him gradually fall apart. It's the only thing I did in Hogan's office that I'm really ashamed of. We all knew what we were doing. We used the law to kill him."

Nearly forty years later, on December 23, 2003, New York Governor George Pataki publicly pardoned Bruce in what he called "a declaration of New York's commitment to upholding the First Amendment." He did not, however, call the 1964 prosecution a motherfucker.

In 1974, when Hollywood got around to lionizing Bruce in MGM's adaptation of Julian Barry's 1971 Broadway play *Lenny*, the word *cocksucker* was the plot device that set the awesome powers of the government against him. "Motherfucker" was nowhere to be heard, not even in the "Are there any niggers here tonight?" routine that ended with the punch line: "some motherfucker called him a nigger." In the film the joke ended with a lot less punch as "somebody called him a nigger." According to Barry, the Motion Picture Association of America (MPAA), whose job is assigning ratings, restricted the producers to only one of the words if they wanted an R instead of something worse; they settled on cocksucker because it had led to his first arrest in 1961, and could be worked into Bruce's turbulent personal life with his stripper wife, Honey Harlowe. Nothing was illuminated about his stormy and seductive relationship with his mother Sadie, professionally known as Sally Marr, who had been a stripper herself when Lenny was growing up.

In his memoir *Tough Talk*, Martin Garbus recounted that he used Dorothy Kilgallen's 1964 testimony in another case, this one before the Rating Appeals Board of that same Motion Picture Association of America. "It was as if I had gotten trapped in a time warp, for here in Los Angeles, on a winter morning in 1994, I was reading from testimony I had elicited thirty years earlier in the heart of a New York summer. The cases were vastly different in legal context, but they shared a common thread, which was this nation's obsessive preoccupation with the concept of obscenity."

The MPAA had burdened comic Martin Lawrence's concert film, *You So Crazy*, with an NC-17, "a euphemistic updating of the old X rating," Garbus wrote. It was the kiss of death, "a more insidious form of censorship," because most newspapers and magazines refused to advertise NC-17 films, most theater chains wouldn't show them, and many major video and DVD retailers like Wal-Mart and Target wouldn't stock them.

Garbus saw a through-line from Lenny Bruce to the young black comedian. "[Lawrence's] stand-up routines were laced with a slashing, brutally frank humor, including explicit descriptions of sex and body parts that left little to the imagination. Framed largely as social satire, they were delivered in a vernacular common to the streets, their dialect and themes most accessible to a black audience in the same way that Bruce's routines were often sprinkled with Yiddish phrases and references."

As Garbus studied the film he could see why Bruce's humor had confounded even the more sophisticated listeners of his time. "Bruce and I, in large measure, shared the same roots, our sensibilities tuned by background to a common pitch. But how could he be easily understood by the sons of another time and place? Who would have been bold enough to try to explain to the choirmaster of a Southern Baptist church that when Lenny depicted a black protester telling Barry Goldwater, 'Don't lay that jacket on us, motherfucker,' he was not commenting on style of dress or expressing an attitude toward incest?"

The MPAA's Appeals Board turned out to be even more of a kangaroo court than Murtagh's judicial triad. Mostly middle-aged and nearly all white, the fifteen members were clearly outside the fan base of ghetto-edged comedy. "Kilgallen's testimony, as perceptive and precise as it was, served Lawrence no better than it had Bruce," Garbus said, "The vote went against him, 12 to 3. The producer chose to release the film without an MPAA rating, which meant that its distribution was severely limited. It was shown in selected theaters and did reasonably well. Martin continued to thrive on network television and in MPAA-rated feature films. He went on delivering his stand-up routines unencumbered by legal restrictions or threats of arrest. Lenny Bruce had not fared nearly as well."

And yet, according to comic and sixties iconoclast Paul Krassner, who helped Bruce write his autobiography, Lenny has had the last word. In a 1996 *Utne Reader* piece called "What Ever Happened to Obscenity?" Krassner noted how those four-, ten-, and twelve-letter words responsible for getting the comedian dragged into court are now part of the everyday American scenery. "Lenny Bruce has finally gotten his wish," he said. "Dirty words have been demystified. Taboos, it seems, evolve along with everything else."

In other words, Lenny Bruce gave us the freedom to shout *motherfucker* in a crowded theater.

ROCK’N’ROL
MOFOS!

> "I wanna rock! I'm not bullshitting you motherfuckers, let's go!"
>
> —Ben Folds Five, "For All the Pretty People" (2005)

Popular American music has traditionally revered motherhood, holding mom up as a blessed symbol of faith, love, and intimacy that no mere romantic lover could touch. "I want a girl just like the girl that married dear old dad," the Peerless Quartet harmonized back in 1911, three years before President Woodrow Wilson signed Mother's Day into a national holiday. "A real old-fashioned girl with heart so true, one who loves nobody else but you." Irish tenor John McCormack coaxed many a salty tear into mugs of beer with "Mother Machree," who occupied "a spot in my heart which no colleen may own." In 1916 balladeer Henry Burr spelled out "M-O-T-H-E-R (A Word That Means the World to Me)" on over a million shellac platters, then described the holy meaning of each letter, as in "M is for the many ways. . . ." In the 1920s, George Jessel waxed nostalgically about "My Mother's Eyes" with the opening verse: "I can remember loving caresses showered on me; Mother's eyes would gaze at me so tender, what was their meaning? Now I can see." Willie Howard cherished the memory of "My Yiddishe Momme," singing, "I long to hold her hand once more, as in days gone by, and ask her to forgive me for things I did that made her cry." Al Jolson, best known today for his various "mammy" songs, got down on one knee to sing "Mother of Mine, I Still Have You" in the film *The Jazz Singer*. Even hillbilly star Jimmie Rodgers got in on the act with "Mother, the Queen of My Heart." Every one of these songs was a mash note to mama, a declaration of eternal love for the one woman who put her heart and soul into the welfare of her darling prince, and nobody would have thought otherwise. Not even Henry Burr's "Daddy You've Been a Mother to Me" would have raised a snicker.

It wasn't until blues music came along that singers began to blur the bonds of motherhood and romance, a reflection perhaps of that disturbing matriarchy that white America imposed upon its black citizens. As a man grew up, he carried the word *mama* into his romantic relationships. When Son House recorded "My Black Mama" in 1930, he wasn't singing about the woman who birthed him into the world, but rather the plain and simple woman who had given him such domestic trouble—or so it seemed. Perhaps the most notable example of confusion is Big Boy Crudup's 1946 recording, "That's All Right," the story of a man's indecision about whether to continue putting up with his girlfriend or pay attention to his parents' admonitions: "My mama she done told me, papa done told me too, this life you're living, son, now women be the death of you." But in another verse he's borrowing an old line from Blind Lemon Jefferson's 1927 "Black Snake Moan" in which "mama" is his girlfriend: "Well now that's all right now, mama, that's all right for you, that's all right now, mama, any way you do, but that's all right, that's all right, that's all right now, mama, any way you do." The double use of mama in "That's All Right" creates some serious ambivalence and ambiguity, which may explain why a mama's boy like Elvis Presley later got hold of it.

Of course, these artists had to avoid any overt sexual connection between filial and sexual love when they went into the studio, and it goes without saying that "mother fucker" (still separate words in those days) was strictly taboo, along with every other obscenity. For example, when the great New Orleans jazz pianist Jelly Roll Morton recorded an extended interview for Library of Congress folklorist Alan Lomax in 1938, he played a boastful song called "Windin' Boy Blues" that he had first performed thirty years earlier in New Orleans whorehouses ("winding" referred to the circular motion of fucking). He sang, "I'm the winding boy, don't deny my name, I'm the windin' boy, bred to fame.... I seen that girl, sittin' on the stump, I screwed her till her pussy stunk... I met that gal, met her on the grass, I pulled that snake right from her big ass," and so on. But when Morton decided to record the song for Victor Records' Bluebird subsidiary in 1939, he renamed it the more ambiguous "Winin' Boy Blues" and turned it into an instrumental with only a short vocal refrain, in which he removed everything except the opening line, "I'm the windin' boy, don't deny my name," which he repeated throughout. Likewise, when blues singers Memphis Minnie (Lizzie Douglas) and Speckled Red (Rufus Perryman) recorded their respective versions of "The Dirty Dozen" in the 1930s, they changed the first line, "All you motherfuckers gather round" to "All you menfolk gather round."

The most famous example of a lyric makeover occurred in the 1940s. When Granville "Stick" McGhee was in boot camp in Virginia during World War II, he and his Army buddies sat in their barracks making up a little blues song about drinking cheap wine. They called it "Drinkin' Wine, Mother Fucker, Drinkin' Wine," and tagged it with the line: "Pass that goddamn bottle to me." A couple of years later, when Stick got a chance to record for Harlem Records in New York, he auditioned his song for the owner, J. Mayo Williams, a college-educated black man who had been working for major record companies since the 1920s. But as Stick said later, "You couldn't say *bed* on a record, let alone *mother fucker*." The song would have to be cleaned up. Even the *goddamn* would have to go.

Williams had a solution. He'd once produced a black vaudevillian named Sam Theard, who sometimes recorded under the name Spo Dee O Dee, an appellation he also fashioned into a late 1930s novelty song called "Spo-De-O-Dee." Under various spellings, "spo-de-o-dee"—taken from the word *spode*, slang for semen, probably inspired by the china-white color of Josiah Spode porcelain—was one of Theard's many euphemisms for sexual intercourse: "Adam met Eve in the Garden of Eden, that's where it first begun; Adam said to Eve, 'Let's spo-de-o-dee, come on, let's have some fun.'" Mayo Williams liked the term because he could sneak it past his white bosses, but more importantly, spo-de-o-dee was four unstressed syllables, just like mother fucker. So when Stick McGhee sat down in the recording studio with his guitar, he transformed "Drinkin' Wine, Mother Fucker" into "Drinkin' Wine, Spo-Dee-O-Dee." The song became one of the biggest R&B hits of 1949—and eventually mellowed into both a rockabilly and R&B standard. Jerry Lee Lewis, a crazy motherfucker by any criterion, even had a country hit with it in 1973.

But "Drinkin' Wine, Spo-Dee-O-Dee" wasn't the first time *motherfucker* had to be dealt with before a blues song was studio-ready. A dozen years earlier, on January 10, 1935, the then-reigning queen of the blues, singer-guitarist Memphis Minnie, dealt with the term more directly by recording a song for Decca Records called "Dirty Mother For You," whose title—which appears in every verse—sounds like a slurring of dirty motherfucker:

> I ain't no doctor, but I'm the doctor's wife
> You better come to me if you want to save your life
> He's a dirty mother for ya, he don't mean no good
> He got drunk this morning, tore up the neighborhood.

I want you to come here, baby, come here quick
He done give me something 'bout to make me sick
Awwww, dirty mother for ya, he don't mean no good
He got drunk this morning, tore up the neighborhood.

The song became so popular that other blues singers on major record labels took a stab at it, including pianist-singer Roosevelt Sykes—as "Dirty Mother For You (Don't You Know)," also on Decca—and Washboard Sam on Vocalion, Decca's blues label. Modern blues fans are probably more familiar with a 1947 version by a ragged vocalist named Nelson Wilburn, who waxed it as "Mother Fuyer" under the name Dirty Red. Recorded in Chicago for a Los Angeles company, featuring the legendary Lonnie Johnson on guitar and Blind John Davis on piano, "Mother Fuyer" had a different set of lyrics and verse structure, and was aimed clearly at the under-the-counter party record market:

Squeeze me tight don't you let me fall
Put my mule kickin' in your stall
Kickin mother fuyer don't ya know
Kickin mother fuyer don't ya know
Kickin' mother fuyer
I ain't gonna tell you no lie…
I don't love my woman
Tell you the reason why
Filled my pants full of red-devil lye
Was a warm mother fuyer don't ya know
Funny mother fuyer don't ya know
Smokin' mother fuyer
I ain't gonna tell you no lie.

R&B star Johnny "Guitar" Watson carried the song into the 1970s with a funked-up version called "Real Mother For Ya," included on an album of the same name, with a cover photo of his real mother pushing him in a soapbox Rolls-Royce. The single went to number five on *Billboard*'s R&B charts in mid-1977 and nearly cracked the Top 40, forty-two years after Memphis Minnie's original.

One recording made strictly as a blank-label bootleg disc for stag parties was cut in 1954 by the Clovers, one of the most popular R&B vocal groups of the time, known for "Blue Velvet," "One Mint Julep," and "Devil or Angel." At the end of one of their sessions for Atlantic Records, they sang—a cappella—a rewrite of Shelton Brooks' 1917 minstrel tune

"Darktown Strutter's Ball," retitled "Rotten Cocksuckers' Ball," with an opening lyric of "Cocksuckin' Sammy get your motherfuckin' mammy, we're goin' downtown to the cocksuckers' ball." Apparently variations had already been circulating for a couple of decades as "The Freak's Ball" and "The Motherfucker's Ball," with the lyric: "Oh there's gonna be a ball at the motherfucker's hall…but the best damn piece of all was when I got my mother-in-law, last Saturday night at the motherfucker's ball." Frank Zappa later recorded the Clovers' version—as "Cock-Suckers' Ball"—at a concert that ended up on a live album, *Does Humor Belong in Music?*, released in England in 1986. Zappa dedicated the song to "all the Republicans in the audience." (*Cock*, as noted at various points throughout this book, was a common black Southern word for vagina, not the penis, so cocksucking in this context referred to cunnilingus, not fellatio.)

The inspiration for at least two songs in the late 1960s was a New York group of leftists and anarchists who called themselves Up Against the Wall Motherfuckers, usually shortened to "the Motherfuckers"—perhaps the first public use of the term as a compound word. The Motherfuckers were formed in the late sixties by Dada painter Ben Morea and poet Dan Georgiakis, who took their name from LeRoi Jones's bitter 1967 poem called "Black People." Jones wrote: "you cant steal nothin from a white man, he's already stole it he owes you anything you want, even his life. All the stores will open if you say the magic words. The magic words are: Up against the wall mother fucker this is a stick up!"

The Motherfuckers set up crash pads, free food banks, and legal services for radicals on the run, instigated political demonstrations and riots (including a confrontation at the Pentagon), and forcibly occupied a popular music venue, the Fillmore East, until owner Bill Graham agreed to allow weekly free concerts. Their "Up against the wall, motherfuckers!" slogan became a popular chant after students scrawled it on the walls of the mathematics department during the Columbia University protests in 1968. Mark Rudd, the fiery leader of the Students for a Democratic Society (SDS), even quoted the line in an April letter he wrote to Columbia's president: "We begin by fighting you over your support of Vietnam and American Imperialism…. There is only one thing left to say. It may sound nihilistic to you, since it is an opening shot in a war of liberation. I'll use the words of LeRoi Jones, whom I'm sure you don't like a whole lot: 'Up against the wall motherfucker, this is a stick-up.'" Rudd made "Up Against the Wall, Motherfucker" the logo of SDS's Columbia chapter, explaining later, "It put the administration and the interests they represent on one side, leftist students and the interest of humanity on the other. Those undecided in the middle are forced to choose sides." Abbie Hoffman, cofounder of the confrontational, anti-establishment Yippies, paid the Motherfuckers their highest compliment by calling them "the middle-class nightmare...an anti-media media phenomenon simply because their name could not be printed."

"Up against the wall, motherfuckers!" became a national countercultural rallying cry when the Jefferson Airplane, a San Francisco acid rock band, injected it into the refrain of the song "We Can Be Together" on their best-selling 1969 *Volunteers* album (which RCA-Victor had originally postponed for several weeks as they unsuccessfully negotiated with writer Paul Kantner to drop the offending lyric):

> All your private property is
> Target for your enemy,
> And your enemy is
> We
> We are forces of chaos and anarchy
> Everything they say we are we are
> And we are very
> Proud of ourselves
> Up against the wall
> Up against the wall motherfucker
> Tear down the walls
> Tear down the walls.

On August 19, 1969, following their performance at the Woodstock festival the day before, the Jefferson Airplane hurried into New York City to perform the song, motherfucker and all, on ABC's *The Dick Cavett Show*, for the benefit of the eastern half of the national primetime television audience—before the censors rallied in time to bleep it for the west coast broadcast. Thus was the word introduced to America's airwaves.

That in turn inspired Ray Wylie Hubbard's early seventies hillbilly anthem "Up Against the Wall, Redneck Mother," which I've already covered in Chapter 4.

The word *motherfucker* didn't become a major record label problem until 1969, when Elektra signed a high-energy Detroit rock group that called itself the MC5, short for Motor City 5. Formed several years earlier as a high school band with Dave Clark Five aspirations, the MC5 had recently developed an anti-war, anti-establishment attitude, thanks in part to its manager, a rifle-toting activist and poet named John Sinclair, who enhanced their "fuck you" reputation by booking them on a festival connected with the anti-government protests at the 1968 Democratic National Convention in Chicago.

When Elektra signed the MC5, company president Jac Holzman and producer/engineer Bruce Botnick came up with the idea of introducing them with a live album because they were such an exciting road band. As MC5 guitarist Wayne Kramer told Rick Clark of *mixonline.com*, "[We were] this band without a hit record that could draw 3,000 people a night in the Detroit area. We could do that in Chicago, and we could do it in Cleveland. We played for years all over that part of the country and built up a grass-roots following that couldn't be denied."

Using an 8-track tape machine, Botnick recorded two evening concerts in late October 1968 at Detroit's Grande Ballroom, plus an afternoon sound check without an audience. Culling the best performances, he assembled an album called *Kick Out the Jams*, taken from the title of the opening song. It began with a call to action from vocalist Rob Tyner: "Right now, right now, right now, it's time to [pause] kick out the jams, motherfuckers!" John Sinclair even made reference to the term—spelled "mother fucker"—in his "manifesto" liner notes on the inside of the fold-out album jacket. When Elektra released *Kick Out the Jams* in early 1969, many retail stores refused to carry it, and of course there was no room for MF on the FM dial.

Fortunately, there was an alternate performance to replace the offending one. Bassist Michael Davis told Clark, "Right before the first show, when we got all our levels and everything set, we were asked, 'Can you do one where you don't say motherfucker? Can you do one where you say something else, like brothers and sisters?' We knew that 'Kick Out the Jams, Motherfuckers' would never be a hit single, we weren't stupid, so we had absolutely no trouble with recording another version of the intro with 'Kick Out the Jams, Brothers and Sisters.' We had to adjust that all of the time, because the police would be waiting for us at the gigs telling us that if we sang that song, they would arrest us. Or the promoter would say, 'If you sing that song, you won't get paid.' So we had a hundred different versions: We had 'Kick Out the Jams, Mother Superior,' 'Kick Out the Jams, Mammy Jammy,' 'Kick Out the Jams, Mustard and Ketchup,' and 'Kick Out the Jams, Sap Suckers.' Tyner would just make them up on the spot and we had no problem with it, and that's why we recorded the alternative 'brothers and sisters' version that afternoon at the sound check."

Botkin inserted this cleaner version into the tape so that a new master could be struck for subsequent pressings. The offending liner notes were also expunged. This new *Kick Out the Jams* LP charted for three weeks in *Billboard* in May 1969, but because of the lost momentum it only reached number thirty. A single version of "Kick Out the Jams," using the "brothers and sisters" version, barely cracked the charts.

But Tyner continued screaming "motherfuckers" in concert. The band also lashed out in the local underground press at Hudson's, Detroit's major retail record chain, after it banned their album, and even plastered one store's windows with "Fuck Hudson's!" written on Elektra stationery. When the chain retaliated by boycotting all Elektra artists, including the then-hot Doors, Jac Holzman dropped MC5 from his roster like a hot spud. The group went on to cut two albums for Atlantic Records, but the limelight had already moved elsewhere. By the time they were recognized as a seminal influence on punk rock and heavy metal, MC5 was long defunct and the members scattered to several parts of the world. But "Kick Out the Jams"—with "motherfuckers" intact—became a staple for many other artists, including Jeff Buckley at nearly all his live concerts and Rage Against the Machine on their 2000 album *Renegades*.

Speaking of the Doors, Elektra boss Holzman had already dealt with the problem of mother-son canoodling a couple of years earlier, in 1967, with the release of the group's first album, *The Doors*. One of the songs on the LP was a dark, moody lamentation by lead singer Jim Morrison called "The End," the band's big closer at their shows. Morrison, who longed to be a decadent, absinthe-sipping poet like Arthur Rimbaud, rather than a mere decadent, hotel-room-trashing rock singer, went into a monologue inspired by *Oedipus Rex*:

> The killer awoke before dawn, he put his boots on
> He took a face from the ancient gallery [author's note: there's the Greek tragedy reference]
> And he walked on down the hall
> He went into the room where his sister lived, and...then he
> Paid a visit to his brother, and then he
> He walked on down the hall, and
> And he came to a door...and he looked inside
> "Father?" "Yes son." "I want to kill you.
> Mother? I want to...fuck you!"

Doors guitarist Robby Krieger later told writer Gavan Daws, "[Jim] was on this Oedipus-complex trip and he was saying, 'Fuck the mother and kill the father! Goddamn it! Fuck the mother and kill the father!' and he would just rant on like that for hours. So we finally [got] him in to record and he did it great."

Morrison garbled the last two words in a scream that allowed the album to be released, but the strong implication of incest in "The End" nonetheless stirred up more attention than the group wanted. Morrison tried to soften the outcry by hinting that his kill-the-father-and-fuck-the-mother references meant destroying the male hierarchy and embracing the most basic elements of love—either within one's psyche or in society in general.

There were other stray references to mother love in rock. In Arlo Guthrie's "Alice's Restaurant," an eighteen-minute recitation off his 1968 Top 20 album of the same name, he played on the mental echo of *motherfucker* by saying he'd been tossed into jail with "mother stabbers" and "father rapers."

Three years later, in 1971, a popular blaxploitation film called *Shaft*, about a tough Harlem private dick named John Shaft, introduced a soulfully seductive soundtrack album and a single, *Theme from Shaft*, that topped their respective *Billboard* charts. Every time the theme played on American radio, listeners heard R&B basso balladeer Isaac Hayes refer to John Shaft as "a *baaad* moth—" before his female backup chorus cut him off with "Shut your mouth!"

Two peculiar euphemisms for *motherfucker* that passed muster in the lily-white world of pop music singledom were "motor scooter" and "motorcycle." On the 1960 number one novelty hit "Alley-Oop" by the Hollywood Argyles, lead vocalist Gary Paxton described the dinosaur-riding caveman as "a bad motor scooter and a mean go-getter." A couple of years earlier, sisters Ann and Lillian Storey, recording as the Twinkies on the tiny Philadelphia-based Peak label, had sung about a boyfriend they called a "Bad Motorcycle": "I knew by the way he spoke, he was a bad motorcycle, *voon voon voon*!" Cameo Records picked up the single, renamed the girls the Storey Sisters, and sold enough copies to catch the ear of Brit chick-comedian Tracey Ullman, who echoed the song into a small eighties hit. In 1964 a band called the Crestones elaborated on the theme with a vocal surf ditty called "She's a Bad Motorcycle" on the tiny Markie label. If the word's meaning weren't clear enough, another band, the Lost, recorded "Mean Motorcycle" for Capitol Records in 1966. As late as 1983, the vocal group the Chi-Lites recorded a small R&B hit called "Bad Motor Scooter."

In one of the stranger examples here, a clever poke at sex and all-American motherhood led to everlasting infamy for a ten-piece rock-funk band, even though the musicians had nothing to do with it. In 1972 record producer-promoter-bullshit artist Terry Knight—best known for creating the early hits of Grand Funk Railroad and contributing to the notorious

"Paul [McCartney] is Dead" hoax of 1969—stumbled upon a group of teenagers from Warren, Ohio, who called themselves Mom's Apple Pie. Knight signed them to a contract with his new label, Brown Bag, and put together a devious media campaign. Working with artist Craig Braun (who had designed the Rolling Stones' zippered *Sticky Fingers* LP a year earlier), Knight came up with what he considered the perfect cover parody for an eponymous debut album called *Mom's Apple Pie*.

At first glance, the LP's artwork looked innocent enough. It featured a Norman Rockwell image—contained within an oval mirror—of an attractive Victorian-era housewife offering the viewer a freshly baked pie with one slice removed and hot juices dripping over the side of the pan. But peering closer, you realized that the missing slice revealed not tasty baked apples but a pink vagina with a discernible clitoris. Dear mother was offering you some steaming pussy. Suddenly that expression on Mom's face, with her tongue licking her lips ("Mmm, good!"), wasn't so beatific.

United Artists, *Mom's Apple Pie*'s distributor, recalled the album, as Knight knew it would—which is why he already had a slightly altered replacement cover ready. Craig Braun had walled off the vagina with bricks, surrounded it with barbed wire, and raised an American flag. A tear was now rolling down Mom's cheek. In the background, two cops peered through the window. Mother's sexual sanctity had been restored, and all was well with the world.

Knight later told writer Barry Stoller, "Well, that was some slice of pie, eh?... We sent out piping hot apple pies in brown paper bags to all the deejays throughout New York to promote that record. That was a good campaign." But not good enough: The anti-censorship furor he envisioned never materialized, the album didn't sell, and the band limped back to Ohio, their career as baked as that apple pie. Knight retired from music the following year, and was sliced to death in Texas by a knife-wielding, pie-eyed maniac three decades later.

Roger Force, Mom's Apple Pie's saxophonist, later told Stoller:

> I remember Knight at one of our recording sessions, showing us the cover. He said it was one of his publicity stunts, like the billboard for Grand Funk in Times Square. He had it all planned, the record would get recalled and it would be a big deal. It was 30,000 album covers that were recalled.... I remember *Saturday Night Live* and the host was Geraldo Rivera, and he flashes the album cover over the air, live. I also remember Knight saying, "I can take a piece of shit and turn it into gold." Meanwhile, I'm famous—for an album cover.

In 1989, eighteen years after Janis Joplin died of a heroin overdose, her record company, Columbia, released an album called *Joplin in Concert* that contained her live performance of a blues called "Ego Rock," recorded in early 1970. It was Joplin's own story of her love-hate relationship with Port Arthur, Texas, her hometown that had notoriously scorned her. Several verses into the song, Joplin gave a spoken interlude:

> Mercy! Mercy!
> I hear you talking about my sorrow, you don't know my pain
> You know there's an inside kind of sorrow, Lord, the women are always singin' the blues.
> All right, all right, motherfucker, *you* sing!

By then, however, being assailed by the word *motherfucker* on a piece of shiny vinyl was as common as hearing people say it on the street. Since the late 1970s, rap and hip-hop music from the ghetto, full of black male pride and posturing, had been struggling into the mainstream, trying to get played on radio. Suddenly, in 1988, there was a swaggering quintet from the Los Angeles ghetto-burb of Compton that didn't give two shits about radio. Calling themselves "Niggaz With Attitude" (N.W.A. for short), they introduced a harsh, violent, street-corner version of rap called *gangsta* that managed to chart and sell millions of records without radio play or other mainstream promotion. Their *Straight Outta Compton* album heralded the black voice of South Central Los Angeles in full cry. Front man O'Shea Jackson, who went by the name Ice Cube, later told the *Los Angeles Times*' Geoff Boucher, "We thought our music was going to land on the shelves with the dirty comedy albums. The blue stuff. We never thought our music could possibly get above the underground." One track called "Fuck tha Police" was a mock court scene described as "N.W.A versus the police department," with Ice Cube and fellow members MC Ren and Eazy-E playing the prosecutors and Dr. Dre presiding as judge. At the end of the song, Judge Dre delivers the verdict to the L.A. cop in the dock: "The jury has found you guilty of being a redneck, white bread, chickenshit muthafucker!" The officer shouts, "But wait, that's a lie! That's a goddamn lie! I want justice! I want justice! Fuck you, you black motherfucker!" as he's dragged from the courtroom. The real-life LAPD, along with the FBI, condemned the song as inflammatory and dangerous. *Rolling Stone* magazine later ranked "Fuck tha Police" number 417 on its list of the 500 Greatest Songs of All Time.

Straight Outta Compton's title track, by Ice Cube, was even more tough-guy profane:

The police are gonna hafta come and get me
Off yo ass, that's how I'm goin out
For the punk motherfuckers that's showin' out
Niggaz start to mumble, they wanna rumble
Mix em and cook em in a pot like gumbo
Goin' off on a motherfucker like that
With a gat that's pointed at yo ass....
AK-47 is the tool
Don't make me act the motherfuckin fool
Me you can go toe to toe, no maybe
I'm knockin niggaz out tha box, daily
Yo, weekly, monthly and yearly
Until them dumb motherfuckers see clearly
That I'm down with the capital C-P-T
Boy, you can't fuck with me.

By now every rapper was coming out of the box with a mouthful of *motherfucks*, and to document the use of the word in hip-hop throughout the 1990s and beyond would require a book of its own. Let's just say that after Ice Cube left N.W.A. over a royalties dispute in 1989, the remaining members dissed him with a track called "A Message to B.A." (i.e., Benedict Arnold) that ended with Dr. Dre jeering, "Think about it, punk motherfucker!" And when N.W.A. reunited in the 1990s, Eazy-E and MC Ren teamed up on a song called "The Muthaphuckin Real." Ice Cube himself responded to the destructive 1992 race riots in Los Angeles with "We Had to Tear This Motherfucker Down."

The floodgates had opened, and the ubiquity of words like *motherfucker* prompted the Parents' Music Resource Center, run by the wife of then-U.S. Senator Al Gore, to develop a record industry–enforced parental advisory sticker required for any offensive single or album before national store chains would sell it.

Nowadays the word has become so casual, it pops up in song titles by well-known rock artists, such as Julian Cope's "Like a Motherfucker," Eels' "It's a Motherfucker" (from Steven Spielberg's Dreamworks label), Beck's "Mutherfuker" (with its tagline: "Everybody's out to get you, motherfucker!"), Superchunk's "Slack Motherfucker," Twisted Sister's "S.M.F." (i.e., Sick Mother Fucker—the inspiration for the band's fan club, Sick Mother Fucking Friends of Twisted Sister), Kid Rock's "You Never Met a Motherfucker Quite Like Me," Prince's "Sexy MF" (sometimes billed in concert and elsewhere as "Sexy Motherfucker"), the Violent Femmes' "Dance, M.F., Dance," Six Feet Under's "Die Motherfucker," Dope's "Die

Motherfucker Die," U2's "Mofo," Nashville Pussy's "Go, Motherfucker, Go," White Zombie's "Welcome to Planet Motherfucker," and Sublime's "Don't Wanna Be No MTV Motherfucker." Singer Martha Wainwright, daughter of sixties folkies Louden Wainwright III and Kate McGarrigle, and brother of troubadour Rufus Wainwright, named one of her EPs *Bloody Mother Fucking Asshole*. Los Angeles punk rockers Black Flag called one of their CDs *Bad Motherfucker*, and New York punk legends Johnny Thunders & The Heartbreakers called their only studio album *L.A.M.F.* (Like a Mother Fucker). Then there are the bands that dare to promote themselves under names like Lazy Mutha Fucka, Jackie-O Motherfucker, the Texas Motherfuckers (from Sweden, no less), and the Reverb Motherfuckers.

Somehow it all came full circle when Nick Cave and the Bad Seeds recorded a version of the nineteenth century proto-blues song, "Stagger Lee," on their 1996 album *Murder Ballads*. Though the song had been waxed more than two hundred times since 1924, none of the recordings dared mention Stagger Lee's reputation as "a bad mother fucker," a staple description from the song's informal street versions, and Cave decided to fix this hole in the historical record. "It's the kind of song where you try and outdo all the versions that came before," he told *Rolling Stone* magazine's David Fricke. "I was just reading this book edited by the poet W.H. Auden, a collection of light verse. And he had a great version of Stagger Lee in there; it was a real surprise to see him get into that. He had Stagger Lee going to Hell and fighting with the Devil and winning, which shows Stagger Lee really is a bad motherfucker."

Just then in came a broad called Nellie Brown,
Was known to make more money than any bitch in town.
She struts across the bar, hitching up her skirt,
Over to Stagger Lee, she starts to flirt with Stagger Lee,
She saw the barkeep, said, "Oh God, he can't be dead!"
Stag said, "Well just count the holes in the motherfucker's head!"
She said, "You ain't look like you scored in quite a time,
Why not come to my pad, it won't cost you a dime,
Mr. Stagger Lee.
But there's something I have to say before you begin,
You'll have to be gone before my man Billy Dilly comes in
Mr. Stagger Lee."
"I'll stay here till Billy comes in, till time comes to pass,
And furthermore I'll fuck Billy Dilly in his motherfucking ass,"
Said Stagger Lee.
"I'm a bad motherfucker, don't you know?"

THE WRITTEN WORD!

"Yeah, I shot the motherfucker!"

—Kalamu ya Salaam, in the words of murder defendant
Dessie Woods, in "Hiway Blues" (1975)

Taboo, a word that Captain Cook brought back from the Pacific island of Tonga in the late eighteenth century, refers among other things to words or phrases considered to have such dangerous supernatural powers that simply to utter them under your breath can bring down the wrath of the gods. *Motherfucker* is certainly one such taboo, and you don't even have to speak it aloud. Even spelled out inertly on a flat surface, whether in pencil, ink, or spray-paint, it has the power of an evil incantation.

Motherfucker in one form or another has been around for centuries, but its literary use—if you're not counting the Greek poet Hipponax's *metrokoites* twenty-five hundred years ago—is fairly recent. Oh, you haven't heard about Hipponax? He grew up in a town on the Aegean Sea, in what is now Turkey, until his slander against local bigwigs required him to decamp around 540 B.C. Notably hunched and ugly, Hipponax was one of the first poets to ruminate at length about the repugnance of man—the stink of his shit and the crust of his other bodily functions. (In other words, Hipponax was my kind of guy.) According to the first-century Roman writer Pliny the Elder, Hipponax offended a famous sculptor named Bupalos by asking him for the hand of his beautiful daughter. Bupalos didn't just scoff at this troll's unmitigated gall; in a piece of public art he literally rendered Hipponax's hideousness in stone, with perhaps some unnecessary caricature added just to piss the little fucker off a little more. Hipponax counterattacked by writing a poem accusing Bupalos of having sex with his mother, whose name may have been Arete. According to British translator Michael Schmidt, "In one fragment Bupalos is quite simply a 'mother-fucker' (*metrokoites*) and we witness him about to pull back his 'godforsaken foreskin'. In another fragment, and as insultingly, the poet himself goes to lie, or seems to, with Bupalos' mother or mistress (depending on who we take Arete to be) and she is certainly up for it, bending obligingly towards the lamp so that he can enter her."

The next infamous example of the term comes twenty-two centuries later, and what better source than the French nobleman Donatien Alphonse François comte de Sade, otherwise known as the Marquis de Sade, who gave us the word *sadism*, or cruel pleasure. Educated by Jesuits who fervently believed whippings were an integral part of the Catholic curriculum, young Sade took to his lessons so well that his greatest joy was living—and writing about—the life of a degenerate. In books like *The 120 Days of Sodom*, he described the hundreds of "passions"—all the way up to murder—that anyone rich and powerful enough could indulge in at a whim, without consequence. Unfortunately, Sade himself was not rich or powerful enough to avoid arrest for abusing prostitutes. On October 18, 1765, after paying twenty-year-old Jeanne Testard two gold louis for her company, he bolted the door to his bedroom and demanded to know if she believed in God, Jesus Christ, and the Virgin Mary. When the harrowed hooker said she did, Sade masturbated into a chalice and screamed that Jesus Christ was a motherfucker. Then, predating *Exorcist* writer William Peter Blatty by over two hundred years, he forced her to masturbate with an ivory crucifix, all the while screaming, "If thou art God, avenge thyself!" God happened to be off doing something else, so it was left to the gendarmes to take Mademoiselle Testard's complaint and throw Sade into the boobyhatch.

In *Maledicta*, a 1977 compendium of oaths and swear words, Reinhold Aman writes that in the United States "mother-fucker" in its intensive form dates from the late 1920s and "motherfucking" was first used around 1933. But truth be told, Aman was off by almost by forty years. More recently, Connecticut legal researcher Fred R. Shapiro found the word in a couple of nineteenth century Texas legal cases. *The Texas Court of Appeals Reports* of 1890 detailed a case of slander against one Marshall Levy (*Levy v. State*, 1889) in which a man named McKinney called him "that God damned mother-f---king, bastardly son-of-a-bitch!" The word got its full airing a few years later, in 1897, in *Fitzpatrick v. State*, when the Texas Court of Criminal Appeals heard the defendant's request to have a murder charge against him reduced to manslaughter because "the deceased called the defendant 'a mother-fucking son-of-a-bitch,' and the defendant, on account of said language and under the immediate influence of sudden passion caused thereby, if any, shot and killed the deceased." The court turned him down.

Generally, however, you'd have a very hard time finding *motherfucker* on the printed page; not even the explicitness of the *Fitzpatrick v. State* appeal survived a later reprinting, in which the wording was changed to "a charge that the defendant was 'a mother and sister riding son of a bitch.'" It's not that writers were afraid of using *motherfucker*, but rather that publishers feared punishment from any number of governments—federal, state, and local. The Founding Fathers were apparently a free-thinking, enlightened bunch who enjoyed telling each other off-color jokes and Rabelaisian yarns, so don't blame it on them. Hammering out the First Amendment to the Constitution in 1791, they included several basic freedoms, including the right to speak and publish whatever was on one's mind. Whatever restrictions might apply to obscenity came from British common law. It wasn't a federal government concern until 1873, when a Connecticut Yankee named Anthony Comstock, who had been traumatized during the Civil War by hearing his fellow soldiers' free-flowing profanity, founded the New York Society for the Suppression of Vice. Perhaps emboldened by an English case from five years earlier, *Regina v. Hicklin*, which defined obscene material as that which tended to "deprave and corrupt those whose minds are open to such immoral influences," Comstock lobbied Congress to pass the Comstock Act, which banned the use of the U.S. Post Office to send anything of a sexual nature, including information about birth control. Many states followed with "Comstock laws" of their own, generally slanted toward preventing the transmission of materials that "depraved and corrupted" the minds of adolescents by creating "sexually impure" thoughts. In 1933 the Court of Appeals for the Second Circuit in New York upgraded the standard to "normal adults" when it determined that the U.S. Customs Office had no right to seize imported copies of Irish novelist James Joyce's *Ulysses*. The U.S. Supreme Court didn't get around to the business of dirty words and ideas until 1957, in the case (*Roth v. U.S.*) of a mail-order porn book dealer named Sam Roth, in which Justice William Brennan, writing for the majority, defined obscenity as material "utterly without redeeming value...which deals with sex in a manner appealing to prurient interest" that may "excite lustful thoughts." Obscenity, he said, "is not within the area of constitutionally protected speech or press."

A year after the *Ulysses* case, *motherfucker*, without being completely spelled out, appeared in a genuine American classic: John O'Hara's 1934 *Appointment in Samarra*, a raw little novel from a major publisher, Harcourt Brace & Company, about a businessman's moral disintegration in a Pennsylvania coal town in 1930. After Al Grecco, an Italian factotum of local Irish mobster Ed Charney, lets his boss's mistress slip off with the WASP protagonist, Charney goes into a rage and insults Grecco's mother: "She was a wonderful woman, and she was his mother, and if Ed Charney called him a son of a bitch, all right; if he called him a bastard, all right. Those were just names that you called a guy when you wanted to make him mad, or when you were mad at him. Those names didn't mean anything anyhow, because, Al figured, if your mother was a bitch, if you were a bastard, what was the use of fighting about it?" But what Charney had said to him was, "Why, you small-time, chiseling bastard, you. You dirty lousy mother--------- bastard." The insult was extreme enough to make Grecco start imagining a brick wall, just like the one in the Chicago garage where one gang had gunned down another on a recent St. Valentine's Day. The prestigious *Saturday Review* magazine objected to the novel's explicitness ("nothing but infantilism"), but there were no legal repercussions about the strongly implied *motherfucker*. The fact that the word was confined within an American town's ethnic and criminal element probably mitigated its impact.

Still, publishers treaded lightly. When Chester Himes's bitter first novel, *If He Hollers Let Him Go*, was published in 1945, his black protagonist, a Los Angeles wartime munitions worker named Bob Jones, freely expressed his contempt for whites, and liberally used "nigger" in nearly every context, but the word *motherfucker* always came out as *bastard* or *sonuvabitch*. The closest he came to unclenching his jaw and breaching the barrier was when a white gate guard asked him, "What'd y'all do las' night, boy?" Jones didn't answer: "I started to tell him I was up all night with his mother, but I didn't feel up to the trouble."

Not until after World War II, as over a million Americans came home with their vocabularies substantially salted with mud-grunt profanity, were publishers willing to allow battlefield memoirists to overrun the lines of decency. Norman Mailer's war novel, *The Naked and the Dead*, was the first to create a public sensation in 1948 by offering the barefaced "fug" as a blunted substitute for "fuck." (*Fug* had appeared three years earlier, in *Cannery Row*, but John Steinbeck used it sparingly, whereas Mailer splattered it on nearly every other page, complete with the more shocking "mother-fuggin.") Mailer wasted no time introducing the profane Gallagher and his fellow soldiers on the opening pages, playing seven-card stud: "For several seconds Gallagher was silent, but the dark lumps on his face turned a dull purple. Then he seemed to burst all at once. 'Of all the mother-fuggin luck, that sonofabitch takes it all.'" When another soldier shouts that the poker game is keeping him awake, Gallagher tells him, "Go fug yourself." (Dorothy Parker reportedly later greeted Mailer at a party with, "So you're the man who can't spell fuck.")

But not until James Jones two years later included fifty *fucks* (down from five times that many in the original manuscript) in another battlefield drama, *From Here to Eternity*, did that unadulterated word enter literary discourse.

Along with war recollections, jazz memoirs from both white and black artists seemed to be a field where a writer could get away with saying *motherfucker*, as long as it were put into a form less obvious than mother-fugger. Jewish clarinetist Milton "Mezz" Mezzrow wrote in *Really the Blues* (1946), "And it was in Pontiac [Reformatory] that I dug that Jim Crow man in person, a motherferyer that would cut your throat for looking"; a dozen pages later a black character says, "Man, they'd cut your nuts out for lookin', where these motherferyers come from." In an appendix Mezzrow explained: "Motherferyer is an incestuous obscenity which has its counterpart in every language in the world." Joe "Wingy" Manone, a one-armed trumpet player from New Orleans, wrote in *Trumpet on the Wing* (1948): "When we came out I discovered some mother-robbin' bastard had broken into my car window and taken my horn." Billy Holiday, in her ghostwritten *Lady Sings the Blues* (1956), said: "It doesn't matter how unlikely the [interracial] couple, the mother-hugging squares always figure they're only up to one damn thing."

The world of urban crime and juvenile delinquency was also ripe for the word to be used, but again as long as the writer removed its stinger. Motherjumper seemed to be the most popular. Hal Ellson, a New York City youth worker who turned to writing about rebellious teens in the late 1940s, used it in his breakthrough, million-selling novel *Duke* (1949): "'So what?' I said to Chink. 'That motherjumper ought to get caught.'" He carried the word into subsequent lurid novels such as *Tomboy* (1950) and *The Golden Spike* (1952). Two writers who collaborated under the name Thurston Scott used *motherjumping* in their 1951 marijuana-fueled potboiler *Cure It with Honey*. Even into the late 1960s the strange word showed up in Richard Farina's *Been Down So Long It Looks Like Up to Me* ("'David, baby,' he yelled happily, throwing out his arms, 'you old benevolent motherjumper, I love you.'") and Spanish Harlem writer Piri Thomas's 1967 *Down These Mean Streets* ("I wanna tell ya I'm here—you bunch of motherjumpers"). In another disreputable precinct of the demimonde, heavyweight boxing champion Rocky Graziano was able to flavor his 1955 autobiography, *Somebody Up There Likes Me*, with lines like "Stand straight, you little mother-lover." For groundbreaking young black writers Langston Hughes and Ralph Ellison, the word was *motherfouler*: "Give it to him, Maceo, coolcrack the motherfouler" and "[P]ut up a sign, motherfouler," were two of many examples in Ellison's 1952 classic *Invisible Man*, while six years later, in a play called *Tambourines to Glory*, one of Hughes's characters said, "Sister Laura's going to crack up and all over Buddy Lomax—who everybody knows is a mother-fouler.") For Robert Gover, in his 1961 racial satire *One Hundred Dollar Misunderstanding*, the term was *motherlumping*: "I feel like sayin, Baby way you go off, you musta been saving that one for a motherlumpin lifetime." When Chester Himes began a series of successful Harlem police detective novels, he liberally put *mother-raping* into the mouths of his lead characters, as in "'All I wish is that I was God for just one mother-raping second,' Grave Digger said, his voice cotton-dry with rage. 'I know,' Coffin Ed said. 'You'd concrete the face of the mother-raping earth and turn white folks into hogs,'" from *Cotton Comes to Harlem* (1965). Even as late as 1969, when he felt free to use any other obscenity, Himes stuck with this blunted phrase in *Blind Man with a Pistol*: "Mother-raping cocksucking turdeating bastard, are you blind?" Another black writer of that era, Alice Childress, used *mother-grabbin'* in her 1969 play *Wine in the Wilderness*, when one of her characters said, "I'm independent as a hog on ice and a hog on ice is dead, cold, well preserved, and don't need a mother-grabbin' thing." John Oliver Killens, in his 1971 novel of black bourgeois manners, *The Cotillion*, put "mammy lover" and "mammy-hunching" into his characters' mouths.

These terms were tolerated because the characters were blacks and Puerto Ricans, with an occasional Lower East Side Jewish kid or Sicilian street fighter thrown in for good measure. Dr. Frederic Wertham praised Hal Ellson's *Duke* in the *American Journal of Psychotherapy* because of its "truth—the authentic truth of real conditions, the psychological truth of individual reactions, the artistic truth of presentation, and the moral truth of facing evil that exists right under our noses." But Wertham was not so generous when juvenile delinquency and its sassy lip began to infect white neighborhoods. His 1954 screed against postwar teenage culture, called *Seduction of the Innocent*, led to a Congressional Subcommittee that banned gory horror comic books and attacked "jungle music," i.e., early rock 'n' roll records.

Not until a homosexual element was added to the juvenile delinquent genre in 1956 could "motherfucker" be used in all its gaping, glaring, transgressing glory. Its baptism in American letters came in the literary debut—*63: Dream Palace: A Novella and Nine Stories*—of James Otis Purdy, a thirty-three-year-old gay novelist and short story writer from Fremont, Ohio. In the novella *63: Dream Palace*, two young brothers named Fenton and Claire Riddleway leave Ronceverte, West Virginia, after the death of their mother, and they end up in what is presumably New York City, where Fenton reluctantly becomes the object of desire among several aging queens and turd-thumping pederasts. When Fenton deludes himself into thinking that a rich, love-starved widow wants to remove him from the world of street hustling, he murders his inconvenient sickly kid brother. "You're dead, you little motherfucker," he mutters as he becomes aware of the horror he's committed. "Dead as mud and I don't have no need sitting here staring you down." All that's left is to carry the body up to the attic of their crumbling house and stuff it into an old trunk. "For part of the night he found that he had fallen asleep over Claire's body, and at the very end before he carried him upstairs and deposited him, he forced himself to kiss the dead stained lips he had stopped, and said, 'Up we go then, motherfucker'"—and those were the final words of the story: a send-off, a kiss-off, a fuck-off, and an altogether parting shot. Purdy wrote prolifically and earned lavish international praise from Dame Edith Sitwell (who arranged for *63: Dream Palace* to be published in Great Britain), Dorothy Parker, and Edward Albee, among others, but he remains a fairly obscure writer in his home country.

Purdy was a part of the new cool school of writers and artists, called Beats, who came of age after World War II. They had adopted the detached "cool pose" of black culture, specifically the aesthetic of bebop jazz, a rejection of heated-up postwar American society. In a 1957 essay called "The White Negro" that ran in *Dissent* magazine, Norman Mailer defined these white hipsters as the true American existentialists, reacting to the nuclear age's ever-present threat of annihilation by embracing "death as an immediate danger" and trying "to exist without roots, to set out on that uncharted journey into the rebellious imperatives of the self." If a white man "absorbed the existentialist synapses of the Negro," Mailer wrote, he "could be considered a White Negro." Part of that pose was the language of the ghetto—its jive, its misdirection, its motherfuckers.

Beat writer and junkie William S. Burroughs brought the word further into the light in his disjointed fever dream, *The Naked Lunch*, first published in Paris (in English) by the notorious Olympic Press in 1959. When Grove Press released the novel in substantially different form in the U.S. three years later (as simply *Naked Lunch*), the Commonwealth of Massachusetts immediately banned it as obscene, and several other states followed suit. Most objectionably, Burroughs had touched on pedophilia, but he also used that dreaded mother word. Olympia publisher Maurice Girodias had already excised the line "Cowboy: New York hood talk mean kill the mother fucker wherever you find him. A rat is a rat is a rat is a rat" (it wouldn't be restored to the text until four decades later), but he left intact a short chapter in which two "Negro Bearers" carry "The Man" into a "technological psychiatry" conference where a large black centipede is scurrying around on a table. One of the bearers looks down and screams, "Man, that mother-fucker's hungry." (In the "restored text" edition of *Naked Lunch* published in 2002, another line—a "young hooligan" threatening "I'll cut your throat you white mother fucker!"—that ran in the Olympia version but not the Grove edition, was also put back in.) Since literary critics at the time considered Burroughs to be nothing more than a drug-addled degenerate writing for a cadre of fellow wastrels and arty down-and-outers, nobody but the authorities seemed to take offense. When the Massachusetts Supreme Judicial Court finally overturned the obscenity ruling in 1966, the decision marked the end of major literary censorship court battles in America.

The word's popular introduction to American literature came in 1964 in *Blues For Mister Charlie*, a play by a young Harlem writer named James Baldwin. (Baldwin had already had a run-in with the leftist literary quarterly *Partisan Review* after the editor, fearing the magazine would lose its second-class mailing rights, garbled several words with asterisks in Baldwin's "Any Day Now," in the spring 1960 edition, including "You've got to fight with the elevator boy because the motherf*****'s white!") Fully aware of *motherfucker*'s incantational power, Baldwin stayed with its short form, *mother*, and saved the force of its full expression for one pivotal scene. *Blues For Mister Charlie* was a bitter tale based loosely on the 1955 bludgeoning and shooting of a fourteen-year-old Chicago kid named Emmett Till, who was visiting his relatives in Money, Mississippi, without having been properly schooled in Jim Crow's rigid decorum. Three days after the boy allegedly whistled at a white woman, his swollen, weighted-down, barbed-wire-wrapped body was fished out of the Tallahatchie River. When his mother brought his bloated corpse back to Chicago, she held an open-casket funeral that put the brutality of the South's racial terrorism into the national limelight—creating what *New York Times* reporter David Halberstam called "the first great media event of the civil rights movement." Till's murderers were tried and acquitted; a year later they boasted of what they'd done in a national magazine.

In Baldwin's retelling, a young man named Richard Henry returns to his Southern hometown after eight years of living in New York, where his preacher father had sent him after his mother mysteriously died inside a white man's home. Like Emmett Till, Richard appears oblivious "to the way we do things down here," according to one white character, but in fact he knows the unspoken ordinances of segregation all too well because he grew up there. He's simply too enraged to care. He flaunts his contempt for whites and their disregard for the worth of black people. "Jive mothers," he tells a friend. "They can rape and kill our women and we can't do nothing."

Baldwin uses *mother* freely throughout the play, mostly to express the anger blacks feel toward whites and their own powerlessness and accommodation. At the very beginning, during a mock fight that gets serious, one student assails his friend with "You mother—" before Richard Henry's father cuts him off in mid-word. A minute later another young man says, "You feel like a damn fool standing up there, letting them white mothers beat on your ass."

In a soliloquy, Richard's girlfriend Juanita tells a symbolic courtroom of whites, "I hope I'm pregnant. I *hope* I am! One more illegitimate black baby—that's right, you jive mothers!" Richard's friend Lorenzo tells the same court, "And I *know* ain't no heroin in this town because none of you mothers need it. You was *born* frozen." Richard himself, facing a storekeeper who's ready to shoot him, says, "You sick mother! Why can't you leave me alone? White man! I don't want nothing from you."

Several black townspeople, speaking as a Greek chorus, call out to the black preacher they suspect of being too tight with Mr. Charlie (i.e., the white man): "Tell the truth, mother—tell the truth." Later they wonder aloud, "Why we always got to love *them*. How come it's *us* always got to do the loving? Because you *black*, mother."

Even the play's one sympathetic white character, newspaper editor Parnell James, exclaims, "Richard would say that [I've] got—black fever! Yeah, and he'd be wrong—that long, loud, black mother."

Baldwin pulls out the stops and releases the full power of the word only once, when Richard willfully sets up a confrontation with the storekeeper who will later kill him: "You don't own this town, you white mother-fucker. You don't *even* own twenty dollars. Don't you raise that hammer. I'll take it and beat your skull to jelly." In that single outburst the insolent young man seals his fate by challenging a white man's authority, scorning his economic situation, and—by calling him a "mother-fucker"—making perhaps the worst allegation a black man could lay upon a white Southerner. After all, the bedrock of segregation seemed to be Mr. Charlie's need to protect the honor of his womenfolk: wife, daughters, and mother.

In fact, Baldwin touches upon the sanctity of the white mother. Parnell James, bored with his marriage and the "dull calisthentic called love," recounts his wife accusing him of speaking another woman's name in his sleep. "What name could I have called? I hope it was—a *white* girl's name, anyway! Ha-ha! How still she became!... And she was just looking at me. Jesus! To have somebody just looking at you—just looking at you—like that—at such a moment! It makes you feel—like you woke up and found yourself in bed with your mother." It's a curious simile. His wife has taken the role of his disapproving, judgmental mother, but the phrase "found yourself in bed with your mother" also has a deeper implication.

The Actors' Studio production of *Blues For Mister Charlie* opened at the ANTA Theatre on Broadway on April 23, 1964 (just a couple of weeks after Lenny Bruce had been arrested for saying "motherfucker" in Greenwich Village), and it was printed as a Dell paperback book six months later. Unlike James Purdy, James Baldwin was already famous, the author of *Go Tell It on the Mountain* (1953) and *The Fire Next Time* (1963), but *Blues For Mister Charlie* vaulted him into the firmament of great American writers, just as many of the nation's black neighborhoods were exploding. The previous September, four little black girls had been killed in a Birmingham, Alabama, church bombing. Three months before that, Baldwin's friend, Medgar Evers, head of the Mississippi NAACP, had been murdered after investigating the shooting of a black man by a white store owner who coveted his young, light-skinned wife. In the year after the debut of *Blues For Mister Charlie*, several gunmen assassinated Malcolm X, Alabama state police shot civil rights activist Jimmie Lee Jackson, and a white Los Angeles traffic cop set off a devastating race riot in the suburban ghetto of Watts. The *New York Times* called *Blues For Mister Charlie* "A play with fires of fury in its belly, tears of anguish in its eyes and a roar of protest in its throat.... It is like a thunderous battle cry." Under the circumstances, any critical or censorial objection to Baldwin's use of *motherfucker* would have seemed both churlish and petty and most likely inspired an indignant backlash from black America's intelligentsia that nobody wanted to deal with at the time.

The following year, Claude Brown's *Manchild in the Promised Land*, the gritty and profane story of a young Harlem criminal, became a literary sensation, but the author used *mother-fucker* (hyphenated) in rare instances to catch the narrator's anger: "I was going to find that nigger, and I was going to beat him and beat him until he stopped breathing. I was going to beat that mother-fucker until he realized what he was doing.... I wasn't even going to tell him why. I was just going to tell that mother-fucker to throw up his hands."

But the writer who really put *motherfucker* on the map, in perhaps its most enraging and inflammatory context, was a former Beat poet and sometime playwright named LeRoi Jones. No, I'm not talking about his 1967 book *Tales*, in which the publisher bowdlerized the word to motherfouler. I refer instead to his 1967 poem called "Black People" that exhorted the American Negro male to take back what had been robbed from him over the past three centuries:

> You cant steal nothin from a white
> man, he's already stole it he owes you
> anything you want, even his life. All
> the stores will open if you say the magic
> words. The magic words are: Up against
> the wall mother fucker this is a stick
> up!… Let's get together and kill him my man.

"Black People" would come back to haunt Jones a year later, after he returned to his hometown, Newark, New Jersey, and was arrested during a ghetto-wide conflagration. When Jones was dragged into court for weapons possession, Judge Leon W. Knapp "amazed me by prefacing my sentencing by reading a poem of mine, 'Black People,' with the lines that became ubiquitous: 'Up against the wall, motherfucker, this is a stickup!' He read this to show that I was guilty," Jones wrote in his autobiography. "When he read the poem, he left out the profanity, and as he read I supplied it." The all-white jury returned a conviction, and Kapp sentenced Jones to jail for two and a half years—though he soon won release on appeal. Another one of Jones's 1967 poems called "Black Dada Nihilismus" didn't help his cause either:

> A cult of death,
> need of the simple striking arm under
> the street lamp. The cutters, from under
> their rented earth. Come up, black dada
> nihilismus. Rape the white girls. Rape
> their fathers. Cut the mothers' throats.

What had happened in the year between the publication of "Black People" and Jones's sentencing was that student protesters at Columbia University had turned his passage into a revolutionary catchphrase, amplified with bullhorns over the barricades at riot police. As for LeRoi Jones himself, like many black prisoners all over America he took a new African name (Amiri Baraka) to reflect his recent Muslim conversion and his rejection of Western society.

Now that *motherfucker* was out of the closet, jazz musicians no longer had to salt their memoirs with stilted creations like motherferyer. Throughout his quirky 1971 autobiography, *Beneath the Underdog*, bassist and composer Charles Mingus peppers *motherfucker* in several contexts. On the very first page, during a bout with his psychiatrist, Mingus describes the average put-upon, victimized Negro as "any black motherfucker on the street." But mostly he makes the word a weapon and a talisman to ward off threats. At one point he turns on a bully and "screams with rage…'Come on, do that again you sonofabitch! Swing, dog! Motherfucker!'" In high school Mingus is set upon by a bully who shouts to his buddies, "Get that motherfucker with the cello!" Years later, when a former tormentor tells him, "Go hide behind your cello like you used to, you motherfucking coward," Mingus tears into him and stomps him badly, and as other boys try to pull him off, he shouts, "Die, motherfucker! Stop breathing!" It's his announcement to the world that no longer will he let anybody push him around. In a screaming match with his mother, he tells her, "You killed your own blood mother, you overholy Bible-quoting witch! Now I'm going over the playground and think of you and beat every motherfucker on earth!"

He also puts the word into the mouths of women drawn to the exotic world of the jazz musician. As he's sexually teasing a beautiful black girl named Rita at the beach, she complains softly, "Oh, Mingus, come back, you dirty motherfucker, damn you, come back in—what are you doing to me?" Even the rich white women who hang out at the clubs on Central Avenue and buy gifts for black musicians have dirty mouths, as when a lady named Cindy accosts him as he's coming off the bandstand with, "Where are you going, you beautiful, independent motherfucker?" When he tells her that maybe she should buy him a Rolls Royce, she playfully says, "Wow, you're a crazy little motherfucker." But later, outside in her car, when he takes her purse and rifles through it for money, she gets a little more resentful. "All right, take it, motherfucker. You bastards are all alike." But then, as he starts loving her, she moans, "Oh, you…! My! You fine motherfuuuu…! Kiss me again like that!"

On the bandstand the word binds the musicians together in a special fraternity. Playing at Billy Berg's in Hollywood with Miles Davis, Lucky Thompson, and Charlie Parker, Mingus recounts the interplay as they riff together:

> "Blow, Miles."
> "I done blew, motherfucker…"
> "Whewee! This motherfucker can play…"
> "When are you motherfuckers going to stop talking and start playing?"

"Ladies and gentlemen, will you all shut up and just listen to this motherfucker blowing."

"Miles! Careful, man, you can't say that."

"Shit, man, I put my hand over the mike on 'motherfucker.' Remember Monk calling the club owner in Detroit a motherfucker seven times on the mike 'cause he didn't have a good piano?"

Mingus recalls a time in 1947 when he and other members of Lionel Hampton's band greeted their new trumpet player, Fats Navarro, in New York's busy Grand Central Station. "[I] felt embarrassed as the band walked out. There were strangers, women and children, all around, and the guys were laughing too loudly and joking and words like motherfucker and cocksucker echoed through the station." (Sometimes *cocksucker* and *motherfucker* meant exactly the same thing: a despised, contemptible person or situation. But unlike *motherfucker*, *cocksucker* has never varied much. In Northern black culture especially, performing oral copulation on another man was far worse than fucking your mother. Or as Fats Navarro, during a bitter harangue against white oppression of black musicians, tells Charles Mingus, "Show me where that atomic power button is and I'll give them cocksuckers liberty." *Motherfuckers* was too soft a word in that context.)

Mingus also shows how the intensity of the word can range from affection to hatred. When he wises off to a black club owner, the man threatens him: "Don't get smart with me, motherfucker. You can be replaced, you know." Mingus is so incensed that he goes for the man's gun and dares him to kill him on the spot, until the owner apologizes. Later the man's tone is softer when he tells Mingus and the other musicians, "When you motherfuckers gonna play some music and stop using my time for your escort bureau?"

(Not all jazzmen or their publishers preferred the rawness of *motherfucker*, however. Though bandleader Preston Love wrote his autobiography nearly twenty-five years later, in 1997, he spelled the word "mother—ker" and kept its use to a minimum, usually to describe the buses his band depended on to get them from one gig to another throughout the Midwest. "Count, if that big mother—ker breaks down again, I'm gonna put a bomb up under its ass." Later, a more dependable bus is a "a sweet little mother—ker." In Love's case, the deletion of the word's most offensive syllable reflected both his personal modesty and the decorousness of the Methodist publisher, Wesleyan University Press. Other jazz musicians avoided it altogether when they wrote their memoirs, feeling that jazz's demimonde reputation didn't need any further reinforcement.)

In 1969 Leonard Gardner, writing about the prize fighting business in his novel *Fat City*, put the word bluntly into the mouth of a black boxer named Buford Wills: "It don't matter if you dead drunk, you got two hands you can beat that motherfucker. I don't care who he is. It all in your mind.... I going kick his ass so bad, every time he take a bite of food tomorrow he going think of me. He going *know* he been in a fight. I get him before he get me. I going hit him with everything. I won't just *beat* that motherfucker, I going *kill* him."

In his 1969 autobiography *Nigger*, comedian and activist Dick Gregory dropped the word sparingly into what was otherwise a glaring study of how casual racism in mid-twentieth-century America wore black people down, and he was later upset to discover that his Jewish collaborator, Robert Lipsyte, had hyphenated it. After knocking a whore off a bar stool, Gregory's father tells the other customers, "Dare any mother-fucker in this place to come and stop me from stomping this bitch." And when Gregory himself later curses out a waitress, she shakes with anger and says, "Just give me my money, you dirty little mother-fucker."

That same year, Cecil Brown loaded the word into his stream-of-consciousness novel *The Life and Loves of Mr. Jiveass Nigger*. "At that point George looked out the window, out past the railroad track, and saw his mother and father and the hired hands hoeing in the field. He could tell by the color of the clothes which speck was his mother and which was his father. Dumb motherfuckers always digging in the dirt." That was the same year his friend, Claude Brown, published as a follow-up to his best-selling *Manchild in the Promised Land* a spoof of Westerns and the Old West itself called *Yellow Back Radio Broke-Down*, whose outlaw antihero, a black man called the Loop Garoo Kid, seared the bodies of such white authorities as sheriffs and preachers with his cracking whip. In one scene, after the good Reverend Boyd insults him, the Kid sends him crawling across the floor. "(CRACK!) Whenever you say something like that. (CRACK! CRACK!) In the future. Check out some sources. (CRACK! CRACK!) Motherfucker! Ask you mama! (CRACK!)"

Also in 1969 (a banner year for motherfuckery in literature), former criminal Robert Beck, using his street moniker Iceberg Slim, wrote a brisk-selling memoir called *Pimp: The Story of My Life* for a Los Angeles paperback mill called Holloway House that specialized in badly edited black fiction. Though his prose was graphic, Beck generally restricted "mother-fucker" (with a hyphen) to heightening the anger or modulating the calculated coolness of a situation, as when a gigolo is trying to frighten the thirteen-year-old narrator into leaving his own mother: "Mama worked long hours as a cook, and Steve and I were alone quite often. At these times he would say, 'You little mother-fucker, you. I'm going to beat your mother-fucking ass. I am telling you, if you don't run away, I am going to kill you.'" Not long afterward, Steve kills the boy's kitten. "Where is that little mother-fucker?" he demands, before yanking the kitten from beneath a couch and smashing its head against a wall. In many ways Beck's story of his life as a mack daddy running whores on the streets of Chicago echoed the pimp years that Malcolm X, with his co-writer Alex Haley, had described so vividly four years earlier in *The Autobiography of Malcolm X*, published by Grove Press not long after his assassination. But the difference between them was that, though Grove was known for pushing the edges of bourgeois decency with such books as *Ulysses* and *Naked Lunch*, Malcolm X, a devout Muslim, kept his otherwise gritty memoir free of obscenities, even though he admitted that Harlem nightlife had once turned him into "an uncouth, wild young Negro. Profanity had become my language." In that regard he was following the example of Ethel Waters, the top black recording star of the 1920s and later an actress. An observant Christian when she dictated *His Eye Is on the Sparrow* (1950) to her ghostwriter, Waters let it be known on the first page that "[b]y the time I was seven I knew all about sex and life in the raw. I could outcurse any stevedore and took a sadistic pleasure in shocking people." Then, having made her point, she avoided even the whiff of an obscene euphemism. But Iceberg Slim felt no such compunction in the more lenient environment of 1969. Though he was not gratuitous, he faithfully captured the salty speech of the desperate, low-down people he had done business with. For instance, Phyllis, one of his first whores, tries to fend him off after they meet with: "I ain't no bitch. I'm a mother-fucking lady. The stud ain't been pulled outta his mammy's womb that kicks my ass." But later, after he plays a few mind games on her, she purrs, "You cold-blooded sweet mother-fucker, I go for you."

In *No Name in the Street* (1972), James Baldwin's sequel to *The Fire Next Time*, he talks about visiting his old friend from junior high, who had grown apart from him in many ways. When the conversation turns to the war in Vietnam, Baldwin says that Americans, and more specifically black people, "had no business there, aiding the slave master to enslave yet more millions of dark people, and also identifying themselves with the white American crimes." At that point his friend rises to his feet and says, "Wait a minute, let me stand up and tell you what I think we're trying to do there." Baldwin is livid. "'We?' I cried. 'What motherfucking we? You stand up, motherfucker, and I'll kick you in the ass!'"

With the word commandeered by black writers or black characters, hardly anybody noticed that Jewish writer Bernard Malamud pointedly used it in the novel *The Fixer* (1966), based on the historical account of a Jew in czarist Russia accused of murdering a Gentile child. Well, I'll take that back. Though *The Fixer* won a Pulitzer Prize and a National Book Award, one local school board on Long Island, New York, did pull it off the shelf of a high school library because it objected to the lines "What do you think goes on in the wagon at night: Are the drivers on their knees fucking their mothers?" and "Who else would do anything like that but a motherfucking Zhid?" Nine years later another Jewish author, Saul Bellow, used the phrase—as two words, which seemed retrograde in the mid-seventies—in his Pulitzer Prize–winning novel *Humboldt's Gift*, when he described a spoiled young companion named Louie Lutz on a Kenyan safari: "The payoff was when he got after [the guide] Theo to teach him Swahili words and the first thing he asked for, naturally, was 'mother fucker.' Charlie, there is absolutely no such thing in Swahili."

The so-called sexual revolution of the swinging sixties had changed and polarized America since the U.S. Supreme Court had last determined the definition of obscenity in 1957 with the *Roth v. U.S.* case. Men's newsstand magazines, books, recordings, and films were more flagrantly graphic than ever. And now, in response, a conservative groundswell was rising up all over the country, with local and state governments protesting not only the spread of pornography but also the fallout from the Supreme Court's 1964 *Jacobellis v. Ohio* decision, which had determined that federal standards trumped community standards when it came to judging what was obscene. (*Jacobellis* was the case in which Justice Potter Stewart famously wrote, "I shall not today attempt further to define the kinds of material I understand to be embraced within that shorthand description [hardcore pornography]; and perhaps I could never succeed in intelligibly doing so. But I know it when I see it.") In 1973 a new Supreme Court obscenity case, *Miller v. California*, tried to settle these problems, with mixed results. The new hypothetical arbiter of what was obscene was an "average person, applying contemporary community standards" as to what might appeal to prurient interest. Applicable state laws governed "patently offensive" sexual conduct. So far so good, as far as the simple word *motherfucker* was concerned, unless a writer used it in a graphic mother-son sex scene. But what really opened the door for the word and others like it was the third prong of the Miller decision: "The work, taken as a whole, [is obscene if it] lacks serious literary, artistic, political, or scientific value." In other words, if the writer could claim even a shred of literary or artistic intent, he was free to use dirty words to his heart's content without them being obscene or actionable in a court of law.

That's why nobody pays much attention to a writer salting and peppering his prose with *motherfucker* anymore. As usually happens with shock-value words, it lost its shock value. There's no price to pay, no outrage from honest citizens that's worth listening to. It's become just another word, raggedly gratuitous. Only now and then is its presence powerful enough to merit mentioning. For example, one of my favorite poems is Charles Bukowski's "The History of One Tough Motherfucker" (1984), an ode to one of those indestructible tomcats—his tail missing, his back legs nearly crushed, his skin nicked with gunshot pellets, working on what seems to be his second set of nine lives. Somehow his determination keeps Bukowski's own spirit from sinking too low.

> and now sometimes I'm interviewed, they want to hear about
> life and literature and I get drunk and hold up my cross-eyed,
> shot, runover de-tailed cat and I say, 'look, look
> at this!'
> but they don't understand, they say something like, 'you
> say you've been influenced by Celine?'
> 'no,' I hold the cat up, 'by what happens, by
> things like this, by this, by this!'
> I shake the cat, hold him up in
> the smoky and drunken light, he's relaxed he knows...
> it's then that the interviews end
> although I am proud sometimes when I see the pictures
> later and there I am and there is the cat and we are photo-
> graphed together.
> he too knows it's bullshit but that somehow it all helps.

And then there's Dessie Woods channeled through poet Kalamu ya Salamm. On February 12, 1975, Woods was sentenced to twenty-two years in a Georgia prison for shooting a white man in the head with his own gun, supposedly after he tried to rape her while she was hitchhiking. She was unrepentant at trial, telling the judge and jury, "Yeah, I shot the motherfucker." Her incarceration inspired a "Free Dessie Woods" campaign that brought to national attention the plight of women, especially black women, who were imprisoned simply because they fought back against men who raped or assaulted them, and eventually led to her freedom in 1981. Her comment inspired Salaam to write "Hiway Blues" (1975) in Woods' feminine voice.

ain't it enough
he think he own
these hot blacktop hiways,
them east eight acres,
that red Chevy pick up
with the dumb bumper stickers
and big wide heavy rubber tires,
two sho nuff ugly brown bloodhounds
and a big tan&white german shepherd
who evil and got yellow teeth?
Ain't it enough
he got a couple a kids to beat on,
a wife who was a high school cheerleader,
a brother who is a doctor,
a cousin with a hardware store,
a divorced sister with dyed hair,
a collection of Hustler magazines
dating back to the beginning,
partial sight in his left eye,
gray hairs growing out his ear,
a sun scorched leathery neck that's cracking,
a rolling limp in his bow legged walk,
and a couple of cases of beer in the closet?
Ain't it enough
he got all that
without having to mess
with me?
Yeah, I shot the
motherfucker!

Ishmael Reed had this to say in a 2000 review of novelist Paul Beatty's *Tuff*:

> When Claude Brown wrote his brilliant *Manchild in the Promised Land* (1965), hood material was fresh. But now, with television's repetitive parade of the kind of characters found in this book—their roughly textured Ebonics, their life on the "existential" edge (think 24-hour installments of *Cops*, and the exposure to the brothers and sisters who appear on *Jerry Springer*)—and with the commercialization of rap which has resulted in a glut, a novelist who covers this familiar territory

had better be original.... But, for the most part, many of [*Tuff*'s] situations and images belong to the cliché hall of fame: 'Rats scaled mountains of trash bags.' Also, the book should gain an entry in the *Guinness Book of Records* for the number of times the words nigger and motherfucker are used. After a white woman psychiatrist used the terms in Woody Allen's *Deconstructing Harry*, maybe the words should be retired.

BURN, MOTHERFUCKER, BURN!

"They talkin' about nuclear war, it's a motherfucker don't you know; if they push that button your ass must go!"

—Jazz legend Sun Ra, in his 1984 song "Nuclear War"

In 1969, at the height of his popularity, science fiction writer Kurt Vonnegut Jr. kicked up a firestorm of controversy with his fiercely anti-war satire *Slaughterhouse Five*. Despite its depiction of 100,000 innocent German civilians, mostly women and children, being incinerated by Allied bombers, what really offended critics was a scene early in the novel (Chapter 2) in which the protagonist, Billy Pilgrim, by failing to duck when German snipers opened up on his unit, provoked a fellow soldier to shout, "Get out of the road, you dumb motherfucker!" As Vonnegut later explained, he used "motherfucker" to show the extremity of the situation because the word "was still a novelty in the speech of white people in 1944. It was fresh and astonishing to Billy, who had never fucked anybody."

In a 1999 paperback called *Palm Sunday: An Autobiographical Collage*, Vonnegut discussed one small town's reaction to the word—and his response:

> My novel *Slaughterhouse-Five* was actually burned in a furnace by a school janitor in Drake, North Dakota, on instructions from the school committee there, and the school board made public statements about the unwholesomeness of the book. Even by the standards of Queen Victoria, the only offensive line in the entire novel is this: "Get out of the road, you dumb motherfucker." This is spoken by an American antitank gunner to an unarmed American chaplain's assistant during the Battle of the Bulge in Europe in December 1944, the largest single defeat of American arms (the Confederacy excluded) in history. The chaplain's assistant had attracted enemy fire.

On November 16, 1973, Vonnegut wrote a letter to Charles McCarthy, the chairman of the Drake School Board. "The news from Drake indicates to me that books and writers are very unreal to you people," he said. "I am writing this letter to let you know how real I am."

He pointed out that neither he nor his publisher was using the Drake burning to create media controversy to sell books. No radio or TV interviews, no editorial-page harangues. Even the very letter he was writing was personal. "You now hold the only copy in your hands. It is a strictly private letter from me to the people of Drake, who have done so much to damage my reputation in the eyes of their children and then in the eyes of the world." Chairman McCarthy was free to toss it into the furnace atop the ashes of *Slaughterhouse Five*.

Vonnegut introduced himself as a fifty-one-year-old combat veteran with a Purple Heart, six kids, and a popular reputation among students. He often spoke at high school and college commencements. He had taught at Harvard, the University of Iowa, and the City College of New York.

> If you were to bother to read my books, to behave as educated persons would, you would learn that they are not sexy, and do not argue in favor of wildness of any kind. They beg that people be kinder and more responsible than they often are. It is true that some of the characters speak coarsely. That is because people speak coarsely in real life. Especially soldiers and hardworking men speak coarsely, and even our most sheltered children know that. And we all know, too, that those words really don't damage children much. They didn't damage us when we were young. It was evil deeds and lying that hurt us.

Vonnegut admitted that the citizens of Drake had the right to decide which books they would allow to be taught to their children. "But it is also true that if you exercise that right and fulfill that responsibility in an ignorant, harsh, un-American manner, then people are entitled to call you bad citizens and fools. Even your own children are entitled to call you that."

He told them that most Americans considered their behavior uncivilized because "books are sacred to free men for very good reasons, and that wars have been fought against nations which hate books and burn them. If you are an American, you must allow all ideas to circulate freely in your community, not merely your own." Teaching children to burn books was "a rotten lesson…in a free society."

In a 1991 collection of essays called *Fates Worse than Death*, Vonnegut facetiously summed up the Drake brouhaha with: "There is the word 'motherfucker' one time in my *Slaughterhouse-Five*, as in, 'Get out of the road, you dumb motherfucker.' Ever since that word was published, way back in 1969, children have been attempting to have intercourse with their mothers. When it will stop no one knows."

Fortunately, Vonnegut's use of "motherfucker" didn't prevent the Modern Library from ranking *Slaughterhouse Five* eighteenth on the list of the twentieth century's top novels.

Kurt Vonnegut had one more fling with the word in his 1997 science fiction novel *Timequake*, in which the character of Vonnegut himself is joined at a writer's retreat by his alter-ego, fictional sci-fi writer Kilgore Trout. Mr. Trout, we learn, has written a short story called "No Laughing Matter" about an alternate universe in which the pilot who dropped atom bombs on Hiroshima and Nagasaki in 1945 was "ordered to drop yet another one on Yokohama, on a couple of million 'little yellow bastards'" The *motherfucker* is this instance was the atom bomb itself. "Up there in the sky all alone," wrote Vonnegut/Trout, "with the purple motherfucker slung underneath their plane, they felt like the Boss God Himself, who had an option which hadn't been theirs before, which was to be merciful." More merciful, certainly, than the civic leaders of Drake, North Dakota.

By then, however, the Supreme Court, in the 1982 case of *Board of Education, Island Trees Union Free School District No. 26 v. Pico*, had already smacked down busybody officialdom that didn't approve of *Slaughterhouse Five*. It was one of nine books that a board in Nassau County, a dozen miles east of New York City, had removed from the local high school library shelves, along with Eldridge Cleaver's *Soul on Ice* (because he talked about white men letting black men fuck their wives), Alice Childress's *A Hero Ain't Nothing But a Sandwich* (because of the words *fuck* and *fuckin'*), Bernard Malamud's Pulitzer Prize–winning novel *The Fixers* (which contained the passages "What do you think goes on in the wagon at night: Are the drivers on their knees fucking their mothers?" and "Who else would do anything like that but a motherfucking Zhid?"), anthropologist Desmond Morris's *The Naked Ape* (for its clinical descriptions of sex), and novels by black authors Langston Hughes and Richard Wright because of their sexual descriptions and racial epithets.

The Court decided that school boards couldn't remove books from school library shelves simply for being "indecent; extol violence, intolerance, and racism; or degrade the dignity of the individual," because students had a Constitutional right "to receive ideas" at a school library. Such a place should give them unlimited choice, and a school board's "discretion may not be exercised in a narrowly partisan or political manner."

The Court referred to an earlier case, *Keefe v. Geanakos*, that had arisen when a Massachusetts high school English teacher named Robert Keefe, during a discussion of radical politics, protest, and dissent in America, assigned his senior class an article written by psychiatrist Robert Lifton in the September 1969 issue of *Atlantic Monthly*, which included several examples of "a vulgar term for an incestuous son," i.e., motherfucker. When members of the school board asked Keefe if he would agree not to use the word in the classroom again, he said no. The board suspended him and proposed terminating his contract. Keefe sought an injunction from the federal district court and, upon its refusal, appealed to the U.S. Court of Appeals for the First Circuit. Considering the relevance of the word in the article, the relevance of the article for the class, and the age and maturity of the students, the court granted Keefe's injunction prohibiting his termination.

But various nefarious do-gooder groups are still out there, ready to march into schools and libraries and pull offensive books off the shelves. Aside from the courts, the main line of defense is a vigilant and snarky gaggle of free-thinkers called The Society for Librarians Who Say "Motherfucker" (http://community.livejournal.com/library_mofo). Since 2004 it's been a community sounding board "for all of those times when the gatekeepers of the world's knowledge are called upon, in their professional capacity, to use the word motherfucker. Or at least to seriously consider it."

Perhaps Supreme Court Justice William J. Brennan said it best in his dissenting opinion of the 1978 *FCC v. Pacifica Foundation* case (i.e., the "Seven Words You Can't Say on TV" decision) when he wrote: "A word is not a crystal, transparent and unchanged, it is the skin of a living thought and may vary greatly in color and content according to the circumstances and the time in which it is used.... The words that the Court and the Commission find so unpalatable may be the stuff of everyday conversations in some, if not many, of the innumerable subcultures that compose this Nation."

So shush your mouth—and take *that*, motherfuckers!

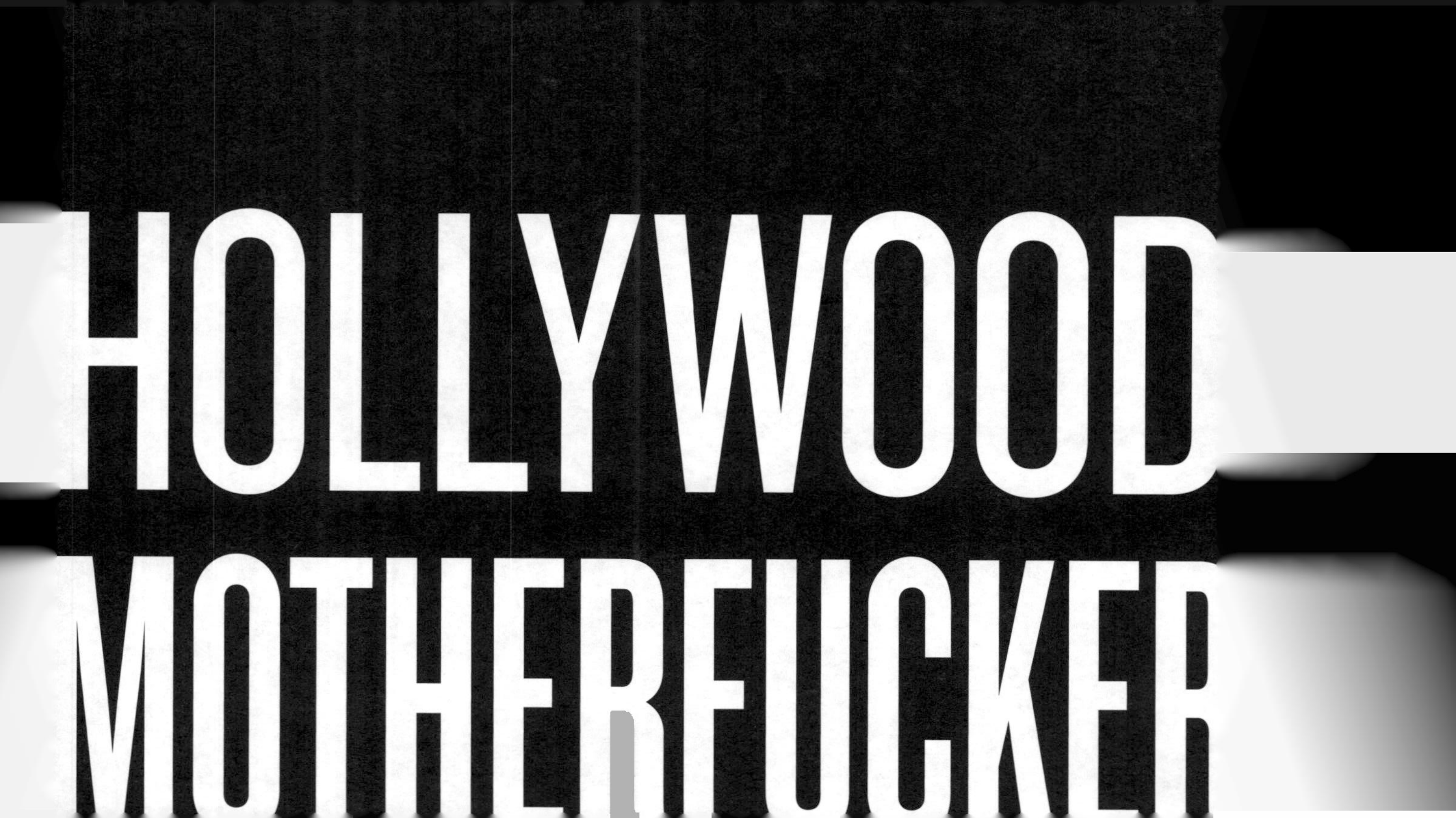
HOLLYWOOD
MOTHERFUCKER

"You're an actor, motherfucker, *act*!"

—Det. Cody Nicholson (Tom Sizemore), *True Romance* (1993)

As I mentioned in Chapter 4, Barbara Stanwyck, in what *New York Times* critic Pauline Kael would later call that "memorable moment," may have broken Hollywood's motherfucker barrier, or at least the *implied* motherfucker barrier, in 1931, when she spat out the words "You *mother*!" in Warner Bros.' *Night Nurse*. But that was in the so-called "pre-Code era," when the studio watchdogs at the Production Code Administration—better known as the Will Hays Office—were still napping with their feet up on the desk.

By 1934, however, there was a new Puritan in charge at the PCA named Joseph Breen, and he took its catalog of "Dos and Don'ts" quite seriously. Actually, Breen was a Catholic, not a Puritan, because in the early thirties Protestantism's moral authority was in tatters, thanks to a recent overthrow (by Constitutional amendment) of fifteen repressive years of alcohol prohibition, along with several high-profile scandals exposing Protestant evangelism as a huckster's game. Breen was, more specifically, the front man for the Catholic Church's Legion of Decency, a censorship wing that held sway over the municipal licensing boards that sanctioned theatrical entertainment in several cities, including Boston, Chicago, and New York, which all had large Irish, Polish, and Italian populations. Once the studio moguls—nearly all Jewish immigrants who were deathly afraid of offending the Christian majority—gave in to the new "Catholic Breen office," nothing but filial piety and Madonna-worship would find its way to the screen again until Breen was in his grave and Hollywood abandoned the Code in 1968.

During those years, writers had to sneak implications of dirty words past the gatekeepers. W.C. Fields, whose personal spin on the English language was a big part of his act, would burst out with exclamations like "Godfrey Daniel!" or "Mother o' Pearl!" More commonly, a character might mutter something under his breath to an authority figure and then, when challenged, repeat it in a cleaned-up form that nonetheless revealed his original intent. For example, in screenwriter Robert Riskin's classic *Mr. Deeds Goes to Town* (1936), when a newspaper editor growls, "What did you say?" at one of his disgruntled reporters, the guy innocently points to the ceiling and says, "I said, 'You've got some dirty plaster.'"

Even the writers of low-budget, all-black films that were made outside of Hollywood's aegis had to be stealthy in making their snickering inserts. For example, in a 1948 film called *Miracle Harlem*, comic Lincoln Perry, who was famous for playing addled layabouts under the name Stepin Fetchit, displays his insouciance when a policeman asks him if he's good at handling a knife. "I knows lots about a knife," Fetchit mumbles in his slow whine, "but I ain't gon' tell ya. But I knows I cain't eat my mash potatoes without a knife." When the black cop interjects with "Stop the foolishness," Fetchit adds, "I ain't foolin', Mister, 'cause I have to have a fo'k [fork] for everything I eat. If I cain't fo'k it, I cain't... uh, I just don't bother with it myself."

On rare occasions, if properly set up ahead of time, a "mother" could be insinuated into the script, as in the 1950 RKO film *The Narrow Margin*, when noir vamp Marie Windsor hisses "So long, *mother*!" to a Chicago bodyguard who's been keeping her in a claustrophobic apartment. Even the much more restrictive universe of television wasn't immune, thanks to a few beloved comedians (like W.C. Fields before them) who were given some leeway in matters of taste. For example, Jackie Gleason, whose variety shows ran continuously on CBS from 1952 to 1970, was infamous for his outrageous characters that walked the edges of network censorship. One of them was an oily late-late-night TV pitchman named Stanley R. Sogg who relentlessly flogged mail-order junk from a shady company called Mother Fletcher. A program booklet from a Jackie Gleason exhibit at the Museum of Radio & TV in Beverly Hills notes that he performed one of his Mother Fletcher sketches as early as May 28, 1955. In the early sixties, when the half-hour program was stretched into an hour, Sogg popped up even more frequently to pitch Mother Fletcher's dubious goods, including "a three-pound wedge of Mother Fletcher's Fotchamarra Motzaroni cheese"—which became Gleason's gag-line for years as a sure laugh-getter, even when he was out of character. Sogg later inspired Johnny Carson's sleazy "Tea-Time Movie" hypester Art Fern, whose most popular line—"Then take the Slauson [Avenue] cut-off [pause] and cut off your slauson"—was also vaguely dirty. By that time mildly salacious catchphrases—such as Dick

Martin's "Look it up in your Funk & Wagnall's [Dictionary]" on *Rowan & Martin's Laugh-In*—had become a television staple.

Another early TV comic and mimic known for his loopy characters was Jonathan Winters, whose fifteen-minute sketch variety show ran on NBC during the 1956–57 season and returned in an hour-long format ten years later on CBS. Probably his most lasting creation was a randy old Whistler's mother on a toot, with a bottle of gin in her apron, a shawl around her shoulders, and a pin through her Victorian bun—Winters in full, giggling drag. He based her on his own Aunt Lu Perks, but he called her Maude Frickert, and the censors never seemed to notice how closely the name resembled "ma frigger." At the beginning of the 1970s, Maude Frickert was the advertising "spokeswoman" for the Target retail chain.

By then, the social upheavals and cultural insurrections of the sixties, not least of which was the "sexual revolution," had soured the younger half of the American public against their elders. They distrusted the old system of proprieties as a mask concealing greater evils. They realized, or at least sensed, that Lyndon Johnson's Vietnam boondoggle had been a lie from the beginning, that Richard Nixon's presidency was rotting from the inside, and that the postwar American Dream had in fact been the American Snooze. Hollywood's traditional feel-good fluff was yesterday's stale hypocrisy. Screaming "fuck!" in a crowded theater sounded more and more like a fiery political statement. Meanwhile, the old Hollywood studio system had been unraveling. The original moguls had mostly shuffled off to fancy mausoleums, and a court-ordered divestment of their theater chains had broken their monopoly over what people could see. As Jack Valenti, the president of the new Motion Picture Association of America (MPAA), would later put it, "the slippage of Hollywood studio authority over the content of films collided with an avalanching revision of American mores and customs.... It would have been foolish to believe that movies, that most creative of art forms, could have remained unaffected by the change and torment in our society. The result of all this was the emergence of a 'new kind' of American movie—frank and open, and made by filmmakers subject to very few self-imposed restraints."

Valenti had seen Old Hollywood's coming demise just weeks after he assumed the original Production Code Administration's leadership in 1966, during nitpick sessions with studio executives at Warner Bros. and MGM over the words "screw" and "hump the hostess" in *Who's Afraid of Virginia Woolf* and full-frontal nudity in *Blow-Up*. "It seemed wrong that grown men should be sitting around discussing such matters," Valenti said. Worse, he envisioned "an unsettling new era in film, in which we would lurch from crisis to crisis, without any suitable solution in sight."

Producers began circumventing Valenti by using subsidiary film companies and independent distributors. When the censorship boards in Chicago and a number of other cities tried to restrain local "art houses" from screening these unrated movies, the U.S. Supreme Court stepped in and delivered the final blow in 1968 with the *Teitel Film Corp. v. Cusack* decision, which enjoined on constitutional grounds any municipality from interfering with private theaters, unless it first got a court order from a judge. With one fell swoop, a stake pierced the MPAA's censorial heart. But like Dracula, Jack Valenti immediately rose from his grave condition in November 1968 and revamped the organization into a ratings board. From then on, the MPAA alerted parents to any troubling content by assigning films a letter designation, from G (general audiences) to X, according to their intensity of sex, violence, drug use, or really bad taste. When the nascent porn industry appropriated X as a badge of honor, especially with high-profile grind-house product like *Deep Throat* in 1972, the MPAA replaced it with NC-17 (no admission for anyone under seventeen).

But during the couple of years while the MPAA's X was in force, Hollywood actually made a handful of well-respected X-rated films, including *A Clockwork Orange*, *Fritz the Cat*, *Midnight Cowboy*, and the high-camp *Myra Breckinridge*. What earned these movies their X certificate, however, wasn't so much bad language but rather nudity, aberrant sex, and graphic violence. *A Clockwork Orange* didn't even contain any recognizable obscenities, unless one considers "the old in-out" an offense to the ear. Not even *Myra Breckinridge*, which probably contributed the first utterance of "motherfucker" in a mainstream American studio movie, got its branding from its language. According to the MPAA guidelines, "A motion picture's single use of one of the harsher sexually-derived words, though only as an expletive, initially requires at least a PG-13 rating. More than one such expletive requires an R rating, as must even one of those words used in a sexual context." But not even what it called "hard language" rated an X. What had raised the MPAA's ire was Raquel Welch anally raping a strapping cowboy with a strap-on-dildo—even though the scene was tastefully—er, non-explicitly—staged. (Likewise, a cowboy's anal rape, compliments of some good ole Texas boys, helped put the X on 1969's *Midnight Cowboy*.) But the word *motherfucker* certainly alerted *Myra Breckinridge*'s 1970 audience that it was in for a rough ride. That ride, unfortunately, was an incoherent, butt-aching journey through Gore Vidal's Tinseltown nightmare starring both Welch and Rex Reed as the feminine and masculine sides of the title character. Only a few minutes into the film, Welch addresses the camera with "Who is Myra Breckinridge? What is she? [*Cut to close up of her face.*] Myra Breckinridge is a *dish*, and don't you forget it, you motherfuckers—as the children say today." The word is bleeped in the middle, but its enunciation is clear nonetheless. (Three decades later the full word was overdubbed back in for the DVD version.) The dialogue in *Midnight Cowboy*, adapted from James Leo Herlihy's novel in 1969, was relatively tame in comparison. Jon Voight's character, Joe Buck, never got much more foul-mouthed than admiringly telling a bus driver that his Greyhound "[s]ure is a powerful mother, ain't it?"

Likewise *Fritz the Cat*, Ralph Bakshi's animated salute to Robert Crumb's comic book character, got its X from its priapic explicitness, not the lines "You're a motherfucking bitch!" (by Fritz) or "You think being a crow is a big motherfucking ball!" (by Fritz's friend Duke). It's hard to say if the word would have even rated an R on its own, because it always accompanied the hard-edged stories and foul-mouthed anti-heroic characters that had suddenly become popular at the beginning of the cynical seventies. Take, for example, *The Friends of Eddie Coyle*, an R-rated 1973 Robert Mitchum film based on George V. Higgins's novel about tough-talking Irish American gangsters in Boston who can barely get a sentence out of their mouths without an intensifying *fuckin'* or an exclamatory *shit*. *Motherfucker* pops up only once, when an undercover federal agent (Richard Jordan) surprises a gang of home-invasion bank robbers with "April fool, motherfuckers!"

(Probably the earliest use of the word in an exhibited movie—one that was actually screened in theaters and recognized as cinema-worthy by fans and critics, even though it wasn't MPAA-rated—was Andy Warhol's *Chelsea Girls*, a 16-mm, three-and-a-half-hour-long art film shot mostly inside Manhattan's famous Chelsea Hotel in 1966 and shown at a funky two-hundred-seat basement theater on W. 41st Street. Consisting mostly of split-screen close-ups and long stretches of improvised dialogue, *Chelsea Girls* starred a flamboyant twenty-nine-year-old homosexual speed freak named Ondine—née Robert Olivio—as the Pope. As soon as either Warhol or fellow director Paul Morrissey pushed a young actress named Ronna Page into the scene, she sparked the temperamental Ondine into an hysterical rant: "You dumb bitch! You filthy whore! How dare you? How dare you? You motherfucker! I'm a phony? So are you!" It hardly seems like landmark material, but then again, the first cinematic motherfucker wasn't likely to tumble from the lips of Jimmy Stewart or Gary Cooper.)

Americans wanted cinematic realism that matched the literary realism of the previous decade, which may account for why these early seventies films were adapted from novels. Take for example *The Last Detail*, an R-rated 1973 film based on Darryl Ponicsan's novel about two Shore Patrol petty officers escorting a young seaman from Norfolk, Virginia, to the naval brig in Portsmouth, New Hampshire. In the old days of Pentagon-approved Hollywood fare, the sailors would have been idiomatically colorful but relatively chaste in speech and behavior. Yet anyone who's been in the naval services knows that sailors and Marines use salty language (itself a reference to "old salts," veterans of the sea) as casually as they breathe; there's a reason why "swearing like a sailor" is a figure of speech. No wonder that in this new film environment Jack Nicholson netted his first Academy Award for saying stuff like, "I *am* the motherfuckin' shore patrol, motherfucker! I am the motherfuckin' shore patrol! Give this man a beer!" and "Aw, motherfucking Jesus H. Christ." His black costar, Otis Young, wasn't so lucky, not even with timeless material like "I'm taking you to jail, motherfucker," "You're a motherfucking menace!" and "I hate this motherfucking chickenshit detail!"—but it wasn't for lack of trying. As for *The Last Detail*'s restricted rating, well, maybe the repeated use of *motherfucker* was a big consideration, but then again, maybe Carol Kane's bare boobs had something to do with it.

If any film introduced the general public to Hollywood's new profanity-laced realities, it was director William Friedkin's *The Exorcist*, a graphic tale of demonic possession that William Peter Blatty adapted from his own bestselling novel. It was an instant blockbuster, with people lined up around the block when it opened on the day after Christmas in 1973. Newspapers reported instances of religious hysteria, fainting, screaming, pallid-faced men and women fleeing the theaters. *The Exorcist* was the ideal test of moviegoers' tolerance for what might be considered abominable language because it was, in effect, a Christian morality play dressed up as a horror movie. At a time when many people were questioning organized religion and the mysteries of faith, *The Exorcist* clearly took the Catholic Church's anti-rationalist worldview and cast medical science as impotent and childlike in the face of evil. Moreover, like vampire films, it conceded the Church's veracity by taking for granted the potency of its symbols (the crucifix, holy water, liturgical incantations from the *Rituale Romanum*, the sanctity of the Virgin Mary). And, like Dante's *Inferno* and *Purgatorio*, it led a man who had lost his faith (priest Damian Karras, played by Jason Miller) into the tormented bowels of Christianity before finally delivering him to salvation. The movie's profanities, obscenities, and transgressions, such as Satan shoving a mother's face into the bloody vagina of her thirteen-year-old daughter, could be forgiven because Satan, after all, is likely to say or do anything to achieve his nefarious designs. And since the power and purity of the Church can only be measured against the pure evil of its arch villain, there was only a (pea-green) soupçon of public outcry, even from the clergy, when Satan (voiced by veteran actress Mercedes McCambridge) brutally told Father Karras, "Your mother sucks cocks in Hell" and screamed "Stick your cock up her ass, you motherfucking worthless cocksucker!" at the eponymous exorcist himself, Father Merrin (Max von Sydow). From then on, motherfuckers were let loose upon the land like the hounds and locusts of Hell itself. A plague on all our movie houses!

One genre that certainly benefited from this tongue-loosening was blaxploitation, a rash of violent, low-budget black movies starring super-bad urban motherfuckers in what were essentially updated toasts. The progenitor was Melvin Van Peebles's incomprehensible *Sweet Sweetback's Baadasssss Song* (1971), billed as "The film The Man doesn't want you to see." Rated X (and later R) for nudity, sex, and violence but not for language (which was fairly chaste), *Sweetback*'s grind-house success convinced schlock producers that there was money to be made in the ghetto. One man who took up the challenge was comic Rudy Ray Moore, who transformed his Dolemite character to the screen in 1975 with a $100,000 bankroll from his party records and stage performances. Though amateurish in every aspect of filmmaking, *Dolemite* had its own outrageous charm, thanks in part to such dialogue as "You no-business, insecure, rat-soup eatin', junkyard motherfucker!" and "Man, move over and let me pass, or you'll have to be pullin' these Hush Puppies out yo muthafuckin' ass!"

(Many years later, in 1993, Moore recounted his dealings with the MPAA to *shockingimages.com*: "'Rat-soup-eatin', no-business, low-life, decrepit, insecure, junkyard,' none of those words are bad. They are not four-letter words. So when we gave the movie to the MPAA to judge it for language, they didn't know what it meant. They come back to Dimension Pictures and said, 'We don't know what Mr. Moore is talking about. We know what motherfucker means, but we don't know what rat-soup-eatin', insecure, peppergut, junkyard means. So what we're gonna do, we gonna rate this picture R for language.'")

Writers and producers came to realize that the word *motherfucker* not only improved a movie's hipness factor, but added toughness to tough guys and humor to humorous ones, and even made tough guys funny, as in *Predator* (1987), when humorless mercenary commando "Dutch" Schaefer (Arnold Schwarzenegger) tells a hideous-looking alien creature, "You're one ugly motherfucker!"

One actor who has always had a way of enhancing the menace of the word by the way he spits it out is Joe Pesci, who has specialized in playing foul-mouthed Italian thugs. For example, in Martin Scorsese's *Casino* (1995) he punctuates the basic nastiness of his character Nicky Santoro with such lines as "Get this through your head, you Jew motherfucker, you! You only exist out here because of me!" or "You're fucking warned. Don't ever go over my fucking head again, you motherfucker, you! " or "You know you're a lying, lowlife motherfucking degenerate prick!"

It could also be a sight gag, as in *Foul Play* (1978), a Goldie Hawn–Chevy Chase comedy, in which two old ladies play Scrabble. One of them lays her tiles out on the board, spelling M-U-T-H-E-R-F-U-C—but the word isn't completed, or spoken.

It's also good for a catchphrase, as when convict Virgil Cane (F. Murray Abraham), in *An Innocent Man* (1989), more than once sums up everyone's predicament behind prison walls with "Ain't life a motherfucker." Or when Charlene (Geena Davis) in *The Long Kiss Goodnight* (1996) shouts in a blaze of gunfire, "Die screaming, motherfucker!" Or is that "Die, screaming motherfucker!"?

In the comedy *Trading Places* (1983) Eddie Murphy's character fends off a big, bass-voiced cellmate (Ron Taylor) by bragging that he got arrested for kicking some guy's ass. Asked why he doesn't have any marks on him, Murphy says, "'Cause I'm a karate man, see. And a karate man bruises on the inside. They don't show their weakness. But you don't know that because you're a big Barry White–looking motherfucker!" Next day, when that same guy runs into Murphy in a black bar, he says, "Hey, you're that jive-ass turkey motherfucker I was gonna carve in prison last night." Murphy, no longer obliged to put on a mean face, acts offended: "Motherfucker? Moi?"" Director John Landis later discussed how the script called for Taylor to call Murphy a "jive turkey," which Landis thought was ridiculous—"no one would say that; it was a white writer's idea of what a black man would say." So he turned to the roughly seventy-five black extras on the set and asked them what the character would say in that situation. They all agreed he'd call Murphy a "motherfucker," so that's how they did the scene.

Another type of joke was to elicit the word from someone you'd least expect to say it. In the black-themed comedy *Friday* (1995), a couple of Jehovah's Witnesses arrive at Ice Cube's front door and ask, "Are you prepared for Jehovah's return? 'Cause if you're not, we've got a pamph—" When Ice Cube cuts them off by slamming the door in their faces, one of them shouts, "Well fuck you, half-dead motherfucker!"

Likewise, in the Wayans Brothers' 1996 parody *Don't Be a Menace to South Central While Drinking Your Juice in the Hood*, young Shawn Wayans's grandmother (Helen Martin) blasts him with dialogue like "You little bitch-ass motherfucker, come over here and give your grandma a hug!" When Wayans slaps her, she berates him with "You still hit like a bitch, motherfucker." Later, when he greets a dignified minister (Chris Spencer) with "Hey, Preach, what up, nigga?" the older gentleman upbraids him for using a word "the white man uses to take away the self esteem of another race." The preacher then adds, "Oh yeah, remind me to pick my laundry up from that chink motherfucker up the street." Almost sounds like Noel Coward wrote it.

The word can also heighten the reality of a situation. When Spike Lee made his *Malcolm X* biopic in 1992, he based it on the bestseller *The Autobiography of Malcolm X*. But the book, despite its raw depiction of Malcolm Little's early years as a thief and a pimp, was free of obscenities, which Malcolm himself considered immodest and undignified by the time he set his story down with writer Alex Haley in 1965. Take for example a scene where a friend chemically straightens young Malcolm's kinky hair for the first time by applying a home remedy called congolene—a mix of mashed potatoes, eggs, and deadly lye that could scald a guy's head if he wasn't careful. "My eyes watered, my nose was running. I couldn't stand it any longer," Malcolm wrote. "I bolted to the washbasin. I was cursing Shorty with every name I could think of when he got the spray going and started soap-lathering my head." But in Spike Lee's dramatization of that scene, actor Denzel Washington leaps out of the chair shouting. "You motherfucker! You're killing me! I'm burning up! My damn head is on fire!" Playing the scene without that word would have sounded false to a 1992 black audience.

Only rarely over the years has the word been held in reserve, saved for just the right scene, to achieve maximum dramatic effect. Take the Oscar-nominated *Pan's Labyrinth* (2006), Mexican director-screenwriter Guillermo del Toro's cruel but magical tale about a girl who escapes into her fantasies during the Spanish Civil War. When del Toro, through one of his characters, launches his sharpest barb—"You motherfucker!"—against a fascist officer who has threatened the life of the child, the word seemed so harsh, so out of place, so transgressive, that it crystallizes the vileness of the man.

But not everyone in filmdom has been comfortable enough with the word to be willing to take it all the way for a joke. For example, back in 1983, when *motherfuckers* were flying like bullets in Hollywood action movies, the producers of *Sudden Impact*, Clint Eastwood's fourth *Dirty*

Harry film, were looking for a new catchphrase to succeed the franchise's earlier classics like "Make my day," but it had to be relatively clean so as not to offend Eastwood's older, more law-and-order demographic.

> Dirty Harry: I really should quit. Then I can handle the law my own way.
> Fellow cop: Yeah, but then you'll be a JAMF.
> Harry: Uh huh. And what is a JAMF?
> Cop: Jive ass mother—
> Harry [cutting him off just in time]: Forget I asked.

When host James Lipton later asked Eastwood on cable TV's *Inside the Actors Studio* what his favorite curse word was, he answered in full, "JAMF—jive ass mother fucker." But the line never caught on at the movies.

If anyone has leaned on *motherfucker* for dialogue fodder, it's writer-director Quentin Tarantino. Just as Al Pacino's 1983 version of *Scarface* holds the record for the number of times it threw "fuck" at the audience, Tarantino's *Pulp Fiction* (1994) is a shrine to motherfucker; it even launched an ancillary product, the Bad Mother Fucker Billfold, which can be purchased even today from dozens of websites, not to mention the motherfucking career of Samuel L. Jackson. In fact, the word reached its apotheosis in Jackson's 2006 gore fest, *Snakes on a Plane*, after *Pulp Fiction*–besotted Internet bloggers convinced the producers to shoot extra scenes in post-production of Jackson spouting a last-minute catchphrase. (For more on *Snakes* and Samuel L. Jackson, go to the next chapter.)

But now, after nearly forty years of motherfucker-at-the-movies, audiences are suffering motherfucker overload. You know the end is near when several producers put the word into the titles of their low-budget movies. All right, maybe *Motherfucker: A Movie*, a 2008 documentary about New York's Motherfucker party scene (see Chapter 18), is justified, but what about the 2004 Italian horror movie short, *Merry Christmas, Motherfucker!*, featuring Santa Claus in scary mode? Or the 2003 cable TV documentary *Richard Pryor: I Ain't Dead Yet, Motherfucker!*? Or the ultra-cheapo *Colonel Kill Motherfuckers* (2008), about a group of role-playing nerds in Alton, Illinois, who accidentally kill an Army veteran and then have to deal with his animated, half-rotted corpse after his mother, a sorceress, brings him back from the grave? (That one is purportedly based on a true story, I'm told.) The tagline says it all: "Revenge is a motherfucker!"

And yet, despite their freedom to say pretty much whatever they want, Hollywood producers have never touched *Oedipus Rex* or any other stories with a prominent theme of sexual love between mother and son. You'll have to visit Pier Paolo Pasolini's 1967 Italian film *Edipo re* for a full treatment of the Greek motherfucker and his mama, or French New Wave director Louis Malle's *Le Souffle au Coeur* (1971), released a year later in the U.S. as *Murmurs of the Heart*, for an innocent coming-of-age story about a confused French teenager (Benoît Ferreux) who has a two-minute romance (shot completely above the shoulders) with his vivacious, lovelorn Italian mother (Lea Massari). In a February 13, 1972, conversation with *Chicago Sun-Times* critic Roger Ebert, Malle said, "When we are young, the Oedipus complex thing is like a joke. It takes years to discover that it is real, that there is a dream ideal, an initiating mother, in our subconscious. The movie is about that sort of childlike dream." Malle treated as dreamlike

When Ebert pointed out that "the moment of incest…is so unsensational, so quiet, that it can almost be described as a moment of fondness," Malle said, "I didn't feel like going any further in this scene with the boy. He was not a professional actor, his reactions were sometimes unpredictable, and, besides, if I had pushed the scene any further it would have destroyed the tone of the movie.… The problem was to somehow de-dramatize the highly charged emotional materials we were working on. They were so loaded they could have destroyed the whole balance, the whole structure of the movie."

Americans are much more uncomfortable with the subject. Mel Brooks, in his *History of the World: Part I* (1981), dismisses it as a joke by having a character ask Oedipus, "What's up, motherfucker?" Our idea of an acceptable motherfucker film is *The Graduate* (1967), in which a young man (Dustin Hoffman) finds himself rutting with his girlfriend's mother (Ann Bancroft, the wife of Mel Brooks). In *The Grifters*, Steven Frears's 1990 adaptation of the Jim Thompson novel, the powerful undertow between a con artist mother (Anjelica Huston) and her grifter son (John Cusack) ends in murder. And in writer-director David O. Russell's quirky little independent comedy-drama *Spanking the Monkey* (1994), he tamps down the sexual undercurrent between an attractive but unhappy woman (Alberta Watson) who's recovering from a broken leg with the help of her repressed medical student son (Jeremy Davies).

The only attempt to explicitly deal with the mother-son taboo comes courtesy of the underground porn industry, in a 1980 film called *Taboo*, starring Mike Ranger as a young man attracted to his seductive mother (Kay Parker), who's going through the aftermath of a messy divorce and the confusion of an experimental night with swingers. To put *Taboo* in its proper context, director Kirdy Stevens filmed it at a time that's now considered to be porn's golden age, when the growth of several X-rated theater chains, including the Pussycat Theaters, created a demand for fairly sophisticated porn movies with "production values"—scripts, semi-professional acting, and competent cinematography. Long after home video destroyed the ambitious theatrical X-rated movie, *Taboo* remains a steady seller and is now available on DVD from Standard Digital.

Ultimately, the effect of the mother of all dirty words on the big or little screen (including video games, which have adopted all the qualities of R- and X-rated movies, including the liberal use of "motherfucker") relies on the wit and delicate touch of the writer. You know you're in trouble when *Othello* is rewritten as a basketball movie under the title *O* (2001), credited to "William Shakespeare & Brad Kaaya." Peter Ritter, film critic for Minneapolis/St. Paul's *City Pages*, liked the idea that *O*'s filmmakers "adhere closely to the play's Machiavellian plotting," but had a problem when Kaaya transformed Shakespeare's "Keep up your bright swords, for the dew will rust them," into "I'll fuck your punk ass up, motherfucker." Ritter deemed it "a questionable improvement." But then again, in modern English as it's spoken in America, one *motherfucker* can express more words and ideas in heaven and earth than are dreamt of in your philosophy.

COME TO ME,
MY MELON
FARMER BABY!

"Yippie-ki-yay, Kimosabe!"

—John McClane (Bruce Willis), in *Die Hard* (1989 TV version)

In the early 1960s, when commercial television began rerunning last year's Hollywood films as this year's "movie specials," bad language wasn't a problem because the film studios' longtime culture cop, the Will Hays Office, washed everybody's mouth out with soap before the script went before the camera. But suddenly, in 1968, after several state courts had put the Hays Office and its censorship Code out of business on constitutional grounds, the TV networks' Standards & Practices Boards were forced to take up the slack—and they've been ordering studios to cut or cover up cuss words ever since. There were several ways a producer could comply. If the offending language were unnecessary to the story, he eliminated the scene, the shot, or the line altogether. He could also bleep the word(s) or create a dropout in the sound. If he had been thinking ahead to that important secondary TV market, he would have already filmed alternate takes with PG-rated dialogue. But most often he simply hired either the original actor or a voiceover specialist to overdub a new line that, ideally, matched the actor's lips and made sense besides. Problem was, the overdubs were too often stupid and clumsy. Some people still laugh at what a numbskull network censor did to Linda Blair's—or should I say Mercedes McCambridge's—famous line from *The Exorcist* (1973), turning "Your mother sucks cocks in Hell!" (Satan's version of the dozens) into the inane "Your mother sews socks that smell!" (a fourth-grader's version of the dozens).

The word *fuck* is easy to replace. "Fuck you" morphs painlessly into "forget you," and "freaking" or "frigging" supplant "fucking" without sounding too ridiculous. But *motherfucker* is more difficult to cover. Since most people instinctively read the way the lips form Ms and Fs, you need a two-syllable M-word followed by a two-syllable F-word.

So the folks in charge of obscuring language started coming up with replacements like "mickyficky" (for Spike Lee's urban black comedy *Do the Right Thing*, 1989), "maggot farmer" (*Platoon*, 1986), "Yippie-ki-yay, Kimosabe!" (*Die Hard*, 1988), "Yippie-ki-yay, Mr. Falcon" (*Die Hard 2*, 1990), "mother-loving" (*Full Metal Jacket*, 1987), and "one bad mother-crusher" (*Robocop* (1987). But the term that seems to have become the "rhubarb standard" (*rhubarb* being film extras' traditional murmur to create an agitated background rumbling) is "melon farmer."

The guy who came up with *melon farmer* is Alex Cox, a maverick British director and scriptwriter who created the 1984 apocalyptic cult film *Repo Man*. On his website (*alexcox.com*), Cox explains that Universal, the studio that owned *Repo Man*, did such a botched job trying to re-edit the film for television that an abashed executive begged him to salvage it. Along with adding a couple of theatrical outtakes and recutting several scenes, Cox took a special interest in replacing the film's obscenities. With tongue in cheek, he transformed "Fuck you, motherfucker" into "Flip you, melon farmer" as a subtle dig at the whole idea behind this kind of bowdlerization. As Cox recalled, "By then I'd made *Sid & Nancy* and I was sick of swearing," but he knew that dubbing an inoffensive oath or a nonsense word onto the soundtrack could subvert a character or the tone of the film—you can't have a hardened killer say "golly darn" and expect the audience to take him seriously after that. "If you must water down a movie for broadcast, what's so wrong with a bleep or unobtrusive simple silence?" Cox asks. "I find that much less distracting than allegedly tough grownups calling each other melon farmers. We all know what they're saying anyway, so it's pointless to pretend they said something else. Delete the expletives if you must, but don't substitute stilted playground hokum."

Cox may have been inspired by the term "Maryland farmer," which had popped up in the 1960s as an entry in the MF substitute sweepstakes, along with Mary Frances, Mr. Franklin, and others. A pedantic history major aware of the plantation owner who wrote several anti-Federalist essays to the Continental Congress in 1788 under the signature "A Farmer," later referred to as "A [Maryland] Farmer," may have come up with it. Who knows? There's an apocryphal tale of an offended (and clueless) Maryland Farmers Association writing a letter of protest to a prominent black activist who called a Capitol Hill politician a "jive Maryland farmer."

Cox's soft cut of *Repo Man* has attained a cult status of its own, especially in Great Britain where the eccentric film played on the BBC, because its fans are wonky enough to appreciate "melon farmer" as a way of giving the censor the finger. Before long, in the British television versions of *Die Hard 2* (1990) and *Die Hard With a Vengeance*, i.e. *Die Hard 3* (1995), Bruce Willis was mouthing "Yippie-ki-yay, melon farmer" instead of the first *Die Hard*'s TV-sanitized "Yippie-ki-yay, Kimosabe."

A couple of British bloggers who rail against this silliness have set up "an anti-censorship campaigning website" called the Melon Farmers (*melonfarmers.co.uk*). "It is not a traditional campaign or political organization," they explain on their main page. "There are no members, no subscriptions and no constitutions." Contacted recently, Melon Farmer Dave (his partner is Melon Farmer Phil) said they formed the website around 2001 to inform the public about TV and film censorship, but since then they've expanded to blowing the whistle on political and economic meddling in the arts all over the world. What makes their name ironic, Dave claims, is that *motherfucker* is not a common term in the UK. "I think motherfucker in Britain alludes to the American use. I would use it only in reference to what an American may say. I don't think Brits would use it at all if it wasn't for Hollywood." British comedians Harry Enfield and Paul Whitehouse drove the point home on Channel 4's *Saturday Live* show in a spoof of Martin Scorsese's *Goodfellas*, called *Badfellas*, in which they uttered lines like "Kiss my knees, muddy funster."

Meanwhile, there's a four-piece "hardcore indie rock" band from Bristol, England, that calls itself the Melon Farmers. And the Northern Ireland alt-rock group Ash recorded a 2002 song called "Melon Farmer," in which "melon farmer" does not appear; in fact, its opening line is: "Motherfucker! What's going on in my head?" But who knows, maybe they've got an alternate "melon farmer" version stashed away just in case they ever want American airplay.

HOLLYWOOD'S BADDEST MOTHERFUCKER!

“Welcome to New York—now duck, motherfucker!”

—The slogan on a Big Apple T-shirt, beneath a photo looking down the barrel of a revolver

If any Hollywood action star should have a franchise on the word *motherfucker*, it's Bruce Willis, whose catchphrase throughout the R-rated worldwide hit *Die Hard* (1988) and its sequels was “Yippie-ki-yay, motherfucker.” The setup came in an early scene when Willis's character, New York cop John McClane, phones über-criminal Hans Gruber (Alan Rickman) after Gruber and his cadre of international terrorists take a high-rise office building hostage.

> Gruber: You know my name but who are you? Just another American who saw too many movies as a child? Another orphan of a bankrupt culture who thinks he's John Wayne? Rambo? Marshall Dillon?
>
> McClane: I was always kind of partial to Roy Rogers, actually. I really dig those sequined shirts.
>
> Gruber: Do you really think you have a chance against us, Mister Cowboy?
>
> McClane: Yippie-ki-yay, motherfucker.

The line was inspired by a song called “I'm an Old Cowhand (From the Rio Grande)” that Roy Rogers crooned in a popular 1943 Western called *King of the Cowboys*. Each verse ended with “yippie-i-o-ki-yay,” but since the *Die Hard* producers probably wanted to avoid copyright problems—composer Johnny Mercer was dead, but his music publisher was still a force to be reckoned with—they shortened Willis's line to “yippie-ki-yay.” Or maybe “yippie-ki-yay” just sounded snappier, especially when Willis attached *motherfucker* to it.

Later in the film McClane says, "You would have made a pretty good cowboy yourself, Hans."

Gruber answers in what seems like a gratuitous setup from the screenwriter: "What was it you said to me earlier? 'Yippie-ki-yay, motherfucker'?"

Willis dropped MF bombs all through *Die Hard*, including "Geronimo, motherfucker!" but none of them stuck like "yippie-ki-yay, motherfucker." And yet poor Bruce never got to be Hollywood's baddest motherfuckin' dude. That honor, appropriately enough, went to a tall, lanky black actor named Samuel L. Jackson, who just happened to be Willis's costar in *Die Hard With a Vengeance* (1995), the third film in the *Die Hard* series. No, Jackson's character, a Harlem shopkeeper named Zeus Carver, didn't utter a crispy aphorism about mother love, nor did he tell John McClane anything more memorable than "Don't fuck with me or I'll shove a lightning bolt up your ass!" He didn't have to, because he was already Hollywood's main mofo, thanks to the film he'd done with Willis the previous year called *Pulp Fiction*.

Samuel Leroy Jackson was born in Washington, D.C., in late 1948 and raised in Chattanooga, Tennessee. He spent his young adulthood engaged in civil rights and student activist movements. By the time he got the acting bug and joined the Negro Ensemble Company in the 1970s, Jackson was already in his late twenties. After he put in several years as a character actor playing addicts and villains, his career got a bump with several memorable parts in Spike Lee's *Do the Right Thing* (1989), *Mo' Better Blues* (1990) and *Jungle Fever* (1991). Then came his breakthrough in 1994, when Quentin Tarantino tapped the then-forty-six-year-old veteran for the role of a vicious yet philosophical criminal named Jules Winnfield in *Pulp Fiction*, a film that itself probably takes some kind of award for more muttered, uttered, spit, and sputtered *motherfucker*s in a movie. Winnfield isn't content to just *be* a bad motherfucker; he advertises it every time he whips out his leather billfold embossed with the letters BMF, which he identifies when he tells his buddy Ringo (John Travolta), "I want you to go in that bag and find my wallet.... It's the one that says bad motherfucker." And after he quotes Ezekiel from the Old Testament, he tells Ringo, "Now I've been saying that shit for years, and if you've ever heard it, it meant your ass. I never gave much thought to what it meant, I just thought it was a cold-blooded thing to say to a motherfucker before I popped a cap in his ass."

Here's another scene:

Jules: What country you from?
Brett: What?

Jules: *What* ain't no country I ever heard of. They speak English in What?

Brett: What?

Jules: English, motherfucker, do you speak it?

Brett: Yes.

Jules: Then you know what I'm saying.

Brett: Yes.

Jules: Describe what Marcellus Wallace looks like.

Brett: What, I—?

Jules [pointing his gun]: Say what again. Say what again, I dare you, I double-dare you, motherfucker. Say what one more goddamn time.

Or:

Jules: I don't wanna hear about no motherfuckin' ifs. All I wanna hear from your ass is, "You ain't got no problem, Jules. I'm on the motherfucker. Go back in there, chill them niggers out and wait for the cavalry, which should be coming directly."

Marsellus: You ain't got no problem, Jules. I'm on the motherfucker. Go back in there, chill them niggers out and wait for the Wolf, who should be coming directly.

Jules: You sendin' the Wolf?

Marsellus: Oh, you feel better, motherfucker?

Jules: Shit, yeah, Negro, that's all you had to say!

Or how's this for something that sounds like it came from the Book of Revelation: "I'm a mushroom-cloud-layin' motherfucker, motherfucker."

Granted, *Pulp Fiction*'s quota of *motherfucker*s fell far short of the 226 fucks in Brian De Palma's 1983 *Scarface*, but let's face it, when it comes to impact, one motherfucker equals at least a dozen fucks, even when the master thespian seething with "fucks" happens to be Al Pacino with a bad, coked-out Cuban accent and an even worse hairpiece.

Now that Sam Jackson was Bad Negro Number One, he landed the lead in *Shaft*, the 2000 remake of the 1971 blaxploitation classic, playing private-eye John Shaft, who, according to Isaac Hayes's theme song from the original, was "a bad mother—" ("Shut your mouth!" a female chorus interjected before he could get the word out.)

Among Jackson's memorable quotes from *Shaft* are:

- To a perp: "April Fool, motherfucker!"
- "Got that, motherfucker!"
- "You knockoff-wearin' motherfucker!"
- To a dirty cop: "How does a third-rate, pencil-pushin', apple-stealin' dickhead like you afford a four-bedroom colonial in Nassau motherfucking County?"
- "I'll get that silver-spoon motherfucker, and I'm gonna get him my own way!"

By the time Jackson began playing Jedi Master Mace Windu in George Lucas's *Star Wars* prequels, beginning with *The Phantom Menace* in 1999, his MF reputation was so solid that bloggers and e-wags submitted lines adapted from his other movies that they wanted him to say, including:

- "I'm a bad-ass light-saber-wielding motherfucker, motherfucker!"
- "Womp rat may taste like pumpkin pie, but I'll never know, 'cause even if it did I wouldn't eat the filthy motherfucker."
- "This is your father's light saber. When you absolutely, positively have to kill every motherfuckin' stormtrooper in the room, accept no substitutes." (This one was inspired by Jackson's line in Tarantino's 1997 blaxploitation opus *Jackie Brown*: "AK-47, the very best there is. When you absolutely positively gotta kill every motherfucker in the room. Accept no substitutes")
- "Feel the Force, motherfucker."
- "Hand me my light saber. It's the one that says 'Bad Motherfucker.'"

As it turned out, Internet bloggers succeeded in supplying Jackson with the catchphrase for his 2006 high-concept adventure from New Line Cinema called *Snakes on a Plane*, and they generated more buzz than New Line's promotion department when the movie came out in mid-August, during the summer blockbuster period just before kids headed back to school. His one-liner was "Enough is enough! I have had it with these motherfucking snakes on this motherfucking plane!" His voice repeated it over the end titles, but substituted "That's it!" for "Enough is enough!" (He also told a newly deputized airplane pilot, "Turn this big motherfucker left, Troy!")

According to the *Hollywood Reporter*, here's how this serpentine tale uncoiled. In March 2006, six months after *Snakes on a Plane*'s principal photography wrapped in British Columbia, director David R. Ellis took his cast and crew back into the studio for five days in Los Angeles to shoot additional scenes—not to fix any story problems (well, maybe that too), but to address the intense fan interest in the project.

In the film, FBI agent Neville Flynn (Jackson) is transporting a witness from Honolulu to Los Angeles on a red-eye flight to testify against a mobster in a Federal case. (So far it's basically an airborne version of the 1951 film *The Narrow Margin*, in which Marie Windsor told a guy, "So long, *mother*"—but wait!) The bad guy doesn't want the flight to arrive on time, or ever, so he smuggles aboard several crates of poisonous snakes with air-pressure devices that will set them free at thirty thousand feet.

Three years earlier, when New Line picked up the script in turnaround from Paramount Pictures, nobody had envisioned it as anything more than a dumb B-movie idea with an even dumber title. Though four professional screenwriters had already retooled the original draft, *Snakes on a Plane* still needed something to get it green-lighted. That something was Samuel L. Jackson. The moment he signed on, New Line upgraded the title to the less lurid, less campy *Pacific Air Flight 121*. "Who wants to be in a movie called *Snakes on a Plane*?" said a talent agent at the time.

But as soon as production began, movie fans picked up on the original title from Tinseltown tastemaker Harry Knowles's Ain't It Cool News website (*aintitcool.com*) and created *Snakes on a Plane* blogs, songs, poems, even T-shirts. "The title is so clear and so straightforward," *snakesonablog.com* creator Brian Finkelstein told the *Hollywood Reporter*. "You know exactly what you're going to get." New Line executives, figuring that all those crazy young fanboys—their primary constituency—couldn't be wrong, reinstated the old title.

By then, computer geek Chris Rohan in Bethesda, Maryland, had created an R-rated mockup of an audio trailer for the film on his website. "It's a genius title," Rohan said. "It's so stupid it's great." One of the lines Rohan came up with, shouted by a Samuel L. Jackson sound-alike in Jules Winnfield mode, was "I want these motherfucking snakes off the motherfucking plane!" It wasn't long before the growing legion of chattering *Snake*-ophiles demanded that Rohan's bon mot come tripping off the cobra-sharp tongue of the real Jackson. New Line duly ordered director Ellis to do the reshoot. And since Jackson's added dialogue was going to push the film's rating from PG-17 into harder R territory, he might as well add more gore and death and bare tits and, yes, more snakes to *Snakes on a Plane* while he was at it. As a joke, Ellis even shot a clip for the very end of the picture, after the rolling credits, of Jackson staring into the camera, telling stragglers, "Movie's over! Get your asses out of the motherfuckin' theater!"

Jackson seemed to enjoy the reshoots as much as anyone. Chris Morris of *moviehole.net* later asked him, "How do you feel having to say 'motherfucker' just because the fans want that?"

Jackson answered, "Fine. I demand that I say it too. 'Hi, how are you—Hi, motherfucker.' But that's cool, that's what they expect. It's that kind of movie."

When *Snakes on a Plane* opened in August 2006, however, it wasn't quite the event movie that New Line expected. Critics hissed and gave it two motherfucking thumbs down. Box office was okay, but not spectacular.

Reviewer James Berardinelli remarked on *reelviews.net*: "Samuel L. Jackson is in fine Samuel L. Jackson form, kicking ass and taking numbers. He has his big speech moments, his bad-ass moments, and he gets to utter the coolest line in the film.... At no point does he yell, 'Die, motherfucker!' which is a shame because it's just the kind of clichéd dialogue that would fit right in."

One critic who called himself Dorkafork told *indcjournal.com*: "Samuel L. Jackson could have said 'muthaf*&#@in' a little more. And Christopher Walken should have been in it: 'Wow! There's a lot of... snakes...on this muthaf&^%#in plane...I can't believe it!'"

Others began to worry about Jackson's ever-shrinking pigeonhole. In a July 2007 article on *mediabistro.com* titled "Sam Jackson! Now with 40% More Motherfucker!" someone called Fishbowl Los Angeles, Geekdom worked himself into a hissy fit:

> [I]f he keeps playing to his lowest common-denominator fans, he's going to start to sound like a played-out SNL bit. It's not enough that *Snakes on a Plane* filmmakers followed bloggers' demands to add more "motherfuckers" to Jackson's dialogue, but when he addressed 6,500 freaks and geeks at Comic-Con [a comic book convention] today, our sources tell us he tossed around "motherfuckers" like a 1980s Billy Crystal saying "you look mahvelous."
>
> True, Jackson has a legitimate bad motherfucker quality that might shield him from becoming the butt of his own joke. After all, a group of kids at the *Snakes on a Plane* panel did offer to make him a "human throne." But catchphrases have a way of undoing careers.
>
> Maybe Jackson's keen to this. When one 15-year-old asked him, "What's it like to be a bad motherfucker all the time?" Jackson answered, "I appreciate that you think that about me,

> but I certainly don't feel like a bad motherfucker all the time. Some days, I'm just trying to get through it."
>
> You can almost hear him, 15 years from now, telling some blogger at gunpoint to "reach in the bag, and hand me back my career. It's the one that says Bad Motherfucker on it."

On his own MySpace page, Jackson billed himself as a "Motherfuckin' Movie Star." He said he doesn't do television: "None of that shit, motherfucker."

When one interviewer asked Samuel L. Jackson what the "L" stood for, he replied, "Motherfucker."

Meanwhile, Bruce Willis was still trying to get some mileage out of "Yippie-ki-yay, motherfucker." On April 30, 2007, as if he were promoting his upcoming PG-13-rated *Die Hard 4.0*—i.e., *Live Free or Die Hard* (in which the garbled catchphrase was barely audible over a gunshot)—Willis showed up at an NBA playoff game between the Toronto Raptors and the New Jersey Nets and, with a couple of beers under his belt, told an on-air Canadian TV reporter, "Yippie-ki-yay, motherfucker!" In the wake of the outcry that followed, a mock-contrite Willis said, "Next time I'll clean up my language. Instead of saying 'yippie-ki-yay, motherfucker,' I'll just say 'motherfucker.'"

That sounds awfully passive-aggressive. Samuel L. Jackson would have simply told everyone, "Get the fuck out of my motherfucking face, motherfuckers!"

UP AGAINST THE GREAT WALL, TURTLE EGG!

"If, for three years [after your father's death] you do not change from the ways of your father, you can be called a pious son."

—Confucius (c. 500 B.C.)

Since *motherfucker* has many definitions, trying to determine its translation into another language seems almost impossible. Do you want an exact translation of the exact meaning, i.e., one who fucks his mother? Do you want an idiomatic term that generally means the same but whose literal translation makes no sense? Or will you settle for a word or a term that within the culture packs the same wallop as *motherfucker*, even though it means something else altogether?

For example, in Polish the literal translation for motherfucker is *matkojebca*, but the word that carries the insult of the concept is *skurwysyn*, or "son of a bitch." Likewise, "son of a whore" is the greater insult in most Romance languages, including Italian (*figlio di puttana*) and French (*fils de pute*, though the more mother-humping *nique ta mere*—"fuck your mother"—is sometimes used). The Swedish *mammaknullare* is literary and rarely used in daily life. The Dutch *moederneuker* is never used except for humorous effect. And the German *mutterficker* is such a literal translation that it likely comes directly from the English *motherfucker*.

In China the stand-in for motherfucker is *wangba dan*, which literally means "turtle egg" or "turtle's egg." Don't ask me why. Calling someone any kind of egg in Mandarin slang doesn't seem to be an endearment. You may be a stupid egg (*ben dan*) or a rotten egg (*huai dan*), but never a good egg. So we can't be surprised that turtle egg is also an insult. For instance, in the mid-forties, U.S. envoy Patrick Hurley heard Mao Zedong call the Nationalist Government leader Chiang Kai-shek a *wangba dan*. Apparently it wasn't a one-time tirade, because Colonel David D. Barrett, head of the U.S. Army Observer Croup, later noted that "[Mao] was not discourteous to me but several times he flew into a violent rage" and called Chiang "that turtle's egg."

Businessweek magazine (July 28, 2003), in an article called "A Thorn in China's Side," reported that Jimmy Lai, one of Hong Kong's major media bosses, called former Chinese Premier Li Peng a "son of a turtle's egg" and "a turtle's egg with a zero IQ." And *New York Times* correspondent Nicholas D. Kristof (April 26, 1993) noted that on Radio Orient, Shanghai's number one talk radio station, producers took callers' phone numbers and then called them back to make sure "that no one calls the mayor a turtle's egg on the air." Kristof added, "Station officials say that callers are normally on their best behavior, and so they have no formal policy about whether to bleep out such Chinese insults as turtle's egg or baby rabbit." Another phrase is "lower than a turtle egg," because a mother buries her eggs and then abandons them to hatch on their own. And let's face it, if your mother sticks her ass in the sand and shits an egg, what does that make you?

According to Lao Wai, a Chinese-American woman blogging in 2007 during her time in China, "This one I knew for a long time, but *wangba dan*, which means 'turtle egg,' is usually translated as bastard, but occupies essentially the same place in the language as motherfucker—questioning someone's parentage is generally pretty serious in China."

Stanford University professor Youqin Wang says a more literal Chinese equivalent of motherfucker is the common obscenity *ta ma de*, pronounced tah-MAH-duh, which is literally "his/her/its mother," but figuratively means "(fuck) his/her/its mother"—sort of like a third-person version of English's second-person "Yo' mama." In an essay called "Oedipus Lex: Some Thoughts on Swear Words and the Incest Taboo in China and the West," Wang writes that "the renowned writer Lu Xun once jokingly claimed that, just as the peony was his country's 'national flower,' *ta ma de* should be considered the 'national swear word' of China. The phrase is close enough in meaning to 'motherfucker' that at least one leading American translator of Chinese literature has rendered it this way in his English language version of Lu Xun's stories." *National Review* writer John Derbyshire calls *ta ma de* Mandarin's "all-purpose expletive," but then asks, "His mother's what?" The term, he says, "somehow manages not to be offensive at all. You hear *ta ma de* all the time in Chinese street talk." It's like "Fuck!" or "Oh shit!"—something you'd blurt out if you smashed your thumb or stubbed your toe. Another problem is that motherfucker is literally an accusation that someone might be screwing his own mother, whereas with *ta ma de* the person delivering the insult is taking the credit for fucking somebody else's mother, or blaming it on someone else. In other words, says Wang, "the 'equivalent' Chinese vulgarity has nothing to do with the mother-son incest taboo."

Similarly, *wangba dan* is a stretch if you want to call someone a motherfucker. According to Wang, "By calling Chiang a [turtle's egg], Mao was suggesting that the father of his rival was a turtle, an animal that in Chinese popular culture is often linked to cuckoldry. To a certain extent, then, 'turtle's egg' functions as a kind of implicit version of *ta ma de*. Both of these common Chinese swear words refer to adultery or fornication; the emphasis is on illicit sex taking place outside of marriage and there is no connotation in either case that incest is involved in any way."

The only link, then, is that *wangba dan* was the most vicious and insulting term that Mao had in his vocabulary, and that the precise meaning was secondary. In English and most other European languages, motherfucker, by implying carnal knowledge between mother and son, is the ultimate insult because it suggests a breaching of one of society's most serious taboos. And yet, though the Chinese also consider this particular form of incest a terrible thing, they don't seem to have anything directly equivalent.

Wang explains that profanities and obscenities help shape social boundaries. "If an action considered despicable is referred to in a commonly used swear word, this accusation will continually remind people that the action is shameful. When people swear in contempt…to release their anger and resentment, they can simultaneously repeat and reinforce moral taboos, such as that associated with mother-son incest. In this sense, the swear word can operate in part as a form of public control."

Searching through China's mythology and classical literature, Wang couldn't find any references to mothers getting it on with their sons. "While I would hesitate to claim that there are no references at all to parent-child incest in the vast body of more than two thousand years of Chinese literature, it is safe to say that incest has never been a common theme for Chinese writers. In other words, there is nothing in traditional Chinese literature comparable to the Oedipus story." Furthermore, Freud's theory of the Oedipus complex as an explanation for human sexual motivation seems to have had no effect on modern Chinese writers. And yet, writes Wang, "[I]ncest has not run rampant in Chinese society.… Why did this kind of story not exist in Chinese imagination or fantasy?"

Wang guesses that the Confucian concept of *xiao*, or "filial piety"—one of the basics of Chinese family ethics for thousands of years—negates the need for an incest taboo. Described in the ancient texts as "the foundation of virtue and the root of civilization," *xiao* encompasses the respect and the debt each child owes his parents. "There is no common specific term for *xiao* in English," says Wang, "since words such as filial tend to have something of an artificial ring to them. In Chinese, the term designates only the love of children for their parents, and cannot be used in other contexts."

All of Chinese literature's protagonists had *xiao*. As opposed to Oedipus being punished by the gods for violating the ultimate taboo, Chinese heroes "are assisted by gods because of their service to their parents and their willingness to sacrifice themselves," says Wang. "The message of the story of Oedipus is a negative injunction: Do not do what Oedipus did! Do not commit parricide or incest! The message of these Chinese stories, on the other hand, is a positive one: Follow the examples of the filial sons! Be a filial son to your parents!"

Lao Wai, the female visitor to China I quoted earlier, notes another bizarre family-related curse: *wo cao ni zu zong de ba1bei*, which translates as "I fuck your eight generations of ancestors." Now *that's* a real motherfucker.

CHINGA TU
MADRE!

"Tua madre si da per niente!"

—Italian expression meaning "Your mother gives it away for free!"

In Mexican American neighborhoods, where a public jeer of disapproval is the singsong *culero!* (asshole) and two commonly shouted epithets are *cabrón* (asshole) and *pendejo* (asshole), one word that seems most disdainful of all is *madre*, or mother. Latin culture is a notoriously macho world where women are categorized as either mothers or whores, but Mexican men often seem to confuse and conflate the two in their curses. According to California reporter Gustavo Arellano, who writes a syndicated column for the *Orange County Weekly* called "Ask a Mexican!", *madre* is "one of the most vulgar words in Mexican Spanish."

In Arellano's Sept 5, 2006, column, reader "Gabacho Grosero" (vulgar white guy) asked, "Is there a Mexican phrase that means 'motherfucker'?" Arellano replied: "The closest Mexican Spanish equivalent to motherfucker is *Chinga tu madre* ('Go fuck your mother'), but that's not the same. Truth is, there are no proper *calques* [word-for-word translations] for motherfucker in Mexican Spanish."

That sounds fairly reasonable, considering that the most iconic figure in Mexico is the Virgin of Guadalupe, an Indian girl who claimed she saw Mary the mother of Christ outside her village several hundred years ago. The Virgin is, oddly enough, Mexico's national symbol of motherhood, abiding in nearly every Mexican and Mexican America home in the form of a velvet painting or statuette. Mexicans hold their own mothers sacred. And they consider everyone else's mother fair game.

Still, like the English *motherfucker, chinga tu madre* has many other meanings that range from offensive to friendly and funny. Since it has the dual meaning of "fuck you," it's probably the worst thing you can say to a Mexican or a Chicano you don't know. But *chinga tu madre* can also be blurted as a shocked reaction, as when a friend rudely awakens you ("*Chinga tu madre! me despertaste!*"—or "Damn it, dude, you woke me up!"). It's an expression of disbelief to what somebody tells you, sort of like "Holy shit!" It's a way of dismissing someone ("*Ha ha ha! chinga tu madre!!! si como no!*"—"Yeah, right, ha ha ha, fuck off, dude!"). It all depends on the emphasis, the voice tone, and the context.

In formal Spanish it's expressed as *chingue su madre!*—meaning to hurry things up or to finish a task in a half-assed way ("*Chingue su madre! asi como quede lo hago!*"—or "Fuck it, who cares?"). Or it can be a reaction to seeing something disturbing ("*Chingue su madre! ese estuvo duro!*"—"Holy shit, that was tough!").

All over the world, mothers seemed to be reviled in the oaths a man throws at other males or simply shouts out when he stubs a toe. One Arabic expression that basically means "Shit!" or "Fuck you!" is *koos emek*, which literally means "your mother's cunt." In Hebrew the term for "You asshole!" or "Fuck you!" is *kus ima shelcha*, which also means "your mother's cunt." (Could this be where cooze, an English slang word for vagina, comes from?) In Italian, Portuguese, Spanish, French, and other Romance languages, "son of a whore" is a common epithet to throw at someone or simply ejaculate as an expletive, and it is much more serious than the English equivalent, "son of a bitch."

As Arellano points out, Mexican Spanish has "more than enough curses" that use *madre*.

> As a noun, *madre* can mean anything from "shit," as in "*No vale madre*" ("It isn't worth shit") to "ass," in which "*Te voy a partir la madre*" translates literally as "I'm going to split for you the mother" but really means "I'm going to kick your fucking ass." *Madre* is also an adverb: "*Te voy a dar un chingazo en la madre*" translates to "I'm going to give you a fucking blow in the mother" but really means "I'm going to give you a fucking blow where it hurts the most." You can also tell *cabrones*, "*Vete a la madre*," which doesn't mean "Go to the mother" but rather "Go to hell." Add an "-ar" suffix to *madre*, and you have the verb *madrear*, which means "to fuck someone up." For example, if you tell your mom "*Te voy a madrear*," you're not telling her that you're going to mother her but are letting *mamí* know that "I'm going to kick your fucking ass." Shame on you.

That's only the beginning. *Hijo (hija) de tu madre* means "Son (or daughter) of your mother," but it's a phrase that parents, especially fathers, use to express disgust for their children. "You can even turn the most benign form of mother, *mamá*, into a crude insult," said Arellano. "Take off the accent, and you're left with *mama*, the present indicative form of *mamar*, which means 'to suck.' And when you say that, you ain't telling a baby how to get the milk out of the bottle."

But of all these curses, *chinga tu madre* is the bedrock, so ingrained in Mexican culture that there's even a whistle for it. That's right, according to the 1976 book *Whistled Languages* by René Guy Busnel and A. Classe, Mexican Spanish has a sharp whistle to catch someone's attention, a longer whistle to boo performers, an extended double-note 'wolf whistle' to harass pretty girls, and most spectacular of all, 'five rapid trills' for '*chinga tu madre*.'

One wonders why Mexican women even bother to bring such ungrateful little motherfuckers into the world.

CRAZY MOTHERFUCKER!

"I'm crazy as a motherfucker!"

—Britney Spears, from her 2007 *Blackout* album track "Get Naked (I Got a Plan)."

There's crazy, and then there's motherfucking crazy. Patsy Cline was "Crazy." Bill Haley was "Crazy, Man, Crazy." The Wilson sisters in the rock group Heart went "Crazy on You." We're talking just standard-issue crazy with those. But if someone tells you, "Don't mess with him, he's a crazy motherfucker," you'd better back off. He just might fuck you up.

That's why—even within a universe of brassy, irritating comics standing in front of brick-wall backdrops (suggesting the need of a firing squad) in late-night comedy joints with names like Chuckles—the Crazy Motherfucker immediately catches your attention. Dressed in a bright yellow tracksuit, with his cap turned backwards and his eyes hidden by wraparound shades, he bounds out upon the stage with a surplus of energy and an overload of in-your-face attitude that's supposed to dazzle you.

"Ooooooooohhhhhhhhhh yeahhhhhhhhhhhhhh!

"Look out now! Look out, y'all, 'cause I'm a crazy motherfucker! Uh-huh, a crazy motherfucker! *Crazy* motherfucker! Crazy! Mother! Fucker! I'm a crazy motherfucker! I'm fuckin' crazy, people! A crazy motherfucker! I'm a crazy muhmuhfuhfuh! A crazy mamafafa! A fuckin' crazy motherfucker!"

He's spouting into the microphone in several volumes and intonations as he bounces around the stage, delivering karate kicks and jabs like an urban Elvis high on Red Bulls. At times his words drop to indistinct mutterings, but mostly they're clear and piercing.

> Any other motherfuckers out there? Oh yeah, I thought so! Why did the crazy motherfucker cross the road? Because he was a *crazy* motherfucker! No reason...he was just a fuckin' crazy

motherfucker! He just ran out there into the road, he showed no regard for traffic, he didn't give a shit. He was a crazy motherfucker!

How many crazy motherfuckers does it take to change a lightbulb? *None!* They won't change it! They're fuckin' crazy! They don't care, they'll live in the dark—because they're fuckin' crazy motherfuckers! Crazyyy motherfuckerssss!

Knock knock.

[Audience: "Who's there?]

Crazy!

[Audience: "Crazy who?]

Crazy motherfucker! Don't answer the door! He's fuckin' crazy! He'll come in and fuck up all your shit! He'll jump on your bed and break all your dishes…he's a crazy motherfucker! Cra-zy muh-ther-fuh-ker!

What do you get when you cross a crazy dude with a motherfucker? That's right…*me*! A crazy motherfucker! A crazzzzzy motherfuckerrrrrrrr! Craaaazy motherfucker!

You begin to notice that he's losing energy, he's running down, as if his batteries are getting low.

"Crazy…….mother…..crazy mother fuck…. Motherfucker. Crazy mother……. I'm a crazy……..okay….uh…."

He drops his shoulders, his voice, and then the character altogether. He scratches his head and looks around sheepishly.

Um…look…um…I'm not…I'm not actually a crazy motherfucker. I…I was given the chance to perform here tonight, I wasn't really prepared. I don't really have it together. I just happened to have this suit in my car, and I guess I thought I'd come up with something. But now I'm just embarrassed, ashamed. This is fucking pathetic.

So I'm just gonna end it. I…I just want to say I'm sorry and I want to say…..I want to say that…I'm…I'm….

Suddenly he gets a jolt of manic energy, as if those Red Bulls he chug-a-lugged are kicking in.

"Just *fuckin'* with you! 'Cause I really *am* a crazy motherfucker! I just fucked you up! Yes! Fuckin' crazy motherfucker! [At the top of his lungs:] *Crazy Motherfucker!* Ohhhhhhhh yeahhhhhhh! Cra-*zy* motherfucker!"

He leaps into the wings and disappears.

"What the hell was that?" somebody asks. A few young guys near the front cheer for his return.

Backstage, a less hyper Mark Fite is sitting in a busy dressing room at the Steve Allen Theater in Hollywood. He's an actor and voiceover specialist, with credits—including *Seinfeld*, *Fight Club*, and the animated cable show *SpongeBob SquarePants*—going back to the mid-nineties. But mostly he performs with comedy ensembles. Over the years he has sat in the audience or in the wings and suffered through plenty of Crazy Motherfuckers trying to bludgeon the audience into laughter with dirty words.

"My Crazy Motherfucker character began as a transition piece within a three-man show called Two-Headed Dog," he says. "It was intended to be an obnoxious spectacle, a spoof on high-energy, no-act comics. The humor comes through the energy and the absurd nature of the performance, the repetitive dialogue, and the twist at the end. Usually it's fairly well received."

But Fite admits that his Crazy Motherfucker works best as part of a larger comedy show. "The whole point of the Crazy Motherfucker is you don't want him hanging around very long, because he gets on everybody's nerves and wears out his welcome after about the second or third motherfucker. I think we all know somebody like that."

CLUB MOTHERFUCKER!

"It ain't nothin' but a motherfuckin' party, yo!"

—Singer-rapper Kid Rock, "Live" (1996)

During the first six years of this century, if New Yorkers were looking for the mother of all parties, they could find it at various club-hopping rock 'n' roll blasts called Motherfuckers, notoriously outré affairs that were definitely not your mother's parties. The first one was put together on Memorial Day Weekend 2000 by four promoters—Georgie Seville and DJ triplets Justine D., Johnny T., and Michael T. (all unrelated)—who collectively called themselves Motherfucker. "The MF fetes are eclectic, itinerant affairs," gossip maven Brian Niemietz blogged at the end of 2006. "They happen about six to eight times a year, usually on the eve of holidays. The most recent was a Halloween bash at the Roxy; the next is tomorrow night, a New Year's Eve Dance Dance Dance party at Club Rebel on West 30th Street." Tickets at the door were fairly cheap. The New Year's Eve Motherfucker was only $30 before midnight, $25 until 4 a.m. and $15 thereafter.

Along with the DJs there were bands of every stripe, making for a mash-up of several decades of rock influences. Among the talent were the voodoo rockabilly Cramps, the proto-punk New York Dolls, and various electronica dance-punk outfits like ESG, The Rapture, Bloc Party, The Bravery, and Theo & The Skyscrapers. A Motherfucker event—whether at Meow Mix, Heaven, Rebel, Spirit, Eugene, or any other trendy underground nightspot in Lower Manhattan—was reasonably democratic. Celebrities, celebutantes, and celebutards had to stand in line with every other dickhead, and once inside they couldn't retreat to roped-off VIP areas because there weren't any. So they rubbed shoulders and who knows what else with "the rocker glittery glitterati and bisexual bad boys from the boroughs," said Niemietz. Personal style defined the caste system. As one New Year's Eve flyer put it: "Motherfucker is a dictatorship at the door and a democracy on the dance floor—so work a look or New York's #1 doorman, Thomas Onorato, will send you straight to the New Year's gulag, whether that be McSorely's or in a time machine back to Xenon." Among the well-knowns who showed up at the end of 2006 and grooved to the sounds of electro-hop-pop were Debbie Harry, Mike Myers, Chloe Sevigny, Boy George, Jim Dawson (hey, how did he get in there?), and members of the Strokes and Interpol. One no-show was Paris Hilton. Georgie Seville joked that he and his co-hosts had thought of actually paying her to stay away from the New Year's Eve bash. "Don't get me started on Paris Hilton," he semi-dished to Niemietz. "She's so gross," Justine D. added bitchily.

But then, after the 2007 Halloween Night spookfest-a-rama, came the final email from Michael T. stating that, because of irrevocable strains in the promoters' relationship, the party—and "an era of clubland"—was "OVAH!"—as in hangovah. "Motherfucker is no more." Mr. T. thanked "all of you sick and crazy Motherfuckers who attended the party throughout the years, come rain, come shine, long lines outside, long lines for the bathrooms."

The Motherfuckers had become an institution. New York's newspapers, from the *Post* to the *Times*, had remarked or reported on the parties, though of course they had to tread around the name by using abbreviations or asterisks or simply omitting it altogether. Filmmaker David Casey shot an in-depth documentary with all four hosts called *Motherfucker: A Movie* that screened at the Sundance Film Festival in January 2007. But none of that mattered in the end. "I don't know if there will ever be another Motherfucker," T. lamented. "Will all the stars be that aligned again…doubtful."

Meanwhile, out on the West Coast, a vintage Hollywood bar turned nightclub called Boardner's has been holding Rock 'n' Roll Motherfuckers karaoke nights every Thursday on its back patio, where people can sing along with a live band.

I don't know what drinks were favorites at the Motherfucker parties, but believe it or not, there are some motherfuckers I can recommend for the next time you're out clubbing. It's amazing how many drinks are actually called motherfuckers. For example, there's the Blue Motherfucker:

Three ounces Absolut Citron®
Three ounces Blue Curacao
Three ounces sweet-and-sour mix

Shake ingredients in a cocktail shaker, strain over ice in a highball glass, and serve.

Mmm, so good you might want to chase it with a Blue Motherfucker #2:

Half-ounce vodka
Half-ounce gin
Half-ounce rum
Half-ounce tequila
Half-ounce Blue Curacao
One and a half ounces sweet-and-sour mix
Four or five ounces 7UP®
Shake ingredients, strain into a Collins glass filled with ice cubes, and serve.

There's also a Blue Motherfucker #3, but if by now that's too much blue for you, why not move toward the red part of the spectrum and try a Purple Motherfucker:

Half-ounce Southern Comfort®
Half-ounce vodka
Half-ounce Amaretto
Half-ounce 7UP®
Half-ounce raspberry liqueur (preferably DeKuyper's Razzmatazz)
Half-ounce sweet-and-sour mix
Put liquors in a mixing glass half-filled with ice. Shake and pour into a Collins glass. Top with 7UP and serve.

While we're talking about colors, how about a simple Green Motherfucker, a shot & shooter mix:

Half-ounce Bacardi® 151
Half-ounce green crème de menthe
Pour ingredients into a shot glass and serve.

The website *webtender.com* suggests you try the Adios Motherfucker and say goodbye to sobriety—and perhaps even consciousness.

Half-ounce vodka
Half-ounce rum
Half-ounce tequila
Half-ounce gin
Half-ounce Blue Curacao

Two ounces sweet-and-sour

Two ounces 7UP®

Pour the alcohol and mixers into a chilled glass filled with ice cubes, then top it with the 7UP. Stir gently and serve.

From jolly old England comes the Rocky Mountain Motherfucker #1:

One ounce Amaretto

Half-ounce Heublein's Yukon Jack® Canadian whiskey (100 proof in the U.S., eighty proof in Canada) or Rose's Triple Sec® orange liqueur

Half-ounce lime juice

Combine ingredients in a shaker over ice and chill. Strain and pour into a shot glass.

There are also Rocky Mountain Motherfucker sequels, but you can go get those recipes yourself.

If you want to get so drunk that you babble like a Mongoloid, try the Mongolian Motherfucker:

Half-ounce Absolut Citron®
Half-ounce Malibu Coconut rum
Quarter-ounce Blue Curacao
Quarter-ounce peach schnapps
Splash of Midori Melon Liqueur®
Splash of Grand Marnier
Splash of banana liqueur
Splash of orange juice
Splash of pineapple juice
Splash of lemonade
Splash of piña colada mix

And yes, of course, there's a Mongolian Motherfucker #2:

Quarter-ounce vodka
Quarter-ounce gin
Quarter-ounce rum
Quarter-ounce sloe gin
Quarter-ounce Bacardi® 151
Quarter-ounce Southern Comfort® peach liqueur
Quarter-ounce triple sec
Splash of Grenadine syrup
Splash of orange juice

Splash of cranberry juice
Put all ingredients in a cocktail shaker. Shake well, strain into a glass filled with ice cubes, and serve.

My favorite is the Fucked Up Motherfucker:

Half-ounce Bacardi® 151
Half-ounce Jägermeister®
Pour ingredients in equal parts into a shot glass, stir, and serve.

Next up is the MMF, or Mean Motherfucker:

Half-ounce Amaretto
Half-ounce gin
Half-ounce melon liqueur
Half-ounce raspberry liqueur
Half-ounce light rum
Half-ounce Southern Comfort
Half-ounce white tequila
Half-ounce triple sec
Half-ounce vodka
Half-ounce Grenadine
Pineapple juice as needed
Half-ounce banana
Two whole maraschino cherries
One slice orange
Mix all the alcohols into a shaker on ice. Then pour into a Collins glass, fill the remainder with pineapple juice, and add the orange slice and cherries. (It tastes like fruit punch!)

Naturally, since New York was the home of Club Motherfucker, there had to be a NY Motherfucker:

Quarter-ounce vodka
Quarter-ounce rum
Quarter-ounce gin
Quarter-ounce coffee liqueur
Half-ounce cream
Pour the vodka, rum, gin, and coffee liqueur into a cocktail shaker half-filled with ice cubes. Shake well and strain into a cocktail glass. Top with cream as desired, and serve.

And finally there's the Mudda Fucka, which calls only for two ounces of Beefeater gin and four ounces of Captain Morgan rum mixed in a flask. Like blunt-force trauma to the head, it's likely to make you as dizzy and dopey as a mudda fucka.

Inventing new cocktails is big business in the bar trade, and with such a glut of experimental concoctions, sometimes the name means everything. Just as the porn biz relies on ever more clever and outrageous DVD titles, the alcohol industry thirsts for sexy names with the sort of cachet one might expect at singles bars. That's why, along with the various motherfucker cocktails, there are drinks like the Hot Screaming Orgasm, the Cumshot, the Blowjob, and the classic Sex on the Beach.

Since so many cocktail recipes are label-specific—with the registered trademark icon attached—you have to wonder who's actually inventing them. For example, rather than generic triple sec (a liqueur flavored with orange peelings) or sweet-and-sour mix, some drinks call for Rose's Triple Sec and Rose's Sweet & Sour. (Rose's, a subsidiary of the Texas-based Cadbury Schweppes Americas Beverages, specializes in non-alcoholic mixers, including Grenadine and other syrups.) Alcohol companies spend billions of dollars annually to advertise their products, and liquor salesmen—like pharmaceutical representatives—often get creative when it comes to dispensing free samples and marketing gimmicks.

At least one vodka manufacturer, Sweden's Absolut, wears its pedigree proudly in a cocktail called the Absolut Motherfucker:

> One and a half ounces Absolut Citron
> One and a half ounces Crown Royal Canadian whisky
> One and a half ounces peach schnapps
> One and a half ounces triple sec
> Splash of orange juice
> Splash of pineapple juice
> Mix all ingredients together and serve over ice.

So, why call a cocktail (a word that goes back at least to 1806 to describe "a stimulating liquor composed of spirits of any kind, sugar, water, and bitters") a motherfucker? Maybe it's the first word you exclaim the moment the zesty taste explodes in your mouth. Maybe it's the last word you mutter before you pass out on the floor. More likely, these drinks are simply so loaded with various liqueurs, cream flavorings, sugar, and artificial sweeteners that they'll give you a headache that hurts like a motherfucker.

MILF DOES A
BODY GOOD

> "Your mama's on the top of my things-to-do list."
>
> —Australian rap group Butterfingers' "Yo Mama" (2004)

As I've pointed out throughout this book, the basic definition of *motherfucker* doesn't require that the fucker and the fuckee be related. If you've ever fucked somebody else's mother, guess what? You're a motherfucker.

These days there's even a new type of mother who, knowingly or otherwise, is luring willing young men into the realm of motherfuckerdom. She's known as a MILF. It's an acronym that entered popular slang after the breakout success of the 1999 teen comedy *American Pie*, a puerile but deftly written story about four high school buddies, including Steve Stifler (Seann W. Scott), who are determined to lose their virginity at the senior prom. In one memorable scene, two of the film's lesser characters, played by John Cho and Justin Isfeld, are looking at a picture of Stifler's blonde, busty mother (then-thirty-five-year-old comedienne Jennifer Coolidge), when Cho exclaims, "Dude, that chick's a MILF!"

"What to hell is that?" asks Isfeld.

"M-I-L-F—Mom I'd Like to Fuck!"

"Yeah dude! Yeah!"

Actually, the Urban Dictionary (*urbandictionary.com*) defines MILF as "Mother I'd Like (to) Fuck," and goes on to describe her as sexually desirable, regardless of her age and current marital status. Compared to your average teenage schoolgirl, a MILF is probably more careful about birth control, knows exactly what she wants, and will bang your brains out with no romantic complications. In other words, a young guy's dream fuck. The prototypical MILF in modern times is Anne Bancroft's Mrs. Robinson, who back in 1967 used her long, stocking-clad legs and husky laugh to entrap young Dustin Hoffman's Benjamin Braddock in *The Graduate*.

In recent years, MILF has become popular in text messages and email, as well as a buzzword for Internet porn sites that feature women roughly between the ages of thirty and fifty. (MILF in this context has nothing to do with the Moro Islamic Liberation Front, a terrorist group in the Philippines seeking to turn the island of Mindanao into an Islamic republic, other than the fact that under this group's brand of Sharia law, mothers would be forced to swaddle themselves in black forehead-to-foot garb to hide any of their MILF qualities, and anyone looking at MILF porn sites would probably be put to death.) Perhaps the most popular and long-running website is MILF Hunter (*milf-hunter.com*), offering hundreds of streaming and downloadable videos and photos of older women. Other sites are MILF (*milf.com*), Poke My Mom (*tour.pokemymom.com*), and I Fucked Your Mother (*ifuckedyour-mother.com*). Naturally there are hundreds of porn DVDs like *MILF Bangers* (Score Group), *MILF Hookers* (Devil's Films), *Mommy Fucks Best* (Platinum X), *Yo' Mama's a Freak* (3rd Degree Films), *Who's Your Mommy* (Combat Zone), *Come to Mommy* (Pulse), and the enchanting *Mother Load* (Zero Tolerance), all giving porn actresses a few extra blessed years of work in what has traditionally been an industry of short careers. The apotheosis of the genre may be a series from Jules Jordan Productions called *Dirty Rotten Mother Fuckers*. There, they've said it, dammit, and it's out in the open.

There's even a mainstream book called *The MILF Anthology: Twenty-One Steamy Stories* (Blue Moon Books, 2006), edited by Cecilia Tan and Lori Perkins, which Amazon describes as "stories of horny young men and the voluptuous older women they crave. For legal reasons, the characters in the stories are all over 18 years of age, but there is plenty of 'Mrs. Robinson' spark. (Think about a hottie like Ashton Kutcher getting it on with sexy mom Demi Moore and you are going in the right direction.) Inexperience meets experience—does the wiser, savvier older woman tame the young buck, or set him free in a whole new way? Or does he teach her some new tricks?"

Besides *American Pie*, probably the biggest media promoter of the acronym has been *Weeds*, Showtime's offbeat program about a suburban mom named Nancy (Mary Louise Parker) who hydroponically grows and sells high-potency marijuana. *Weeds*' final episode of its second season, which aired October 2, 2006, was called "MILF Money," complete with an original rap song by Snoop Dogg called "MILF Weed," his name for the sexy mom's sticky icky. Snoop's blessing of the blend suddenly turns Nancy's MILF weed into a hot commodity around town.

> I'ma gonna tell it to you, to you,
> so you need to know,
> we smokin' MILF weed every day
> on the road.
> We get it crack-a-lackin'
> everytime you see me, doh,
> it's Snoop Dee-oh-double-G
> blaze the endo.

Snoop's video of the song, featuring Mary-Louise Parker dancing like a white girl in Snoop's Crippin' Kitchen recording studio, is available on YouTube.

Before we start worrying that society's traditional respect for motherhood is degenerating out of control, it's best to stop and reflect that the MILF phenomenon is built on the prevailing male perception that the baseline for mothers is not a sexy one. After all, there's no category for Stripper I'd Like to Fuck to separate the lap-dancing wheat from the pole-dancing chaff. Sure, Pamela Anderson has kids, and so do Britney Spears and Angelina Jolie, but even they were considered much more fuckable *before* they earned their stretch marks. The MILF, in other words, exists as an exception to the rule, a rare babe within a general population of women whom few high school lads would consider fuck-worthy on a bright and sober afternoon.

Thus, most horny mommies who yearn to be MILFs are forced to take the initiative themselves if they want some action from sturdy young men. Lately we've seen a new breed of older woman ready to go hunting for SILFs (Sons I'd Like to Fuck). She's known as a cougar, a confident and aggressive *Sex in the City* kind of gal pulling forty or pushing fifty and seeking the pleasure of post-adolescent studs. Maybe she's an executive or a former trophy wife, but this is one mother (whether or not she actually has children) who has trimmed her body at the gym and sculpted her features at a local plastic surgeon's office, and now she's ready for a tiger who can do all night what her aging ex-husband used to take all night to do. According to writer Gendy Alimurung, "The precise age at which a woman reaches cougardom varies depending on whom you ask, but the 45-year-old woman to 25-year-old guy is a typical age differential." Like young MILF hunters, the predatory cougar has plenty of websites to visit for advice, a pep talk, or the location of fair game, including *urbancougar.com* and *cougardate.com*. The term appears to have come from Canada, home of Valerie Gibson, whose 2001 *Cougar: A Guide for Older Women Dating Younger Men* is the bible for this set.

Alimurung asks, "Is it any different from 50-year-old men dating 30-year-old women? Are cougars pathetic or powerful? Are they the next great thing, representing an entirely new dating paradigm, or are they the proverbial mutton dressed as lamb?"

Now that the boomer bulge of America's population is entering its senior and senile citizen stage, can the GILF (Granny I'd Like to Fuck) craze be far behind? If so, will grandmotherfucker be entering the language anytime soon?

NOT WITH MY MOTHER YOU DON'T!

“Taste is not your strong suit, right, Larry?”

—CNN host Larry King, to Larry Flynt, on *Larry King Live*, January 10, 1997

In the early 1980s one of America's most popular magazine advertising campaigns was a series of tongue-in-cheek celebrity interviews for Campari, a spicy Italian aperitif, in which minor film stars like Jill St. John, Tony Roberts, Geraldine Chaplin, and Elizabeth Ashley talked about their “first time.” From 1981 to 1983, the ads ran in all the major magazines, including *Time* and *Newsweek*, usually on the coveted (expensive) shiny back cover. According to Robert Jordan, the head of the ad agency that designed and sold the ad, Campari USA spent three million dollars on the campaign, and well over ten million potential consumers saw it. Jordan explained that Campari, despite its popularity in Europe,

> was not much of a factor in the beverage business in the United States and had not been tried by very many people. It has a rather unique bitter flavor, and as a consequence it is something of an acquired taste. In other words, if you try it, the first time you may be somewhat ambivalent about it. But, perhaps, the second time you drink it you get to like it a little more.... The objective of the copy, therefore, was to really make the point, if you try this, you may feel a little ambivalent about it, but you'll kinda get to like it. And if you take it a second time, you may get to enjoy it even more.

So the agency went for a typical Madison Avenue bait-and-switch: The ads featured glamorous people talking about their “first time,” giving the reader the impression, at first glance, that the topic was sex, not some overpriced concoction of alcohol and bitters.

For example, one of the ads, headlined "Jill St. John Talks About Her First Time" over a photo of the beautiful actress in an elegant setting, had this interchange:

> Jill St. John: My first time was in the Tre Scalini, that adorable sidewalk cafe in Rome.
>
> Interviewer: Oh, really? Right out in the open?
>
> St. John: Sure. You see, I'm basically an outdoorsy-type person.
>
> Interviewer: I see. You must tell me all about it.
>
> St. John: Well, we were just relaxing after a hard day shooting, just me and the crew. It happened with the stunt man.
>
> Interviewer: That stunt man? That sounds a bit risky.
>
> St. John: Oh, it wasn't really. You see, he was Italian and they just seem to know about these things.
>
> Interviewer: Go on.
>
> St. John: He was very romantic. He leaned close....

And then he gave her a charming smile and ordered her a Gingerly—"that's Campari and ginger-ale and soda." The ad was itself a spoof of the pretentious, faux-urbane, ersatz-Continental crap that one generally found stuffing the pages of Hugh Hefner's *Playboy*. In fact, it ran in *Playboy* and fit right in.

But one magazine that Campari didn't have to pay to run its campaign was *Hustler*, Larry Flynt's notorious newsstand monthly known for "showing pink," i.e., "spreading beaver" in gynecological detail. It was the anti-*Playboy*, working-class and proud of it, with back-alley humor, gross cartoons about shitting and farting, and occasionally a subtlety-free advertising parody. For example, its satires of tobacco industry ads showed Marlboro-manly men lying in cancer wards or coughing up blackened lungs. (Full disclosure: I was a *Hustler* editor for a couple of years in the late 1970s and have since worked for Larry Flynt on other magazines.)

One of the columns in *Hustler* was "Asshole of the Month," a screed against someone, usually a public figure, who had either pissed Flynt off or was threatening the right of every red-blooded American to buy porno. Sleazy TV evangelists were especially good targets, and plentiful, too. One of the victim assholes was a Lynchburg, Virginia–based Baptist rabble-rouser named Jerry Falwell, the perpetually smirking honcho of a giant collection plate called the Moral Majority, whose frequent attacks against *Hustler* had begun to get under Larry Flynt's skin. Though Falwell had already rated a couple of previous appearances as Asshole of the

Month (one of which I had written several years earlier), Flynt decided it wasn't enough.

"After several years of listening to him bash me and reading his insults," Flynt said later, "I decided it was time to start poking some fun at him. So we ran a parody ad in *Hustler*—a takeoff on the then-current Campari ads in which people were interviewed describing 'their first time'.... We had Falwell describing his 'first time' as having been with his mother, 'drunk off our God-fearing asses' in an outhouse."

The "Jerry Falwell Talks About His First Time" ad first appeared on the inside front cover of *Hustler's* November 1983 issue (and later in the March 1984 issue). In the interview, Falwell "admitted" that he had been so intoxicated that "Mom looked better than a Baptist whore with a $100 donation," and that he'd decided to fuck her because she had already "showed all the other guys in town such a good time." Finally, when asked if he had tried Campari since that first time, "Falwell" said, "I always get sloshed before I go out to the pulpit. You don't think I could lay down all that bullshit sober, do you?" Overall, if you didn't read too closely, the Falwell ad looked like just another entry in the Campari campaign—right down to the photograph showing a bottle, two glasses, a set of ice tongs in Falwell's hand, and Campari's copyright and trademark symbols. The only hint of a joke was a small-print disclaimer at the bottom of the page: "Ad parody—not to be taken seriously."

The real Jerry Falwell wasn't amused when he saw himself discussing how he doggy-fucked his drunken ma in a shithouse. As he would tell CNN's Larry King fourteen years later, "I was in Washington, and a reporter, as I was leaving a press conference, said, 'Have you seen the current issue—upcoming issue of *Hustler*?' I said, 'No, nor any of the prior ones.' 'Well, you're in there.' I said, 'Nothing new. I have been in it a number of times.' 'But your mother is in this one.' That's when I saw the ad and my mother had not passed just—just shortly passed, and she was eighty-two and a sweet wonderful Godly lady." Falwell sued Flynt and his *Hustler* operation for libel and intentional infliction of emotional distress in the U.S. District Court for the Western District of Virginia. A jury agreed with Flynt that the ad wasn't libelous, but it found in favor of Falwell on the emotional distress charge and awarded him $240,000 in damages.

Falwell might have also sued Flynt under the old "fighting words" doctrine, but the Supreme Court had already shot that down ten years earlier in a couple of cases (*Goody v. Wilson* and *Lewis v. City of New Orleans*) that vacated the convictions of several rowdy citizens arrested for shouting such things as "Motherfucking fascist pig cops!" "There goes the big, bad, motherfucking cops!" and "Goddamned motherfucking police!"

After a federal court rejected Larry Flynt's appeal, he decided to take it all the way to the top. "I wasn't about to pay Falwell for hurting his feelings," he said. In 1988 the U.S. Supreme Court agreed to hear the case (*Hustler Magazine, Inc. v. Falwell*). Flynt's defense was that his portrayal of "the respondent and his mother [being] drunk and immoral" may have been in bad taste and perhaps hurtful, but Falwell was a big boy, as well as a controversial public figure who had stomped on more than a few tender toes himself. *Hustler* was simply filling the time-honored role of the old broadsheets that once mercilessly lampooned political figures under the protection of the First Amendment. Chief Justice William H. Rehnquist, who wrote the Court's opinion, agreed: "The appeal of the political cartoon or caricature is often based on exploration of unfortunate physical traits or politically embarrassing events—an exploration often calculated to injure the feelings of the subject of the portrayal.... The political cartoon is a weapon of attack, of scorn and ridicule and satire; it is least effective when it tries to pat some politician on the back." He cited Thomas Nast's scathing magazine cartoons that skewered New York City's corrupt Boss Tweed and stimulated political discourse at the turn of the century.

As to Falwell's complaint that being accused of drunkenly fucking his own mother was so "outrageous" that it went beyond the scope of First Amendment protection, Rehnquist said that outrageousness was so subjective a standard that it "runs afoul of our longstanding refusal to allow damages to be awarded because the speech in question may have an adverse emotional impact on the audience." Certainly the ad was "gross and repugnant." But since the district court had originally determined that *Hustler*'s ad wasn't libelous, there was no dispute as to whether anyone actually believed that Falwell had fucked his soused-up mother. In other words, the Campari ad didn't make any false statements that were implied to be true. Everybody knew, or should have known, that the whole thing was a dirty joke. The Court, in a unanimous 8 to 0 decision, reversed the earlier judgment, reasoning that if it supported Falwell's position, "all anyone would have to prove is that 'he upset me' or 'she made me feel bad.' The lawsuits would be endless, and that would be the end of free speech."

One would think that after all that rancor, these strangest of bedfellows would have had nothing further to do with each other. But eventually Falwell, like a good Christian, forgave Flynt, called him a "warm-hearted" guy, and debated him on a 1997 college lecture tour. Of course,

Falwell might have simply been doing damage control, because the year previously, director Milos Foreman had documented the publisher's Supreme Court victory in the popular film *The People vs. Larry Flynt*, portraying it as a big win for the Constitution and the American Way. In any event, the preacher, with his loopy smirk frozen in place, subsequently moved on and did great things, like expose the homosexual agenda behind the children's TV show *Teletubbies* (one of the puppets was purple) and the real villains behind the 9/11 terrorist attacks (lesbians, abortionists, the ACLU, et al).

When Falwell died in 2007, Flynt wrote a piece for the *Los Angeles Times* called "My Friend, Jerry Falwell," in which he recounted his own bizarre relationship with the reverend. "Falwell was blasting me every chance he had," Flynt said. "He would talk about how I was a slime dealer responsible for the decay of all morals. He called me every terrible name he could think of—names as bad, in my opinion, as any language used in my magazine." But in the end, Flynt paid him back in spades. And he didn't even have to come right out and say the word *motherfucker*.

AND YOU CAN QUOTE ME ON THAT!

"I keep telling motherfuckers, 'You think *I* cuss. You haven't been to a grade school lately.' Them motherfuckers making new shit up. I'm listening to *them* because I'm still stuck on motherfucker. I ask *them* what the latest is."

—comedian Eddie Griffin, to Daniel R. Epstein of *ugo.com* (2003)

Now that *motherfucker* is loose in the culture, it's coming out of the mouths of people from all walks of fame. Here are some gems from the past and present.

"That motherfucker!"
—Howard Stern, referring to fellow shock jock Don Imus's producer, Bernard McGuirk, who had slandered Stern's girlfriend; uttered on censorship-free Sirius Radio, April 23, 2007.

"In a culture that tries to obliterate female genitals, from the *Times* to Barbie to *Playboy* to the theory that the clitoris is a vestigial penis, the vagina is posited not as a place but as a hole, an entryway. The beaver shots pioneered by *Hustler* were revolutionary and threatening because vaginas were shown to be hairy, red, purple, layered, complex; nevertheless they remained an invitation, a place to stick something into. A beaver shot with something coming out, like menstrual blood or a baby's head or an afterbirth, is not erotic, or we'd see those images in skin magazines. Emissions of the vagina are problematic because they signal the transformation of the sexual object into the mother. That's why motherfucker is such a charged word."
—Eve Ensler, author of *The Vagina Monologues*, in an interview with Blanche McCrary Boyd in the *Village Voice*, February 11–17, 1998.

"I don't talk to you white motherfuckers.... You bitch motherfuckers in the white press.... Fuck you, you motherfucking asshole.... white devils."
—Gus Savage, former Democratic Congressman from Chicago, as reported by Marilyn Rauber in the *New York Post*, June 27, 1991.

"*Donnie Brasco* was a motherfucker of a movie. I spent a lot of time with the real Donnie Brasco.... He lived it. I was just pretending."

—Johnny Depp, who played the title role in the film *Danny Brasco*, to *Vanity Fair* writer Kevin Sessums, 1997.

"You old red-faced motherfucker!"

—Sean Penn (as Jeff Spicoli) to Ray Walston (as history teacher Mr. Hand), ad-libbing during a classroom scene in the 1982 film *Fast Times at Ridgemont High*. The line as scripted was "You *dick*!" but Penn, in Method fashion, wanted to get under Walston's skin, according to director Amy Heckerling. She added, "Ray Walston came up to me [afterward] and said, 'You tell that young man that *that* is not appropriate!'" The "motherfucker" take was left on the editing room floor, and "You dick!" became one of the film's buzz lines.

"I go 3,000 motherfucking miles, sleep on railroad porches, in Starvation flops, eat out of cans—in Hickey, N.C."

—Jack Kerouac, in a letter to John Clellon Holmes, Oct 12, 1952.

"Ali [McGraw] and Jackie Kennedy at the moment were considered the two most admired women in America, and me, I'm sure, the luckiest motherfucker."

—Film producer Robert Evans, talking about his wife, McGraw, after her enormous success in *Love Story*, from the 2002 documentary *The Kid Stays in the Picture*.

"I'll bury you, you son-of-a-bitch motherfucker."

—Frank Sinatra, to Las Vegas Sands Casino executive Carl Cohen in July 1967, after Cohen cut off his line of gambling credit. (Cohen responded by knocking a couple of caps off Sinatra's front teeth.)

"Okay, you cocksuckers, motherfuckers, *and* Mr. DiMucci!"

—Record producer Phil Spector, addressing the assembled musicians at a recording session, after singer and fifties icon Dion DiMucci demanded that Spector show him more respect; as reported by Mick Brown in the 2007 book *Tearing Down the Wall of Sound*.

"A few years before WBAI got in trouble for playing George Carlin's infamous 'Seven Words' routine, I was on that station talking about words that were taboo on radio. 'I can say finger as a noun, but not as a verb,' I said. 'And I can say mother as long as it's not just half a word.'"

—Writer Paul Krassner, in a personal email to the author, June 26, 2008.

"Yeah, I call this one a fuck-you-if-you-can't-take-a-joke comedy.... When you read a script like this, the first thing you think is, I hope to God they don't back off on all this stuff and try to make it so you can take your kids.... I'm not saying it's bad to make those movies, that's great. It's just that it was such a thrill to make an adult comedy and you *know* you were making an adult comedy and you know not to shoot an alternative take where [costar] Robin [Williams] *doesn't* say motherfucker."

—Actor Edward Norton, discussing his 2002 comedy *Death to Smoochy*; to Paul Fischer of *filmmonthly.com.*

"Anyway, [the TV executives] folded like a house of cards, and meanwhile, Bob Saget is on tonight which gives you an idea of the level of comedy they think you can handle. Do you understand the contempt the networks have for us that put on that puerile bullshit and not give me—not just me, but anyone else with a point of view perhaps, maybe even one you don't agree with, on television. They cow-tow to the special interest groups and a couple of deranged motherfucking people, who hear the word Jesus and immediately think you're making fun of Jesus, when I did not make fun of Jesus. They hear the word gay. I did not make fun of gays. What I made fun of was a double standard that exists in this fucking country, they think you're too stupid to see through that and that's exactly what they fucking count on, while they sell the number-two killer drug in this country, fucking alcohol, and they have the gall to do it in your fucking living room with your children there. They don't even lurk around playgrounds. You drug dealing capitalist motherfucker!"

—Comedian Bill Hicks, talking about his segment being cut from *The David Letterman Show* a few days earlier, on Oct 1, 1993, because it was too controversial.

"One of [the cops] put his hand on me and said: 'Hey, boy.' He was armed. I said, 'Motherfucker, if you ever put your hand on me again, you be ready to kill me or be ready to die. You want to say something to me, you know what my name is.'"

—Comedian Dick Gregory, telling Robert Chalmers in 2004 about being harassed by Chicago police officers after one of his shows.

"You can't fire white folk. You fire white folk, you'd best believe somebody gettin' shot that day. 'I'm fired? I'll be right back, you sons of bitches.' You fire a brother, we be mad for a different reason. 'How come you didn't call me at home, motherfucker? You knew I was fired yesterday. Makin' me burn up all my goddamn gas.'"

— D.L. Hughley, from Spike Lee's 2000 film *The Original Kings of Comedy.*

"Fuck you, you Jew motherfucker!"

—Chicago Mayor Richard Daly, to New York Senator Abraham Ribicoff, after Ribicoff denounced the Chicago police department's "Gestapo tactics" against political demonstrators from the floor of the 1968 Democratic National Convention. Daly later claimed he had actually shouted "You fink, you!"

"It hurt like a motherfucker!"

—Entertainer Sammy Davis Jr., recalling being scratched off the guest list for John F. Kennedy's inaugural after he'd worked for Kennedy's 1960 presidential campaign; the reason for the snub was that Davis was dating blonde actress Kim Novak.

"Sammy Davis was one talented motherfucker!"

—Christopher Kennedy Lawford, son of Peter Lawford and Pat Kennedy Lawford, from his 2005 book *Symptoms of Withdrawal.*

"When you're typing this interview, make sure you put it in there that I am the stupidest fighter in the history of the game. Just the dumbest motherfucker ever."

—Mike Tyson, to Greg Leon of *boxingtalk.com*, July 11, 2005.

"You are my friend, my pal, my domino partner, and the funniest motherfucker in the world today!"

—Singer Willie Nelson to Richard Pryor, on Pryor's MySpace page, which is still being maintained after his death.

"You know the worst thing about niggas? Niggas always want credit for some shit they supposed to do. A nigga will brag about some shit a normal man just does. A nigga will say some shit like, 'I take care of my kids.' You're *supposed* to, you dumb motherfucker! What kind of ignorant shit is that? 'I ain't never been to jail!' What do you want, a cookie?! You're not *supposed* to go to jail, you low-expectation-having motherfucker!

—Comedian Chris Rock, *Bring the Pain* (HBO, 1996)

"Haven't we gone far enough with colored ribbons for different causes? Every cause has its own color. Red for AIDS, blue for child abuse, pink for breast cancer, green for the rain forest. I've got a brown one. You know what it means? 'Eat shit, motherfucker!'"

—George Carlin, "Free Floating Hostility," from his 1996 album *Back in Town.*

"This play allowed me to go places, especially with relationships, that there's just no way you could do with kids. With children's theater you always have to censor yourself. You can't call someone a motherfucker."

— Playwright Michael Miller, as his new adult-themed work, *El Paso*, opened in Toronto, Canada, in 2002.

James Lipton, host of the Bravo channel's *Inside the Actors Studio* since 1994, always asks his famous guests a set of questions devised by French TV host Bernard Pivot. Question number seven is, "What's your favorite curse word?" Here are several answers:

"Motherfucker!"
—Michael Douglas
"Motherfucker!"
—Laurence Fishburne
"Motherfucker!"
—Harrison Ford
"Motherfucker!"
—Chris Rock
"Motherfucker!"
—Danny Glover
"Motherfucker!"
—Gene Hackman
"Motherfucker!"
—Jamie Foxx
"Motherfucker!"
—John Cusack
"Motherfucker!"
—George Carlin
"Motherfucker!"
—Ethan Hawke
"Motherfucker!"
—Will Smith
"Cocksucking motherfucker!"
—Jack Lemmon

"Motherfucker cocksucker!"

—Liza Minelli

"JAMF—Jive-ass motherfucker!"

—Clint Eastwood

"Shit motherfucker, cocksucking motherfucker!"

—The cast of *Law & Order*

(The only word that's more popular is "fuck," volunteered by over twenty guests, including Geena Davis, Billy Crystal, Robert DeNiro, Melanie Griffith, and Meg Ryan.)

"You little jive-ass, stupid motherfucker. Do you really think you're gonna catch me on that same shit twice?"

—R&B drummer-bandleader Johnny Otis, on the phone with Count Basie in the early 1940s, recounted in Otis's 1993 autobiography *Upside Your Head*. He had already been pranked with a fake job offer from a famous jazz pianist. But this time the man on the other end of the phone was actually Count Basie (and yes, Otis did get the job).

"I've had my hair like this from day one, mostly because it's much more comfortable and it looks good on my head. I don't want to be runnin' to some motherfucker to straighten the shit out! When I started, I knew I didn't fit any visual that anyone was going to lie down and take their clothes off about. Work doesn't come to me; I go out and look for it. I call motherfuckers up and say, 'Can I have a job? Can I work with you?' Sometimes it works, sometimes it doesn't."

—Whoopi Goldberg, to Wyclef Jean, April 1999.

"My friend Jack Nitzsche got to go to Swinging London early, while he was arranging a lot of the Rolling Stones albums. One night back in 1965 or '66, he ran into the American artist PJ Proby, who he had recorded as Jet Powers here in Los Angeles. By this time Proby'd had nearly a dozen hits in England, he was a big star, right up there with the Beatles. He and Jack went to a club called the Scotch of Saint James. Some blokes were looking at them and making wisecracks to each other and laughing. When one of them walked by, Proby got up and bumped into him pretty hard and said, 'Motherfucker, are you looking to get your ass kicked?' The guy went white and split with his buddies. Proby, who likes to fight, told Jack he hadn't had a good fight since he'd been there. He said the big key to intimidating Brits was to call them a motherfucker, because they'd never heard the word before and it did something to their head. This would have been '64 or '65."

—Former producer-manager Denny Bruce, to the author, in 2008.

"When a young guy heads out to the park sporting a 'Jewcy' or 'Shalom Motherfucker' tee [shirt], he's laying Jewish claim to certain elements of American popular culture while challenging age-old stereotypes. 'I'm not an asexual weakling,' the shirt proclaims, even if the wearer would never be comfortable saying so."

—Brooklyn writer Ellen Umansky, in a 2003 *Nextbook* essay.

"Five Temptations...one mic[rophone]. Whatever they did, they came back to the mic.... Now everybody on the goddamned stage got a mic! Forty motherfucking people! Motherfucker, why? We can't understand what *one* of yo' asses is sayin'!"

—Comedian Steve Harvey, talking about rappers, in Spike Lee's 2000 film *The Original Kings of Comedy.*

"I was sitting beside a youngish white fellow [at a 1967 Amiri Baraka poetry reading of 'Black People' at Fisk University]. He had been very quiet. But when Baraka said at one point 'Up against the wall, motherfucker,' this man jumped to his feet and said 'Yeah, yeah, kill 'em.' And here he was, ordering his own execution. That's how electrified the atmosphere was. 'Kill 'em all!' he said."

—Poet Gwendolyn Brooks, talking to Ida Lewis in the April 1971 issue of *Essence* magazine.

"If you want to save the planet, I want you to start jumping up and down. Come on, motherfuckers, make some noise!"

—Madonna, in the introduction to her song "Ray of Light" from the Wembley concert stage in London during the internationally televised Live Earth concert, July 7, 2007, later called "officially the largest global entertainment event in history" by organizer Al Gore. "Come on, motherfuckers, make some noise!" had been Madonna's usual introduction to "Ray of Light" during her earlier Confessions Tour.

"The doctor smacked me on my ass. I yelled, 'One more time, motherfucker, I'll stick that rubber glove up yo' ass!'"

—Comedian Blowfly, a.k.a. Clarence Reid, recounting his 1945 birth to writer David Waller (*wweek.com*) in 2002.

"Now I can't have no curse show, I mean I gotta throw in a few jokes in between the curses, I can't come out and go 'Hello! Filth flar'n filth, motherfucker, dick, pussy, snot, and shit. Good night!'"

—Eddie Murphy, imitating a Bill Cosby rant against profanity in his 1987 film *Raw.*

"I'm just jokin', motherfuckers. Shit!"

—Comic Chris Rock, after calling the crowd "motherfuckers" during his introduction of the Red Hot Chili Peppers at the Live Earth concert in London, July 7, 2007, which was broadcast live on the BBC and Canadian TV. The BBC immediately cut him off and made several apologies, but the word had already gone out on the air.

"When white people killed all the Indians, who did all the work? Go get the niggers! Then, in the fifties, [blacks] finally said, 'Hey, I ain't doin' shit for you motherfuckers no more.' And The Man said, 'Fine! We'll call Julio and give him a quarter to come pick our fields.'"

—Comedian Carlos Mencia, at the Brea Improve in Orange, California, July 2004.

"You are not going to fuck with the Chinese. There is fourteen billion of those motherfuckers. White people, let me let you in on a little nigger secret. If you motherfuckers fuck with the Chinese, niggaz are not going to help out. I'm sorry. I'm so sorry."

—Comedian Katt Williams, on HBO's *The Pimp Chronicles Pt. 1*, 2006.

"White people can't dance. I'm not being racist, it's true. Just like when white people say black people have big lips, it's not racist, it's true. Black people have big lips, white people can't dance. Some brothers will be in the club and white people are like, 'What are those niggers doing in here?' They watchin' y'all dance. And they're like, 'Look at these crazy muthafuckas.' Y'all be stepping on people's feet and hittin' one another."

—Eddie Murphy, *Raw* (1987).

Britney: Nothing gets to him [Kevin Federline].... Not my man. And that's why I married him, because he's not a shallow motherfucker Hollywood actor-guy....

Details: People think Kevin is with you for your money.

Britney: Well, time will tell, motherchuckers, you know what I mean? We're going to be together forever....

Britney: When I have kids—I think Céline Dion, the way she does it with her show in Vegas is the way to go. Everybody comes to her.

When I have kids, I'm so there. That's what I'm doing: "Come to me, motherfuckers."

—Britney Spears, to *Details* magazine, January 2005.

Eddie Murphy: "Brothers act like they couldn't have been slaves back two hundred years ago. It's like the motherfuckers *liked* that shit. 'I wish I was a slave, I would fuck somebody up! Shit, tell *me* to bale some motherfuckin' cotton! I would been on the street and shit, would've come up and say, 'Eh, yo, nigger, bale this cotton!' I would say, 'Suck my *dick*, massa!'"

—Eddie Murphy, *Delirious* (1983).

"People wouldn't believe that my mom tried to run me over. I told the cameraman, 'Give her two white zinfandels and she'll tell you the whole story.' At the beginning of the film she's all nice, and me and my brother watched that and said, 'Who the fuck is that? That ain't the woman who raised us.' So we shot a family reunion and we gave her a few drinks and boom [she said], 'I ran that motherfucker over.' *That's* the woman I know."

—Eddie Griffin, talking about his 2002 concert film, *Undercover Brother.*

"Get the fuck out of the way, I can't see! There are cars there, motherfucker!"

—*Spiderman* star Tobey Maguire, to a group of paparazzi, as he was trying to drive out of a parking lot, according to *showhype.com* on July 10, 2008.

"Some of these [panhandlers] look healthy but they're just bums. The very idea. They want me to just give them the hard-earned money my folks send to me every week. 'You leech. Get a job, my dad works eight hours a day for this money.' You ever get those bums that turn mental on you? 'Sorry, I don't got any money.'

"'*Motherfucker*!'

"'Whoa whoa, where's my checkbook? Hold on. Is that *Mr.* Bum?'"

—Bill Hicks, The Village Gate, New York City, 1990.

I might as well finish up with jazz great Miles Davis, whose quotes seemingly add up to miles of motherfuckers. Here are a few:

Davis discussing his diet: "I figure if horses can eat green shit all day and run like a motherfucker, why not me too?"

Dissing jazz pianist Cecil Taylor: "Who's that motherfucker? He can't play shit!"

Dissing fellow trumpeter Wynton Marsalis: "That motherfucker's not sharing a stage with me."

Complimenting jazz pianist Chick Correa: "You a motherfucker."

Referring to a cut from Jimi Hendrix's *Band of Gypsies* LP to explain why he liked the rock guitarist: "It's that goddamned motherfucking 'Machine Gun.'"

Writing in his 1989 autobiography, *Miles*, about the combo that backed him on several early sixties albums, including *Seven Steps to Heaven*: "I knew right away that this was going to be a motherfucker of a group.... Man, I could just hear that shit popping all over the place."

Describing his innovative mid-sixties Miles Davis Quintet: "You get the right guys to play the right things at the right time and you got a motherfucker."

Discussing an early mentor named Gustav who played in the St. Louis Symphony Orchestra: "He was a bad motherfucker. He also made great trumpet mouthpieces, and I use one of his designs even today."

Talking about his old pal, saxophonist Charlie Parker: "One time I left him in my apartment when I went to school and when I got back home the motherfucker had pawned my suitcase and was sitting on the floor nodding after shooting up."

www.FeralHouse.com